MIGRATING FICTIONS

Migrating Fictions

Gender, Race, and Citizenship in
U.S. Internal Displacements

ABIGAIL G. H. MANZELLA

THE OHIO STATE UNIVERSITY PRESS | COLUMBUS

Library of Congress Cataloging-in-Publication Data
Names: Manzella, Abigail G. H., author.
Title: Migrating fictions : gender, race, and citizenship in U.S. internal displacements /
    Abigail G. H. Manzella.
Description: Columbus : The Ohio State University Press, [2018] | Includes bibliographical
    references and index.
Identifiers: LCCN 2017036404 | ISBN 9780814213582 (cloth ; alk. paper) | ISBN 0814213588
    (cloth ; alk. paper)
Subjects: LCSH: American fiction—20th century—History and criticism. | Migration,
    Internal, in literature. | Race relations in literature. | Displacement (Psychology) in
    literature. | Refugees in literature.
Classification: LCC PS379 .M295 2018 | DDC 813/.509355—dc23
LC record available at https://lccn.loc.gov/2017036404

Cover design by Andrew Brozyna
Text design by Juliet Williams
Type set in Adobe Minion Pro

Front cover images: (1) Jack Delano, "Group of Florida migrants on their way to Cranberry,
New Jersey, to pick potatoes," Near Shawboro, North Carolina. Library of Congress, July
1940. (2) Clem Albers, "Persons of Japanese ancestry arrive at the Santa Anita Assembly
center from Santa Anita Assembly center from San Pedro, California. Evacuees lived at
this center at the Santa Anita race track before being moved inland to relocation centers,"
Arcadia, California. National Archives, April 5, 1942.

Back cover image: Dorothea Lange, "Cheap auto camp housing for citrus workers," Tulare
County, California. National Archives, February 1940.

Published by The Ohio State University Press

♾ The paper used in this publication meets the minimum requirements of the American
National Standard for Information Sciences—Permanence of Paper for Printed Library
Materials. ANSI Z39.48-1992.

9 8 7 6 5 4 3 2 1

To my parents, Kathy and Joe, for teaching me what is possible

And to Lee for being my safe place when I seek those possibilities

CONTENTS

ACKNOWLEDGMENTS

DON'T LET anyone fool you, it's a slog to write a book, and while much of this writing took place sitting on a sofa with my laptop and giant stacks of books, the contemplation for it often took place surrounded by others in conversations, teaching, and listening. It was a journey that taught me a great deal but also reminded me of the benefits of home via places and people.

Thank you to Elizabeth Ammons for guiding me at the start of this project and for her close, critical, and intelligent eye and to Christina Sharpe for steering me along the way and for her continuing words of encouragement throughout the process; such kindnesses mean a lot. I'd like to thank others at Tufts University for creating a positive atmosphere for me to grow and work, including Modhumita Roy, Joe Litvak, Sonia Hofkosh, and Ronna Johnson, as well as Chantal Hardy, Noah Barrientos, Sue Penney, and Wendy Medeiros during my days working in the front office. Stern College for Women gave me my first full-time teaching position, and I particularly want to thank Linda Shires, Ann Peters, Nora Nachumi, Richard Nochimson, and Manny Weidhorn. At Centre College I found a place that felt like a home even though it was a temporary one. Specific thank yous go to Philip White, Lisa Williams, Mark Rasmussen, Jami Powell, Heather Morton, and Eva Cadavid. When I was at the University of Missouri I found great colleagues, including Joanna Hearne with her kindness and helpful comments, Sam Cohen, Sheri-Marie Harrison, Andy Hoberek, Nancy West, Julija Šukys, Elizabeth Chang, Elisa Glick, Joan Hermsen, and Alex Socarides, among many more.

To my students, I appreciate their taking their educational journey with me. Librarian and office administrators have helped me throughout my career, including Shulamith Cohen, Hallie Cantor, Elinor Grumet, Paula Fleming, Mary Moore, Sharon Black, Vickie Thorp, Paula Donoho, and Anne Barker. Thank you also to my editor, Lindsay Martin, to managing editor, Tara Cyphers, who kindly shepherded me through the end of the project, and to the anonymous readers whose comments greatly helped me to make this book what it is.

In the fall of 2013, the National Humanities Center provided a welcoming environment and my fellow members of the Race, State, and History Working Group, including Julie Greene, Martha Jones, Sylvia Chong, Martin Summers and Tim Marr, gave me thoughtful feedback on a chapter from this work. It's a privilege to learn from others. I also appreciated the invitation to share some of my work at the Americanist Speakers Series sponsored by Duke, the University of North Carolina, and other institutions around the Research Triangle. In the spring of 2014, the Arizona State University Institute for Humanities Research supported me during my fellowship semester. It was a pleasure to work alongside scholars such as Desirée Garcia, Bambi Haggins, and Ersula Ore. My thanks to Sally Kitch for her leadership and Shannon Lujan for her work as my research assistant.

I am grateful for the recognition from the Women's Committee from the American Studies Association for the Gloria E. Anzaldúa Award, which was earned by an earlier version of chapter 4. Similarly, I appreciate the funding to present at the Race and Space Symposium at the University of Alabama because it gave me an opportunity to meet many other young scholars of race studies such as Ashon Crawley, Yumi Pak, Debby Katz, Merinda Simmons, and Brittney Cooper as well as allowed me to meet Queen Quet Marquette L. Goodwine, Phillip Biedler, Trudier Harris, and Houston Baker. That kind of early support matters.

A version of chapter 3 was published by the University of Alabama Press in *Race and Displacement: Nation, Migration, and Identity in the 21st Century*. Thank you to the University of Alabama Press for the permission to reprint that work. The image in that same chapter is from the National Archives, and I value the ability to reproduce Dorothea Lange's photograph. A huge thank you to Julie Otsuka for kindly talking to me about not only her writing but also her family. It is a gift as a scholar to be able to talk to living authors.

I'd also like to give appreciation to my professors at Middlebury College and the Bread Loaf School of English: Deb Evans, Will Nash, Brett Millier, Su Lian Tan, Evan Bennett, Carol Christiansen, and Julia Alvarez, as well as Alan MacVey, Cindy Rosenthal, Arthur Little, Kevin Dunn, Michael Cadden, Oskar Eustis, and Reetika Vazirani, to name but a few who showed me the best in scholarship, artistry, and teaching. To all those who sang with me along the way in choirs, on musical theatre stages, with jazz, classical music, and of course a cappella—particularly the Mischords—I thank you for the music that guides me.

To my friends who listened to my stories about work but helped me to experience the world beyond, your presence in my life gives me joy, specifically Joyce Wagner, Lauren Stewart, Meg Allen Greenhill, and Betsy Goodchild. My first spaces in Wyomissing Hills and the Poconos of Pennsylvania shaped who I am, as did my friends who grew with me. My extended family I thank for the reminders of the benefit of being able to come home again: the Hugheses, the Gallens, and the rest of the family. To Sarah Ballard, I'm glad you have become part of my family, and to the Manions, I appreciate your welcoming me into yours. To my brother, Zach Manzella, thanks for always pushing me in everything as well as for sharing your case law knowledge, and to my parents, Kathy and Joe Manzella, thank you for teaching me to look for ways to make the world a better place.

Finally, Lee Manion's position as my Ursa Major orients me back to my own North Star and reminds me of why I work and why I play. Wherever we are together, I am home.

The "Unprecedented" Internal U.S. Migrations of the Twentieth and Twenty-First Centuries

THE TRAIL OF TEARS (1838–39) is a name used to describe the mass removal of the Cherokee from their ancestral homelands in the eastern United States to Indian Territory in the yet-to-be-established state of Oklahoma. It functions in the popular imagination and in some academic texts as the archetypal example of an internal displacement. While the Removal's forced nature is widely understood, its description as internal is problematic. The Cherokee were removed not from the United States but from sovereign territory within the larger borders of the United States in a forced march that crossed national borders. Yet many textbooks on migration still refer to the Trail of Tears as an "internal migration," which they define as "the movement of people *within* a specific nation."[1] I highlight this discrepancy in order to call attention to the ways in which seemingly fixed terms, particularly "internal migrant," "refugee," and "citizen," develop in relation to governmental practices and manipulations. In this respect, the Trail of Tears anticipates subsequent U.S. internal migrations (without being defined by them) by showing how governmental institutions employ uncertainty regarding moving peoples to promote particular notions of landownership and "American-ness" that would later continue to create a precarious citizenship for racial minorities, women, and the lower classes.

---

1. Henderson and Olasiji, *Migrants, Immigrants, and Slaves*, 2, italics added. See also Bailey, *Immigration and Migration*, 6.

One reason why the Trail of Tears is misunderstood is because of the hegemonic notion of an always already existing United States, a concept produced by the ideology that would become Manifest Destiny, in shaping a particular image of the continent marked by national borders. This hegemonic ideology had direct effects on the Cherokee, since the removal impacted those moved not just because they were taken from their homes and sovereign space but also because of the specific way the Nation was moved—under very harsh conditions that disregarded their humanity. The U.S. army rounded up Cherokee in surprise raids and held them in containment camps that were simple, fenced areas. This approach, often separating family members from each other, meant that many just had the clothes they were wearing, as well as little access to sanitation. Dysentery and other diseases flourished. They then traveled approximately 1,200 miles on foot and by boat; many traveled during the winter with limited food rations. The result was the death of approximately 4,000 of 15,000 Cherokee along the path.[2]

My point is to emphasize not simply that the Trail of Tears was a forced migration, but that its method and logic were intended to assert the dominance of the United States over the Cherokee nation as a people and a place. While it is of course important to recognize the agency of individuals in such instances—the Cherokee resisted and attempted renewal throughout this process—it is equally crucial to see the forces and models that propelled the Removal in the first place and continued to determine subsequent U.S. governmental actions, which promulgated the notion of American exceptionalism and deemed that the United States was worthy of whatever land it wished without regard for those already on it.[3]

In this way, the Trail of Tears is a precursor to the examples that follow in this book. It is a part of an under-examined history of enforced movements that require further theorization because the Cherokee nation, itself a sovereign state but treated as a dependent people by the United States when it was convenient, was, during the march, ambiguously poised between two categories that would only be codified legally by the United Nations (UN) in the twentieth century: refugees and internally displaced persons. A variety of court cases during this time debated the "relationship between the right and obligations of individuals (citizens) and the rights and obligations of nations (states)" in regard to Indigenous peoples and whether they should be treated as part of the United States or separate from it.[4] These rulings reveal that the

2. Sturgis, *The Trail of Tears and Indian Removal,* 58, 60.
3. Ibid., 65.
4. Barker, "For Whom Sovereignty Matters," 2.

interweaving of land, identity, and power have a long-standing tradition in the United States.[5]

Contemporary discussions of migration continue to negotiate the categories of internally displaced person and refugee along with their affiliated concepts. The term "refugee" positions a migrant as an individual who, "owing to a well-founded fear of being persecuted for reasons of race, religion, nationality, membership of a particular social group or political opinion, is outside the country of his nationality, and is unable or, owing to such fear, is unwilling to avail himself of the protection of that country."[6] This definition from Article 1 of the Geneva Convention Relating to the Status of Refugees in 1951 is internationally recognized, granting codified legal protections for refugees.[7] The idea of the refugee is connected intimately to the role of the nation in migration, where individuals leave one citizenship-based space to travel to another space with the goal of eventually being accepted as citizens in this new territory. As human geographer Tim Cresswell states,

> [The refugee] is founded on the organization of the nation-state at the turn of the [twentieth] century in Europe. The drawing and policing of national borders, the firming up of state sovereignty and the construction of national identities were all necessary conditions for the production of the refugee as a person "out of place." The place they were out of was the nation and that was itself a relatively recent phenomenon.[8]

---

5. The Cherokee argued that they should be seen as maintaining their own sovereignty and that the existence of treaties with the United States was proof of their status as an independent state, while the United States sought to show that the Cherokee should not be treated with the legal power of international law by denying that they had been recognized as a political entity among "the general society of nations" (*Johnson v. M'Intosh* [1823]). Instead they claimed that "Indians had no right of soil as sovereign, independent states" (*Johnson v. M'Intosh* [1823]) because Marshall's Doctrine of Discovery states that "the appropriation of the lands for agriculture [. . .] secured the rights of the discovering nation to claim full sovereignty within the lands and against all other claims" (Barker, "For Whom Sovereignty Matters," 7–8). This view created a tendentious definition of how ownership rights worked so that European invaders could secure land rights while also ignoring the agricultural history of the Cherokee (12). See Barker, "For Whom Sovereignty Matters" for more on the court battles over sovereignty.

6. United Nations General Assembly, *Convention Relating to the Status of Refugees*.

7. Historically the document's scope was limited to events preceding 1951 and could be interpreted to relate only to exiles in Europe, since it was created to solve the itinerant problem after World War II. However, in 1967, the United Nations General Assembly Protocol relating to the Status of Refugees removed restrictions based on time and geography so that the language still holds to today. See United Nations High Commissioner for Refugees, introductory note, 2.

8. Cresswell, *Place: An Introduction*, 183.

Until the refugee gains protection from the new state, this "out of place-ness" exposes the refugee to suffering and violence because he or she has no legal rights of citizenship.

Still, to understand migration via the refugee's temporary in-betweenness with an expected resolution is already to accept a false binary, since many migrants actually move within their home country and therefore never technically lose their citizenship rights. Additionally, as Patricia Truitt has argued, by categorizing the refugee as necessarily crossing national boundaries, many who are affected but remain within the nation are vastly overlooked by international protection because of this "exilic bias."[9] In the United States, such internal displacement shapes the modern experience to a far greater extent than typically is understood. The disempowered status of a refugee needs to be seen as having potential commonalities with the disempowerment of the majority of migrants who travel internally within a country. Such migrants fall within the category of internally displaced persons (IDPs)—individuals forced into migration but still presumably protected by their nation state. The United Nations specifically labels them as individuals and groups

> who have been forced or obligated to flee or to leave their homes or places of habitual residence, in particular as a result of or in order to avoid the effects of armed conflict, situations of generalized violence, violations of human rights or natural or human-made disasters, and who have not crossed an internationally recognized State border.[10]

It is important to note that there are legal protections granted to refugees that are not internationally guaranteed for the internally displaced, since the "responsibility for the protection of IDPs rests first and foremost with national governments and local authorities."[11] These internal displacements are acknowledged as one of the greatest humanitarian crises of our time, but since the legal protections of the internally displaced do not exist internationally in the same way as they do for refugees, the question remains, what hap-

---

9. Truitt, *False Images*, 11. As the number of refugees continues to increase, a "source control bias" has begun that looks at the country of origin to try to solve the problems within that nation so that people do not need to flee (Aleinikoff, "State-Centered Refugee Law," 263). This approach that could help many who are unable to cross borders has generally turned into an ideal of containment, since, as T. Alexander Aleinikoff has stated, "refugee law has become immigration law, emphasizing protection of borders rather than protection of persons" ("State-Centered Refugee Law," 265).

10. United Nations High Commissioner for Refugees, *Guiding Principles on Internal Displacement*, 1.

11. Vieira de Mello, foreword.

pens when national and local authorities do not appropriately protect those who are displaced and are perhaps even part of the displacement problem? How do we see that rights of citizenship are often bound up in issues of law, property, and race that undermine the expected protections from the United States and the ideals of American exceptionalism it espouses?

By investigating such displacements at the national level across the twentieth century, this book works to fill in the gap left between international and national law by studying patterns of mass movements that are downplayed because a national boundary is not crossed. A fundamental question that any study of migration and citizenship must address is when and how to apply the term "refugee" as opposed to "internally displaced person." Scholarly views on this question are divided because there are political benefits and shortcomings on either side. Some current discussions of the treatment of many people of color in the United States are attempting to address this gap by eliding the distinction between external refugee and internal migrant in order to show commonalities and thus achieve greater protections. Immigration lawyer and professor Raha Jorjani, for instance, has stated that many African Americans "would be able to demonstrate that they had more than a well-founded fear of persecution at the hands of their government" because of how they are treated by police, in prison, and generally by their own country, which would give them "a strong claim for asylum protection under U.S. law."[12] In her personal experience, writer Edwidge Danticat found that she was treated as someone "in transit," as an unwanted refugee, not because she was an immigrant to the United States from Haiti but because she was black.[13] In Danticat's words, "Ultimately we realize the precarious nature of citizenship here: that we too are prey, and that those who have been in this country from generations—walking, living, loving in the same skin we're in—they too can suddenly become refugees."[14] Both of these invocations approach but do not fully claim the term "refugee" for U.S. citizens; instead, they state that it is a position that might be caused via a rejection by one's own country. Such caution is necessary because claiming the status of refugee due to a failure in state support can paradoxically perpetuate that very failure. At the same time, maintaining a strict legal distinction between refugee and internally displaced person can obscure the ways in which various citizens have felt their sense of safety and protections to be compromised without hope for acknowledgment or redress. In addition, we must consider how natural disasters or other moments marked as "excep-

---

12. Jorjani, "Could Black People in the U.S. Qualify as Refugee?"
13. Danticat, "Message to My Daughters," 207.
14. Ibid., 210–11.

tional," which are followed by states of emergency, affect the legal protections that are supposed to be guaranteed to citizens during migration.

Whereas the refugee is seen by definition as a problem of external migration, of movement from one nation to another that would alter that person's citizenship, the internal migrant theoretically should not face challenges to his or her citizenship when moving, though in fact such often occurs. A primary example of this problematic relationship was the displacement caused by Hurricane Katrina, which made landfall in southeastern Louisiana on August 29, 2005. The storm caused destruction throughout the Gulf Coast region, with an official death toll of 1,833 people, but even the authority behind this number, the National Hurricane Center, acknowledges, "the true number will probably not ever be known."[15] New Orleans, a city with a majority black population and often overlooked minority populations such as Vietnamese Americans and Latino/as, bore the brunt of the devastation after portions of its levees burst, submerging 80 percent of the city and causing the evacuation and displacement of over one million people.[16] Since that time, criticism has begun to reveal issues such as the systemic racism and classism toward and within the city both during and prior to the storm in thoughtful and provocative ways.[17] Displaced people themselves even asked if the degree of flooding of their properties in the Lower Ninth Ward was exacerbated by this lack of concern stemming from historical racial problems.[18] Gender factors are also beginning to be highlighted, such as in sociologist Jacqueline Litt's study that details how New Orleans women, living in a city where their levels of unemployment and poverty far exceed the national average, used community networks to get away from the storm and survive in its aftermath.[19] These are the stories about identity and movement that need to be better understood for the future because, although the city and the region as a whole have been affected across racial lines, the region has lost hundreds of thousands of residents within the African American population, and women with children are the slowest to

15. Knabb, Rhome, and Brown, "Tropical Cyclone Report," 11.

16. Ibid. and Hori, Schafer, and Bowman, "Displacement Dynamics." Importantly, though, there was at least one significantly sized group that had been doubly displaced—the ethnically Vietnamese community in Village de L'Est who had been refugees at the end of the Vietnam War and who were now IDPs because of the storm. See Marguerite Nguyen, "Vietnamese American New Orleans" for more discussion on this community and the fact that many of them took both journeys together (117).

17. See, for example, Dyson, Come Hell or High Water or Bergal et al., City Adrift.

18. Elder et al., "African Americans' Decisions Not to Evacuate."

19. Litt, "'We need to get together with each other.'" Also for data see Willinger, Katrina and the Women of New Orleans, 6 and 33.

return. By contrast, the Vietnamese American community has had a high rate of return and the Latino population has actually grown; the specifics of these disparities should be better understood.[20]

One obstacle in achieving this fuller understanding results from moments when white mainstream views apply the concept of the refugee to nonwhite and lower-class migrants that by definition separates them from their citizenship rights. During Katrina, questions of whether residents were perceived and treated with the rights and care afforded to full citizens can be heard in the diction used to represent their plight. The media repeatedly described hurricane victims as "refugees" when they fit within the historical category of internally displaced persons.[21] Furthermore, during the Katrina catastrophe, both human and natural, reporters spoke as though the situation had no antecedents. They called it "an unprecedented instant migration" with one important difference from some of the migrations that preceded it: "This group didn't get to make the choice about when to leave or where to go for a better life. They were simply wrenched out of their homes, and many had little, if any, say in where they ended up."[22] The media's account became the dominant narrative of Katrina; these stories explained and perpetuated the idea that migration was typically voluntary—and in the distant past—except in the case of seemingly unavoidable natural calamities, for which the only response is pity. On many levels, however, the New Orleans disaster had previous models. The bias of the media and of the national response has precedents, as does the magnitude of human displacement. While it is important to note distinctions, there are many internal migrations with which to compare the Louisiana upheaval, some equally forced. Indeed, the United States was founded on the displacement of peoples: the European immigrants who sailed west, the Africans who were brought forcibly as enslaved people, and the Native Americans who were attacked, evacuated from their homelands, and then sequestered. The initial European invasion led to internal migrations, both forced and chosen, that speak to the spatialized history of the country—one that continues to be reflected in dislocations such as those caused by Hurricane Katrina. Lack of historical knowledge and appropriate terminology indicate the hidden sys-

---

20. See Willinger, *Katrina and the Women of New Orleans,* 30; Groen and Polivka, "Going Home after Hurricane Katrina"; and Geaghan, "Forced to Move," 3. See Leong et al., "Resilient History."

21. See Sommers et al., "Race and Media Coverage of Hurricane Katrina" for its discussion of the "high likelihood that race played a contributing role" in the media coverage of Katrina (50).

22. Mankiewicz, "The New Diaspora."

tems of oppression and the slippage in how the protections of citizenship are not equally meted out in the "refuge" that is supposed to be the United States.

This unawareness of previous events, especially those in the last century, as well as the racialized and gendered implications of the history and politics that went along with them, prompted my writing of *Migrating Fictions: Gender, Race, and Citizenship in U.S. Internal Displacements*. Additionally, the media's narrative about the "unprecedented" nature of Katrina points to a need for awareness about the stories we tell about our past. Who narrativizes such events, and how are the stories contingent upon the teller? From the Massachusetts Bay Colony to Ellis Island, from the cowboy to the prospector, migrations and their retellings—both historical and fictional—appear to represent a journey to freedom and individual self-determination often primarily focused on the white, male experience. This view, however, overlooks the major internal migrations of the last century that were largely compelled, not voluntary, and the variety of participants that were equally a part of U.S. identity and history.

This study seeks to theorize an alternate location that incorporates the acknowledged plight and insecurity of the international refugee (with its accompanying humanitarian, ethical call for action) into the category of the internally displaced person in order to address national constructions of precarious citizenship and their relation to movement; so doing will enable IDPs to seek social justice without inadvertently disenfranchising citizens of their rights. This book shows that the United States has displayed a history of spatial colonization within its own borders that extends beyond isolated incidents into a pattern based on ideology about nation building, citizenship, and labor. Considering some of the major internal displacement of the twentieth century together—the Great Migration, the Dust Bowl, the movement to and from the U.S. concentration camps, and the prevalence of Southwestern migrant labor—reveals a past imbued with (en)forced movements and community disruption that creates, in Zora Neale Hurston's oxymoronic words, "permanent transients" that are often race- and class-specific. Though each is seemingly a distinct regional phenomenon, these events and their fictional representations reveal similar tactics of displacement against the disempowered. This book investigates these events in relation to changing immigration policy; between the Johnson-Reed Act of 1924 and the immigration reform under the Hart-Celler Act of 1965, the number of international immigrants was vastly reduced, and so the nation's attention was turned to those within its own borders. *Migrating Fictions* is the first book-length study to examine all of these movements together along with their literature and shows that one of the trends is how enforced movement is often placed upon the laboring class and people of color. Mobility may mean freedom for the leisure class, but for the working class it often means a precarious life of endless migratory labor and the loss of a home space.

In other words, this book traces how Jeffersonian ideals of independent landownership as the basis for the nation are manipulated by various groups over time to move others—whether women, people of color, the lower class, or those who are seen as not worthy of the full benefits of citizenship for whatever reason—into disadvantageous positions and places. These exclusionary ideals of landownership reveal that the concept of the United States as a site of refuge is a myth. These government constructs, as well as how fiction responds to them by presenting alternative narratives and the possibility of "imagining otherwise," thus become key to the theory of movement and definitions of internal migrants because who is given or loses rights is based on just such stories.[23] Only by first understanding the ways in which internally displaced persons are shaped as such long before any "disaster" occurs can we work toward a theoretical conception of movement and space that balances between the stateless refugee and the ignored internal migrant.

THEORIZING MIGRATION AND CITIZENSHIP

Prominent theorists have addressed the relationship among citizenship, the law, and movement in ways that are illuminating for my examination of internal displacement and the precarious life it tends to produce. My approach to the problem of citizenship and the law for internal migrants draws on work by Alexander Weheliye, Giorgio Agamben, and Judith Butler. Agamben and Butler are themselves responding to Michel Foucault's highly influential discussions of sovereignty, state power, and management. These theorists' formulations of key critical concepts, including the state of exception, bare life, governmentality, and precarity, allow us to see how internal displacement is part of a larger nexus of political and economic forces designed to produce and maintain inequality, particularly in terms of race, gender, and class. At the same time, I suggest that this bare life and precarity are made more fully evident through internal displacement, which exposes the dominant governmental paradigm linking landownership and citizenship. The position of

---

23. See Gordon, *Ghostly Matters,* 5 for her important contribution of this term and its idea of seeing beyond the current situation.

the internally displaced can query the dominant view because displacement demands attention to the transitory spaces of movement.

Agamben's argument about the "state of exception" and the production of "bare life," and Butler's about the application of governmentality help to pinpoint the ways in which displaced peoples tend to have their citizenship rights ignored or revoked in times of movement or crisis.[24] In Agamben's work, the state of exception is the tool through which sovereign power is able to suspend certain laws because of a moment labeled as so unusual that the rules temporarily do not apply, but then makes these unusual moments usual, and bare life, or "life exposed to death," is the potential violence from the state because a person lacks protection under the law.[25] Such concepts are exemplified in Agamben's work about the Nazi concentration camp, which exists outside the normal juridical order and enables all violence against human beings by reducing them to bare life and by making the state of exception the rule.[26] Butler's application of Foucault's term characterizes governmentality as "marked by a diffuse set of strategies and tactics" that "gains its meaning and purpose from no single source" and that "dispose[s] and order[s] populations [. . .] to produce and reproduce subjects, their practices and beliefs, in relation to specific policy aims."[27] My use of Agamben and Butler, however, is filtered through recent work that has questioned the elimination of racial hierarchies from the concepts of bare life and governmentality. Particularly I draw upon Alexander Weheliye, who is himself extending the work of Hortense Spillers and Sylvia Wynter.[28] By expanding the state of exception to include the kind of violence already part of the ordinary functioning of the law—as in slavery or the U.S. prison system—we can see how "different populations—often racialized—are suspended in a perpetual state of emergency."[29] In my view, this governmental system that creates gendered and racial disparities, while operating regularly in everyday life, becomes more fully exposed in the moments labeled as exceptional, especially when those moments occur around movement and migration. In other words, built-in exceptions to the governmental system extend preexisting acts of violence, revealing how controls on movement and freedom work within both the ordinary system and its supposed emergency state.

Bare life and the state of exception are important concepts for understanding the effects of governmental practices on changing notions of citizenship.

---

24. Agamben, *Homo Sacer*, 88; Butler, *A Precarious Life*, 52.
25. Agamben, *Homo Sacer*, 88.
26. Ibid., 167–80.
27. Butler, *A Precarious Life*, 52.
28. Weheliye, *Habeas Viscus*, 74–88.
29. Ibid., 88.

For instance, Agamben usefully points out how citizenship in general has been called into question by repeated invocations of the state of exception, which creates a "zone of indistinction" between the law and its suspension.[30] In his view, the refugee has taken the place of earlier subjects who were denied full inclusion in the state. This new exclusion eventually "introduc[ed] the principle according to which citizenship was something of which one had to prove oneself worthy and which could therefore always be called into question."[31] In this respect, all are equally disempowered by the undermining of citizenship via the state of exception and constructions of bare life, which have been employed in the service of political exclusion and genocide. Weheliye, by comparison, shows how the majority of these structures involve "other forms of political death" that do not annihilate subjects.[32] In other words, rather than using the Nazi concentration camp as the paradigmatic example of bare life, Weheliye suggests that slavery and the space of the plantation epitomize how the nation-state diminishes the rights of its people while still preserving their existence for labor. Additionally, he questions Agamben's "zone of indistinction," which claims that all are equally disempowered by this modern sovereignty. Instead, Weheliye shows how we need to see not only the particulars of how some have their rights withdrawn while they are still forced to serve the state through exploitation, but also that this withdrawal is often made unequally against groups of people who are marked as outsiders through categorizations such as race.[33]

Combining Agamben's argument about the state of exception, Butler's points about the application of governmentality, and Weheliye's awareness of race as a key factor in these decisions lends additional theoretical weight to the distinction between the refugee and the internally displaced person. By applying their ideas to the history of internal displacements and how that intersects with racial discourse in the United States, I suggest that forced movement, rather than being a mere symptom of other repressive forces, functions as a key for defining citizenship.

For instance, Agamben's concept of the state of exception can be applied to some comments by the then mayor of New Orleans Ray Nagin. After Hurricane Katrina, Nagin said on multiple occasions that he had called for martial law, a right not afforded to a mayor; martial law was also invoked by Press Secretary Scott McClellan and only later denied by National Guard Lieutenant

---

30. Agamben, *Homo Sacer*, 37.
31. Ibid., 132.
32. Weheliye, *Habeas Viscus*, 35.
33. Ibid., 36–37.

General H. Steven Blum.[34] Since the city was not being run by the military but the military was doing supporting work for the city, martial law was never officially instituted, but its invocation does show several officials in power stressing that the basic rule of law had been momentarily halted, as in the "state of emergency" that had been declared for Louisiana, Mississippi, Alabama, and Florida.[35] Under the state of emergency, the National Guard was called in to keep the peace, federal troops were brought in to provide humanitarian aid, and certain rights, such as the right to congregate, were suspended. Under a state of emergency in Louisiana, curfews may be called, traffic by vehicle or on foot may be controlled or interrupted, the possession of weapons may be controlled, the sale of alcohol may be prohibited, and the use of sound equipment such as bullhorns may be prohibited.[36] In particular, what this meant was that some police officials in New Orleans told their officers that martial law did exist, which allowed them to "take back the city" by doing things such as shooting looters.[37] In short, a state of emergency is precisely the kind of state of exception that Agamben is discussing that allows authorities to change the law of the land. During Katrina, this idea led to guns being taken from individuals. The thinking goes that this is a necessary adjustment because only police should have guns in such a time. Therefore, the Second Amendment for gun rights was suspended, as was a basic understanding of appropriate punishment—death for the appearance of a petty crime.[38] States of exception can and often are employed by those in power to restrict or reduce the citizenship and rights of already marginalized populations.

Such moments of crisis tend to turn U.S. citizens into rightless refugees, but as Weheliye and Butler make clear, their rights and protections regularly have been eroded by the existing power structure itself long before these extreme incidents. Whereas the sovereign authority can suspend the law and, say, invoke martial law or a state of emergency, the biopolitical manipulations of governmentality can shape subjects unequally, rendering certain groups, such as African Americans in New Orleans, less able to be seen as victims who deserve the freedom of movement. Butler's argument about the overlap between the direct authoritarian action of sovereignty and the diffuse functioning of governmentality gives us a way to understand how the instability of particular citizens is exacerbated during movement and migration.

34. McDonell, "What Is Martial Law?"
35. Ibid. See also "Legal Answers for New Orleans Residents."
36. "Louisiana Laws—RS 14:329.6."
37. McGreal, "New Orleans Police on Trial."
38. Berenson and Broder, "Police Begin Seizing Guns of Civilians."

In other words, I am extending the idea of precarious citizenship explored by scholars such as Butler as well as by Michael Hardt and Antonio Negri.[39] As Butler explains:

> "Precarity" designates that politically induced condition in which certain populations suffer from failing social and economic networks of support and become differentially exposed to injury, violence, and death. Such populations are at heightened risk of disease, poverty, starvation, displacement, and of exposure to violence without protection. Precarity also characterizes that politically induced condition of maximized vulnerability and exposure for populations exposed to arbitrary state violence and to other forms of aggression that are not enacted by states and against which states do not offer adequate protection.[40]

This understanding of precarity shows how particular people are at risk for falling into the category of bare life. While who is found to be precarious may change over time, this vulnerability, as Butler further elucidates, "characterizes such lives who do not qualify as recognizable, readable, or grievable" and thus "is [a] rubric that brings together women, queers, transgender people, the poor, and the stateless."[41] Whereas precarity highlights the ways in which "other forms of political death," as Weheliye put it, tend to be overlooked, it also adds to that understanding by pinpointing the intersections of gender and sexuality with citizenship.[42]

All of this inequality is occurring while the United States continues to present its essence as being a place of refuge for those seeking freedom and equality. One of the key phrases espoused by both liberal and conservative politicians is the idea of American exceptionalism, that there is something special about this place that affords opportunities like nowhere else, which these internal displacements show to be a myth on many levels.[43] The mix of

---

39. Hardt and Negri, *Multitude*.

40. Butler, "Performativity, Precarity and Sexual Politics," ii.

41. Ibid., xii–xiii.

42. Weheliye, *Habeas Viscus*, 35.

43. Sylvia Chong makes a connection between exceptionalism and John Winthrop in American colonial history:

> En route to what would become the Massachusetts Bay Colony, John Winthrop set out the idea of the New World as not merely another refuge for his persecuted religious sect but as a "city upon a hill," a chosen land for a chosen people to enact God's kingdom on earth. Here, the Puritan vision of being "elect" forms the basis for their exceptionalism—a dream that the new American colonies will succeed where the corrupt Old World has failed, which retroactively remakes the New World from a conquered territory into the predestined location for such redemp-

emergency, precarity, and exceptionalism in the Trail of Tears and Hurricane Katrina are just two examples of a more far-reaching phenomenon. The history of U.S. citizenship reveals how race and a lack of access to land and land-ownership become circularly reinforcing concepts that perpetuate precarity.

Therefore, part of my theoretical framework draws on scholarship in critical race studies, which has exposed the long-standing connections between the law and racism in the United States. My analysis shows that internally displaced people have been produced as an operating, unofficial category of precarious citizenship by governmental forces both direct and indirect. This connection between the government and its ability to disempower as well as empower through the unequal distribution of rights is of course not a new one. In 1787, when creating the foundations of the United States at the Constitutional Convention, James Madison said, "Landholders ought to have a share in the government, to support these invaluable interests, and to balance and check the other. They ought to be so constituted as to protect the minority of the opulent against the majority."[44] This view shows not an egalitarian ideal but unequal protections for the minority of the rich at the beginning of the nation, with only landowners having a full voice in the government. As the idea of legal documentation for citizenship developed in the United States, the 1790 Naturalization Act directly tied citizenship to race, requiring that citizens be a "free white person." Over time, "those of African descent" were also included, but this only opened the conversation to a black/white binary. Therefore, as many scholars, such as Ian Haney López in *White by Law*, have shown, early citizenship cases were focused on proving one's race as tied to whiteness. Beyond that, though, as Cathy J. Schlund-Vials has demonstrated, citizenship also became "in part a public, sentimental performance, requiring the 'would-be American' to declare affiliation and loyalty" and is displayed by "demonstrable patriotism and knowledge of U.S. history."[45] Thus, a racialized notion of who was a citizen was also bound up in cultural capital and the need for an ongoing recitation of fealty when one's status was in question.

Even as the state claimed to be becoming more inclusive through ending slavery, Frederick Douglass points out the results of receiving some but not all the rights afforded to other Americans:

---

tion. This New England strain of exceptionalism mobilizes the sacred to justify the protonational, thus marrying a universal logic to a historical particularity. ("Exceptionalism," 306–7)

Thus, even the earliest voices were building up the idea of the New World as justified in its actions because of its special status. (I wish to thank the author for sharing her work with me while still in manuscript stage.)

44. James Madison quoted in Yates, "Notes of the Secret Debates."
45. Schlund-Vials, *Modeling Citizenship*, 7–8.

If I were in a monarchial government, or an autocratic or aristocratic government, where the few bore rule and the many were subject, there would be no special stigma resting upon me, because I did not exercise the elective franchise[; . . .] but here where universal suffrage is the rule, where that is the fundamental idea of the Government, to rule us out is to make us an exception, to brand us with the stigma of inferiority, and to invite to our heads the missiles of those about us.[46]

What Douglass is demonstrating is that in the United States, where there were not fixed social classes, the lack of voting rights pointed to precisely a diminished citizenship meant to keep ideas of superiority and inferiority intact even at the very moment that the Fourteenth Amendment was being passed, which detailed that "all persons born or naturalized in the United States [. . .] are citizens [. . . who are not to be denied] equal protections of the laws."[47]

Mae Ngai continues this discussion of citizenship into the twentieth century, stating that the "race science" of the nineteenth century was adapted in the twentieth century to build power structures not just on a physiognomic difference but also on how that was tied to nationality: "Modern racial ideology depended increasingly on the idea of complex cultural, national, and physical *difference* more than on simple biological hierarchy."[48] Thus, the historically racist idea that some races are superior to others because of physically perceived difference is then compounded with the ideas of cultural difference as the nation-state takes on its own level of power. Ngai also explains how this is enacted through the law with the goal of getting around the equal protection guaranteed by the Fourteenth Amendment:

> On the one hand the law separated public and private spheres, prohibiting racial discrimination by the state but permitting it in private relations. On the other hand Congress and the courts sneaked racial distinction into public policy through doctrinal rationalizations like "separate but equal." During the 1920s the legal traditions that had justified racial discrimination against African Americans were extended to other ethno-racial groups in immigration law through the use of euphemism ("aliens ineligible to citizenship") and the invention of new categories of identity ("national origins").[49]

---

46. Douglass, *What the Black Man Wants*.
47. U.S. Constitution, Amend. XIV, Sec. 1.
48. Ngai, *Impossible Subjects*, 8.
49. Ibid., 9.

Therefore, in the twentieth century the state itself adapted to be able to keep making legal distinctions based on race that undermined access to full citizenship rights.

Since citizenship is also very much bound up with space and since the United States particularly developed with the idea that landownership was a primary way to connect its people to the unfolding idea of the nation, it follows that lacking property demonstrated a lack of connection to that nation state. The right to own land was a foundational element of the development of the United States and the basics of self-sufficiency in this new economy. Therefore, this book will follow how the lack of landownership rights and the removal of even consistent rights to staying in one space become another tactic in the ongoing process of how governmental forces keep power and rights in the hands of a few. *Migrating Fictions* reveals the hidden elements of landownership and precarious citizenship within migrant discourse to show how this disempowerment is tied to movement while that very movement can itself function as a space to open up awareness and critique of such governmentalities.

THEORIES OF MOVEMENT AND THE ROLE OF GENDER

The question of space and movement has received renewed attention since criticism's "Spatial Turn" during the last quarter of the twentieth century, a debate that was shaped by scholars such as Michel Foucault and Henri Lefebvre and that addressed the need for space to be considered alongside the social and historical in humanistic study.[50] This interdisciplinary discussion about movement across space has developed into an area that considers not just the geographic but also the cultural, political, and economic interactions between people and spaces. The work of historic-geographic critics such as Lefebvre, Edward Soja, and Linda McDowell constitutes the theoretical underpinning for my investigation into how the diachronic role of time relates to the synchronic role of space.[51] Lefebvre's work developed the idea that space could be understood through the different aspects of the perceived, conceived, and lived—*une dialectique de triplicité* of material space, representational space, and experienced space. Building upon this idea, Soja reframes Lefebvre's three-

---

50. See work such as Foucault, *Discipline and Punishment* and "Of Other Spaces" as well as Lefebvre, *The Production of Space*.

51. See McDowell, *Gender, Identity and Place* and Soja, *Thirdspace*. As Soja notes, recent critical attention to space and geography attempts to create "a more flexible and balanced critical theory that re-entwines the making of history with the social production of space, with the construction and configuration of human geographies" (11).

part concept into Firstspace, Secondspace, and Thirdspace—the trialectics of the real, the imagined, and the real-and-imagined spaces combined. Both Soja and Lefebvre are interested in thinking about the *relationship* between the physical elements of space and the way that space is imagined to be, with Soja further stressing that this intersection between the real and imagined elements of space is "radically open to additional otherness, to a continuing expansion of spatial knowledge."[52] In other words, he creates a framework that builds on earlier scholarship in the field as well as focusing on cultural studies adaptations. Feminist scholars such as McDowell have done just such cultural studies adaptations by paying increased attention to class and gender, showing that combining the materiality of the space with the imaginings of an individual can create new possibilities and resistance against oppression.

My analysis continues the project explained by these geographers by attending to the specificity of identity markers such as race, gender, and perceived citizenship in relationship to the social construction of space. I draw upon the ideas of postcolonial scholar Homi Bhabha and *mestiza* writer Gloria Anzaldúa because of their gendered as well as ethnoracially specific terminology such as "hybridity," "the borderlands," and "*Nepantla*" to distinguish how Thirdspace, the blending of real and imagined locations to create new spatial and communal possibilities, works for different populations.[53] A sense of self is more complicated than choosing which side of a binary or boundary to claim, since often choices are imposed from outside and since the interaction of a seeming cultural opposition may create a complex "hybridity" of cultures within the individual and the community in which he or she lives that extends beyond an either/or binary. Collectively, all of these theories provide a useful means for showing that spaces and identity categories are inseparable from people's understanding of themselves and of their communities in historical accounts as well as in their literary imaginings.

As Bhabha and Anzaldúa in particular highlight, the effects of internal migration have implications for the relationship of mobility and identity categories such as race, gender, and class. For instance, from a gendered perspective, Doreen Massey discusses the need for women to "keep moving" in order to not be trapped in a static and homebound space because "the mobility of women does indeed seem to pose a threat to a settled patriarchal order."[54] Additionally, Truitt has shown that it is women who are often unable to mobi-

52. Soja, *Thirdspace*, 61.

53. See Anzaldúa, *Borderland/La Frontera* and Bhabha, "Third Space." Soja's spelling of the term "Thirdspace" differs from Bhabha, who spells it "third space." In quotations I will spell it as each scholar does, but when I am employing the term, I will use "Thirdspace."

54. Doreen Massey, *Race, Space and Gender*, 11.

lize during times of human suffering because of their lack of access to funding as well as the number of people who depend on them, and it is this difficulty in crossing national borders that keeps them from being seen on the international scale as refugees.[55] Nevertheless, the history of internal displacements in the United States, which essentially renders invisible the presence of women in movement, labor, and community formation, reveals the pitfalls of mobility. Although a woman may want to escape the clichéd and literal boundaries of the kitchen by showing her ability to move, the loss of a home can equally disempower. Therefore, the *choice* to be stable or in motion should be the larger goal, since as geographers Tim Cresswell and Tanu Priya Uteng have stated about mobility, "On the one hand it is positively coded as progress, freedom or modernity itself; on the other hand it brings to mind issues of restricted movement, vigilance and control."[56] Rather than simply adopting a stereotypical white, male view of individual and unattached mobility as the best challenge to patriarchal society, one must consider the ways in which individuals and communities are empowered or debilitated by movement and the typical invisibility of women.

Women constitute a significant source via their participation in mass movements and in their fictional retellings of those events. The female authors I have selected for this study—some of whom were themselves subject to troubled, gender-biased receptions—have direct personal, familial, or professional connections to the histories they tell, which show the value of women in this quest both in active resistance and through cultural preservation and transformation. They work to save themselves, their families, their communities, and their stories, as they also imagine new ideas and opportunities for the future by constructing Thirdspaces in their literary works.

Migrating Fictions addresses these issues by analyzing constructions of space and movement as inflected by race, gender, and locality in the major twentieth-century historical migrations and, notably, in novels, including Zora Neale Hurston's *Their Eyes Were Watching God* (1937), Sanora Babb's *Whose Names Are Unknown* (written 1939/published 2004), Julie Otsuka's *When the Emperor Was Divine* (2002), Helena María Viramontes's *Under the Feet of Jesus* (1995), and, in an afterword, Jesmyn Ward's *Salvage the Bones* (2011). These representative novels from different historical moments, from different regions of the country, and with different racial and economic concerns can be used to construct a larger lexicon for our understanding of movement in the twentieth century.

---

55. Truitt, *False Images*, 13.
56. Cresswell and Uteng, *Gendered Mobility*, 1.

Each chapter concentrates on one major internal migration, its historical and legal circumstances, and one major textual example, but the capaciousness of these texts and the historical movements means that such analysis has ramifications for other fictional and historical examples as well as for theories of movement and citizenship in general. These selections recognize the intersectionality of the fields of movement, gender, and race studies that too often still disassociate their overlapping interests. They represent a variety of U.S. racialized identities, including African American, Anglo-American, Asian American, and Latino/a to indicate that some elements continuously reemerge no matter who is on the move, but also to uncover the historically and spatially distinct factors of each movement. Additionally, rather than focusing on only one migration-causing event (such as Hurricane Katrina) and its fictional presentations, this book, by looking across the century, more fully identifies the historical continuities that affect seemingly distinct internal migrations. This same choice also recognizes ongoing attempts within the literary tradition to describe the causes of these movements while imagining solutions, something that has been obscured by the periodization that separates critical scholarship on the modern from the postmodern and the early twentieth century from the post–World War II period. In this sense my work is influenced by the approaches of feminist scholars like Rita Felski, who explains in *The Gender of Modernity* how the work of female writers in the early twentieth century has been overlooked because it does not fit into the definition of modernism that privileges white, male authors, as well as by Caren Kaplan, who in *Questions of Travel* expanded scholarship on displacement over preestablished classifications of modernism and postmodernism. By engaging with novels that would be placed under different categories varying from social realist to postmodern, and with areas normally separated into the political and the artistic, this book aims to break down the categorical barriers that still associate migration with white masculinity and that minimize the contributions and struggles, both actual and imaginative, of women and people of color.

The gendered reception of these novels of displacement shows in particular the initial and continued dominance of male authors but also an increasing interest in what female authors bring to the conversation in a way that calls attention to the ongoing devaluation of some women's writing. Male-written fiction on the subject remains the most recognized—with examples including John Steinbeck's *The Grapes of Wrath* (1939), John Okada's *No-No Boy* (1956), Richard Wright's *Native Son* (1940) and *Black Boy* (1945), Tomas Rivera's *. . . y no se lo tragó la tierra* [*. . . And the Earth Did Not Devour Him*] (1971), and even Dave Eggers's *Zeitoun* (2009)—but female voices on internal migration are now attaining more popular and critical attention as their readership grows through mainstream presses and classroom assignments. In the 1930s, Zora Neale Hurston was a well-known author and part of the Harlem Renaissance, but even so, *Their Eyes Were Watching God* received many negative reviews from male writers who objected to her focus on the movement through the rural South at a time when they were espousing creativity focused on travel to the urban North. Therefore, although *Their Eyes* received attention and a wide audience on its release, it received much more acclaim when it was recovered in the 1970s by Alice Walker and other feminist and womanist scholars and is now a largely canonical text for those who study race and gender. Also during the 1930s, Sanora Babb, a professional writer who helped during the Dust Bowl migration, never had the chance to receive contemporary responses to her novel because Steinbeck's publication monopolized her subject matter, and her novel is only now beginning to acquire a readership with its recent publication in the twenty-first century. Conversely, the more contemporary authors have been more quickly accepted, but their treatment of historical displacement has been downplayed or decried. Viramontes's novel is now widely taught, albeit mainly for environmental and racial issues, and Otsuka's work gained notoriety for its painterly style and its unintended timeliness, since readers saw the incarceration of people of Japanese descent as a warning against sequestering Arab Americans after 9/11. The most recent text, Ward's *Salvage the Bones,* received the highest accolades with its winning of the National Book Award and was directly acknowledged for discussing Hurricane Katrina; however, the award itself has been criticized by some prominent critics for, in recent years, nominating too many female authors.[57] Critic Laura Miller also added that the nominees are "the literary equivalent of spinach. [. . . books] you *ought* to read, whether you like it or not."[58] Perhaps not coincidentally, the year following Ward's win, the judges of the National Book Award were given new instructions that overtly stated that it was acceptable to nominate well-known authors, seemingly responding to Miller's criticism and perhaps questioning Ward's merit.[59] Hence, women and

57. James, "Book Award Becomes a Feast of Canapés."

58. Miller, "How the National Book Awards Made Themselves Irrelevant." Julie Otsuka was also a finalist for the National Book Award that year for *The Buddha in the Attic.* She responded to Miller's critique by stating,

> I guess my role as a writer is to make these people [her characters are Japanese immigrants to the United States] visible—to give them a shape and a voice and tell their story to the world. [. . .] And if this makes me sound like someone you ought to read, someone whose books "are good for you whether you like it or not," I don't mind. Because I'm not writing to be liked. I'm just telling the stories I need to tell before my time on this earth is over. I don't think I could live with myself otherwise. (Johnston, "Interview with Julie Otsuka")

59. Kaufman, "Book Awards Seek a Bigger Splash, Red Carpet and All."

narratives about migration-causing events may be gaining more recognition, but with that notice comes a backlash that such authors and their subject matter are diminishing the value of awards and contributing to their supposed irrelevance.

In general, *Migrating Fictions* examines large-scale internal displacements in the twentieth century while acknowledging the voices of women, the laboring class, and various racial groups that narrate and people these incidents, thus contributing to current efforts in ethnic and gender studies to bring a diversity of experiences in from the edges of scholarship on space and place. Such stories provide significant material for exploring the role of space in literature; my chosen authors and their characters teach about the power of the individual, but they also point to the complex logic behind mass movements with causes that are natural, governmental, and societal.

TWENTIETH-CENTURY MIGRATIONS AND THIRDSPACE

This book looks at those outside forces, but it also considers acts of resistance from within the communities affected, which include the developing empowerment of women as a result of different strategies of movement and conceptions of community. All of my chapters deal with such resistance, starting from their basic migratory patterns. These often overlapping mass movements considered here add challenges to a chronological treatment. While I have organized the chapters of *Migrating Fictions* historically, moving through the Great Migration, the Dust Bowl, the U.S. concentration camps during World War II, and the ongoing migrant labor in the Southwest after the Bracero Program, I continually return to different types of migration: environmental, wartime, and economic.⁶⁰ This arrangement unsettles simplistic notions of progress and increasing emancipation by showing the historical shifts in anxieties over race and movement. It also indicates how different female authors, speaking for the activities of distinct disadvantaged groups, have found storytelling and a symbolic identification with the past to offer greater or lesser potential for resistance to displacement and dispossession. Hence, my discussion proceeds through Hurston's fictional reply to the African American migration north, Babb's novel about Anglo-American farmers displaced during the Dust Bowl, Otsuka's narrative about the incarceration of people of Japanese descent, and Viramontes's presentation of Chicano/a migrant laborers. This order follows

---

60. It is important to note that the UN definition of "refugee" does not consider economic displacement as a legal cause for protection or aid. See K. Long, *From Refugee to Migrant?*, 2. Economic displacement is also not part of the UN definition of an internally displaced person, yet there is a vast moving population that requires further consideration.

the interconnections among the historical events as well as the repetitions of imposed governmentality that still do not extinguish female agency.

The historical migrations of the twentieth century are, of course, part of a larger structure. An ideology of American superiority, which would contribute to the removal of the Cherokee and to the notion of Manifest Destiny in the nineteenth century, uncovers patterns of exclusion in later migrations such as the Dust Bowl, U.S. concentration camps, and Southwestern migrant labor—with the first beginning in the same territory to which the Cherokee had been driven, the second built upon Indian reservations, and the third relying upon similar tactics of displacement and land seizure by the U.S. government. Thus, in 1930s California, when "migration anxiety" propelled harsh laws against Dust Bowl farmers moving to the state, the situation should be understood not as an isolated incident but as a reiteration and reconfiguration of earlier immigration policy and a precedent for the Japanese American removal during World War II.[61] This pattern is a pendulum swing that welcomes new inhabitants to live and work in a region and then becomes hostile to that group when they seem to gain any numbers or potential to empower themselves. For instance, after the start of World War I, immigration restrictions were lessened on Mexican workers because the United States needed bodies to replace those abroad.[62] These new workers helped to develop California into the greatest industrialized agricultural market in the country, but as those workers created unions to lessen their harsh working conditions, the immigration restrictions increased, along with "repatriation" back to Mexico.[63] Additionally, the Japanese American removal had ownership-restricting precedents. For example, as Cletus Daniel has commented, Japanese immigrants could not attain landownership because of the Alien Land Law that was formulated and supported by California farm owners who wanted to maintain their profits and who invoked racist ideology to constrain new immigrants from becoming competitors.[64] All was said to be "in the name of selfless agrarianism," the invocation of Jeffersonian ideals for profit, while what is exposed instead is a historical pattern that keeps profit, power, and land in the hands of a few.[65] In general, if we limit our study of communities to those defined only by ownership and static space, we will overlook the multifarious ways in which they thrive or fail during and after migration.

61. Gregory, *American Exodus*, 79–80.
62. Daniel, *Bitter Harvest*, 66.
63. Ibid., 68.
64. Ibid., 63.
65. Ibid.

I analyze how these historical migrations and their fictional representations attempt to produce a resistive Thirdspace beyond and against the ideological manipulations of the dominant governmental, legal, and economic
forces. Thirdspace becomes, in the work of these novels and in U.S. history,
a political site for imagining the collectivity of migratory movements; furthermore, it is a concept that unfolds and develops throughout the chapters
of the book. If Hurston's text, as I argue, shows the utopian potential of the
individual home in relation to the surrounding community, then Babb's novel
locates a Thirdspace created through an environmental and economic disaster outside of the traditional domestic space that embraces—though it fails to
fully realize—a form of social justice based on class that considers collective
stewardship rather than individual ownership. Otsuka's text, by comparison,
extends that economic dislocation from the home to the political and constitutional displacement of people of Japanese descent in the racialized bare life
of the camp; in the process, the novel creates a Thirdspace that challenges the
categorical distinction between international immigrant and internal citizen.
Finally, Viramontes's portrayal of Mexican American migrant labor and the
ambiguous space of the border ultimately produces a Thirdspace that demands
social justice—in effect incorporating the ethical claim of the refugee into the
internally displaced, perpetually migrating citizen. Thirdspace thus opens up
a way of thinking through the refugee–internally displaced person problem
without relieving the state of its responsibility to safeguard all citizens.

My first chapter begins with a brief case study of the history of African
Americans from the time of colonization and slavery through emancipation
and Jim Crow. The removal of their citizenship and landownership rights
highlights flaws in views of American-ness and American exceptionalism.
This history is foundational for my argument, showing a developing governmentality of precarity existing even before the formal beginning of the nation
that would serve as a model for later displacements. The chapter then focuses
more specifically on how this relationship progressed in the twentieth century
and is interpreted and altered in Zora Neale Hurston's *Their Eyes Were Watching God*. This modernist novel is structured as an allegorical road story that
places a female, the main character Janie, as traveler and seeker of knowledge.
She takes a literal journey through the American South and a symbolic, epi-
sodic journey across African American history through slavery, sharecropping, W. E. B. Du Bois's idea of the "Talented Tenth," and Jim Crow in the
beginning of the twentieth century. While many critics, such as Lawrence
Rodgers, say the novel ignores the Great Migration—the northern movement
of over a million African Americans, which overlapped chronologically with

Hurston's writing—I demonstrate, instead, that it invokes a history of the governmental disempowerment of blacks through their inability to control their bodies and movement. Janie's connection to land and movement creates an inverted journey into the South in an economic displacement that leads to an environmental one when the 1928 Okeechobee Hurricane ravages part of Florida. The main character's movement is thus a counter–Great Migration to self and community. That is, *Their Eyes* directly links migration to a way of viewing spatial dynamics that politicizes and genders space, and shows the hope for fully realized citizenship through self-possession and landownership. Janie's precarity throughout the novel shows her searching for a location of black diasporic identity that exists outside the bounds of the northern movement and gendered expectations that can be both lived and imagined. In the end, with Janie in her own home, the novel is able to create a Thirdspace that is not yet understood by the whole community but is realized through knowledge of African American culture, individual landownership, and storytelling.

My second chapter builds upon the first by showing another group's attempt to respond to imposed governmentality in the Dust Bowl and *Whose Names Are Unknown*, in which, conversely, an environmental displacement becomes an economic one. Specifically, I begin by giving an overview of the importance of landownership as a means to develop and expand the United States. This view is exemplified in Henry Nash Smith's representation of the yeoman myth that valorizes the nineteenth-century, white, male farmer while overlooking the farmer's untenable position planting in an area previously labeled the Great American Desert. This history underlies the resulting environmental disaster known as the Dust Bowl, which forced 250,000 people to migrate from the center of the country to the West. During the Dust Bowl, the white migrants themselves try to refashion gender roles by including the voices of women in their political and economic struggle. Historically, some migrants were stopped by California's border patrol because they were considered vagrants and therefore unwanted outsiders even though they were U.S. citizens. Babb's novel reveals the misery created under these restrictions and pressures. I argue that this work exposes what I call myths of possession that equate power and success with landownership and self-possession. By tracing the movement of these "unlanded" yeomen in the 1930s as they attempt to realize this governmentally supported myth, Babb's novel searches for an alternative to these myths by positing her own idealized community united across race and gender in federal camps and on strike lines under the idea of "collective respect," with everyone working together without interest for individual ownership or gain. While they work toward a Thirdspace as a way to social justice, this active attempt is ultimately restricted to class, and fails to bring women and people of color fully into the decision-making process, even at the conclusion of the book. This limited approach to the reorganization of identity relationships parallels their limited approach to spatial reconfiguration of their occupational predicament because it accepts the premise of an already flawed system—they do not use the imagined part of Thirdspace to more fully question the rights of the government and farm corporations to own all of the land and manipulate citizenship laws in the first place.

In the third chapter, I discuss the incarceration of people of Japanese descent and Otsuka's *When the Emperor Was Divine*, which tells the story of a Japanese American family that endures a wartime displacement to and from a U.S. concentration camp during World War II. I contextualize this movement by discussing the history of immigration law and the genre of incarceration narratives over time. I then show that this forced migration, with its different socially constructed spaces, stops Otsuka's characters from being able to arrive "home" ever again. The family's seemingly circular movement removes the safety of their home and alters their relationship with their community and with each other. Gender impacts these relationships in the structure of the historical camps that broke down the nuclear family by taking away the power and, sometimes, the presence of the male head of household. In the novel, this altered gender dynamic is specifically exposed through the mother assuming responsibility for every aspect of her family once her husband has been imprisoned, but this authority has been thrust upon her as the government forcibly assumes the traditional patriarchal role, making her empowerment illusory. This chapter argues that space is used by both the U.S. government and the dominant society at large to "disorient" this racialized group of people that is not seen as "American" enough, confusing them and turning them away from the East, even as they attempt to overcome these influences with imaginative escapist approaches of magical thinking and dreaming. Eventually the alterations imposed on them through space are so great that these controlling ideas become internalized, requiring the characters to (using Lefebvre's spatial terms) "perceive" their lived space as the "conceived space" of the concentration camp. In other words, the government controls the characters' understanding of space on both the "real" and "imagined" levels so that they cannot create their own redemptive Thirdspace or forge new functional gender norms, and their own home comes to represent the prison the United States had placed them in—and will not symbolically release them from—even though the camp barbed wire no longer surrounds them. These concerns continue to resonate with subsequent generations of Japanese Americans, as Otsuka's personal history demonstrates.

While the third chapter concentrates on the exclusionary aspects of a wartime displacement built upon an ideology of foreignness as the enemy, the fourth chapter continues that notion beyond the wartime state of exception in an ongoing economic displacement. Through the analysis of border history and gender oppression via conquest and conversion along the Mexican–U.S. border as well as of Viramontes's *Under the Feet of Jesus,* I show how laborers of Mexican descent are trapped in the cyclical seasonal pattern of movement based on crops, live in a series of interchangeable small shacks with no privacy, retell stories filtered through the lens of the colonizer that disempower on the level of race and gender, and are constantly forced to occupy liminal social and political spaces that deny them a sense of having a homeland on either Mexican or U.S. soil. These governmental practices that mark them with a "disembodied criminality" developed out of the history of U.S. immigration policies. Arguing that Viramontes's characters fight back with their own response, one best explained by Anzaldúa's notion of the literal "borderlands" and the spiritual in-betweenness of "*Nepantla,*" I show how the character Estrella incorporates both real and imagined elements that transform spiritual stories of women from various times, places, and cultural/religious identities, developing an "embodied spirituality" as she searches for a new Thirdspace for her marginalized people. The book's ending should be read as a call for social justice for its permanent transients. In this chapter, Viramontes's novel indicates how narratives of the past—historical and literary—can be redeployed in productive ways with female leadership, particularly by exposing the fraught histories of movement concealed by governmental policies and ideology. Such exposure, because it occurs specifically at the border and in a borderland space, allows us to see how the internally displaced person must be treated with the ethical imperative of the refugee.

The fourth chapter shows Estrella's newly found engagement with her narrative past, but her community remains limited by difficulties in productive movement. In my afterword, I return to this issue of limited movement with a discussion of the mobility poor in Hurricane Katrina and Ward's *Salvage the Bones.* This event and Ward's novel reveal that, contrary to our expectations, the contemporary moment is not the most liberatory for individuals in relationship to movement. This novel follows the Batiste family in a fictional town in Mississippi during the twelve days around the hurricane. These characters do not even consider migration, and instead their story is one of homebound survival when the costs of movement are too high, reminding us of the importance of choice for movement or stasis. Additionally, despite the narrative's focus on an intelligent, fifteen-year-old girl, showing the potential of female roles in the community, her position as an impoverished, pregnant child indicates how women and children continue to be dispossessed in the larger American society and during migration-causing moments. Bearing striking similarities to the 1928 hurricane and Hurston's treatment of it, bringing us full circle, Hurricane Katrina and Ward's novel reveal how earlier interpretations of history continue to be reflected in more recent events. These patterns of displacement will continue to repeat themselves if we do not enact better protections for internally displaced persons by realizing the critical connection between repeated narratives of migration and the dominance of land possession in our stories and lived experiences.

Altogether the history and the novels highlight how outside influences compel movement and identity transformation. They also demonstrate how those impacted individuals create spaces of opposition, imagining alternative histories and futures for themselves through acts of resistance and Thirdspace even as these spaces of resistance are often fractured by gender and racial divides. Thus, these chapters, while looking closely at different migrations and the racial groups they affected, disclose that without a fuller understanding of how governmentality can be imposed in similar ways on various groups (especially those deemed as falling short in their "American-ness") as well as how those people can reappropriate such practices for their own purposes, we will fail to see the new possibilities that extend beyond the historically "fixed" event of movement. Taken together, my analyses of these texts contribute to the contemporary space theory project of exploring and contesting the overriding notion that space is neutral, is accessible to all, evolves organically, and simply provides a background against which various activities, such as racial injustice and gender and class oppression, take place. By investigating narratives of internally displaced people and their relationship to precarious citizenship, this interdisciplinary study reveals how literature can provide alternative histories of space and home, exposes the governmentalities and myths of American exceptionalism that help to construct them, and argues for a conception of Thirdspace that mediates between the legal categories of the refugee and the internally displaced person in an effort for social justice.

CHAPTER 1

The Economic and Environmental Displacements during the Great Migration

Precarious Citizenship and Hurston's *Their Eyes Were Watching God*

LANDOWNERSHIP WAS a dominant force for European methods of colonization, displacement, and control. When the British, French, Dutch, and Spanish came to the Americas, they promulgated the idea that power should be in the hands of those who legally possessed land and were thus capable of holding property rights as a supplement to physical violence. They extended that connection between land and power as they began to conquer the native peoples and spaces around them in order to build what would only later become a new nation. Not only did the colonists claim that their view of land and authority was the only legitimate one, thus marking Native Americans as racially and legally inferior, but they also reinforced racial hierarchies by kidnapping Africans and enslaving them, labeling them as bodies without legal rights, to work on those lands. Yet even with the American Revolution, many of the same tactics and methods employed previously—including the enslavement and dispossession of Indigenous peoples, Africans, and African Americans— would continue to serve as a model for U.S. mythologies and legislations about landownership and movement that extends to other racial groups and later internal migrations discussed elsewhere in this book. The case of enslaved blacks, who existed within the state but were not acknowledged as citizens, in particular exemplifies the problems of the ideology of American exceptionalism as well as the restrictions on who is able to claim American-ness. In other words, the history of space and movement for African Americans in the United States is foundational to the argument of *Migrating Fictions* because it highlights the development of a governmentality of precarity, which utilizes both limitations on movement as well as forced movement without protection. In Alexander Weheliye's revision of the largely deracinated notions of bare life and governmentality put forth by Giorgio Agamben and Michel Foucault, the law is employed to place different racialized groups "in a perpetual state of emergency" that nonetheless preserves their bodies for labor.[1] This revised view of bare life and governmentality that incorporates race allows us to see how the history of unequal subjects began at the very inception of American colonization and evolved through slavery, emancipation, and Jim Crow, to today. This precarious existence, as Judith Butler explains, is a "politically induced condition of maximized vulnerability and exposure for populations exposed to arbitrary state violence."[2] This chapter opens by briefly recounting that history in order to focus more specifically on how this relationship progressed in the twentieth century and is then interpreted and altered in Zora Neale Hurston's *Their Eyes Were Watching God.*

The first recorded Africans in the English colonies are listed as arriving in Jamestown in 1619. While the status of these earliest immigrants is often studied for its complexity, because of a deficiency of clear documentation about such issues like the definition of indentured servitude versus slavery, as time passed the "loose system of African long-term labor [was] turned into codified, perpetual, and inherited racial slavery."[3] This move to enslavement not only gave whites a free labor source but also allowed them to dispossess their fellow inhabitants of what they had accumulated. This happened to Anthony Johnson, who, though a free black man when he died in 1670, had his land seized because he was "a negro and by consequence, an alien."[4] As decided by this case, "negroes" were marked by their race and as such by a lack of citizenship, leading to an inability to own land. From the very start of the English colonies, the notions of landownership, race, and citizenship were intertwined.

Citizenship's tie to spatialization was two-pronged, comprising both spatial possession itself and the ability to move between spaces. Therefore, denial of access to movement was part of being an enslaved person. The mobility of enslaved people was one of the earliest concerns as a means of control via confinement. As Stephanie Camp points out in her work on the "geography of containment" of Southern enslaved women, slave laws were enacted as early as 1680 "for preventing Negroes Insurrection" and slave patrols were used to reinforce these laws.[5] Slave owners wished to control black mobility, and

---

1. Weheliye, *Habeas Viscus,* 88.
2. Butler, "Performativity, Precarity and Sexual Politics," ii.
3. Horton and Horton, *Hard Road to Freedom,* 27.
4. *Image 177 of Virginia, 1665-76, Foreign Business and Inquistions.*
5. Camp, *Closer to Freedom,* 12, 25.

blacks understood the risk to their own bodies if they disobeyed these restrictions. Overall, this historical relationship between the law and African Americans on limiting mobility and landownership has long-term reverberations.

At the end of the Civil War, new promises about landownership and citizenship rights were made and retracted. Some of those soon-to-be citizens,
such as Garrison Frazier, were part of the conversation on how those rights
should develop. Frazier, who understood the connection between these ideals,
explained that the best path to freedom was "to have land, and turn it and till
it by our own labor."[6] After hearing such statements from black leaders, William Tecumseh Sherman established, through Special Field Order No. 15, the
Sea Islands and much of the coastal region in the South for black settlement
with the promise of forty acres and later the loan of mules—the probable
source of the famous offer of forty acres and a mule. Subsequently, this land
was retracted during President Andrew Johnson's attempted amelioration of
the relationship with white Southerners; the explanation was that the order
was said to have been intended for "'temporary provisions' [. . .] not to con-
vey permanent possession."[7] There were also the promises of the Thirteenth,
Fourteenth, and Fifteenth Amendments after the war that granted the rights
of freedom, citizenship, and voting, but with the dismantling of Reconstruction these elements were also not fully realized. Instead what was created was
a devalued citizenship without full rights, one defined by race and a perception of inferiority.

These legal constraints extended into extralegal suppression as well, for
long after the end of Reconstruction, as Grace Hale states, "lynching denied
that any space was black space, [and] even the very bodies of African Americans were subject to invasion by whites."[8] Critics from Ida B. Wells at the end
of the nineteenth century to Sandy Alexandre in the twenty-first century have
commented on how the violence of lynching at the turn of the twentieth century was used to prove that African Americans lacked even self possession—
the legal and physical control over their own bodies—through the public
taking of their lives. Lynching was also used to take possession of their land,
reinforcing that whites still controlled all the land symbolically and literally.[9]

African Americans' bodies, even when they were not slaughtered, continued to be commodities under sharecropping that did not even have slavery's promise of basic sustenance.[10] The dehumanizing effects of sharecropping

---

6. Foner, *Reconstruction*, 70.

7. Ibid., 70–71.

8. Hale, *Making Whiteness*, 229.

9. Alexandre, *The Properties of Violence*, 4.

10. Foner, *Reconstruction*, 106.

overlapped with the restrictive segregation of Jim Crow, which codified the two-tiered system of citizenship that had been implicit all along, where access to landownership and movement between spaces were limited by economic conditions and the racial divide. Yet even as the economic forces of urbanization and industrialization after World War I created a need for labor in the North that gave African Americans an apparently greater possibility of movement, resulting in the Great Migration, this movement was not ultimately liberating. Various forms of governmentality, such as the redlining that limited African Americans' access to credit and therefore equal access to housing and other social and economic opportunities, made the move to northern cities analogous to living in the segregated South, albeit often in more subtle ways. Even to this day, questions about equal access to the legal system and police protection continue, not just with the violence against black bodies taking a dominant position in our political conversations but also with the role of the prison system in controlling these same bodies by diminishing their citizenship rights and freedom of movement. Thus, when viewed through the lens of space and movement, the history of African Americans in the United States, rather than demonstrating a clear narrative of progress toward freedom and equality, reveals an increasingly refined apparatus for control and disenfranchisement that, despite several important legal changes, works to maintain a state of precarity and lack of full citizenship. In general, then, African American history is fundamental to my examination of migration because it reveals how governmentalities of movement and stasis are part of a U.S. mythology that too often connects landownership to those empowered citizens who are seen to embody "American-ness," an abstraction that is tinged with preconceptions about issues such as race, ethnicity, religion, class, and gender.

While the history can describe the changing legal restrictions on movement and citizenship, literary narratives about the black migratory experience are valuable because they provide critiques and alternatives. Harlem Renaissance writer Zora Neale Hurston's *Their Eyes Were Watching God* (1937) offers just such a powerful perspective. Hurston was born in Notasulga, Alabama, and raised in the all-black town of Eatonville, Florida. Through her life and writing she not only provides knowledge of the time but also creates some unrealized prospects for change. She slowly migrated north in the 1920s to become a writer (of fiction and anthropology) and receive her education at Barnard College. Even so, Hurston's movements north and south were complicated, because she often traveled into the South to live and to do research, and, in 1936, as a woman in her forties, Hurston earned a Guggenheim fellowship that she used to do research in Jamaica and Haiti, journeying into black spaces beyond the boundaries of the United States. While in Haiti, she wrote

Their Eyes Were Watching God, a novel about an African American woman, Janie, who does not migrate north but instead travels further and further into the South, living within several communities. In this novel Hurston narrates these historical interactions between African Americans and their relationship to space, movement, and citizenship while presenting some of her own imagined solutions.

Although Hurston too often is read as an ahistorical writer, her most famous novel illustrates and illuminates the larger historical process by which African Americans were denied citizenship. Strikingly, *Their Eyes* encapsulates this history through an allegorical structure that links its main character's movements south to the ways in which African Americans were first denied citizenship through slavery, then denied full citizenship via a precarious existence as sharecroppers unable to afford their own land, then by a class system that divided economically and enabled ownership only for the elite, and finally were further undermined by a migrant laborer structure that made movement, now no longer a sign of liberty, a marker of diminished citizenship rights. This last phase of migratory labor rendered African American workers a category of their own that did not require help when disaster struck and could be imposed upon in a state of emergency. Hurston treats southern migration literally and allegorically to affirm the importance of diasporic black cultural heritage for identity. At the same time, the novel is not simply a mirror of historical occupation and migration patterns. It symbolically inverts the migration to the North to reflect upon the larger history of African American experiences, expanding the conversation about race and space across time, while it searches for ways to connect to black, rural culture. Yet *Their Eyes* is also inverting the gendered expectation of the rugged, male individual with a female traveler, the protagonist Janie. By staging Janie's journey through a counter-narrative that challenges the American myths of exceptionalism and freedom through movement, Hurston exposes the governmental structures that inhibit African Americans while also imagining what several theorists call "Thirdspace," a postcolonial and social geography term that emphasizes how the combination of real and imagined space creates new cultural options and exposes the limitations of the dominant ideology.[11] Hurston's utopian Thirdspace of the individual home indicates how citizenship through self-possession and landownership is possible for blacks but fails to include

11. Soja in *Thirdspace* directly states that Thirdspace is a combination of "a Firstspace perspective that is focused on the 'real' material world and a Secondspace perspective that interprets this reality through 'imagined' representation of spatiality" (6), while Bhabha in "The Third Space" emphasizes postcolonial and historical elements, showing that the intermingling of various cultures can create a positive hybridity. Soja's and Bhabha's spellings of the term differ. In quotations I will spell it as each scholar does, but when I am employing the term, I will use "Thirdspace."

the larger African American community. Her work, though not fully jetti-soning the association of ownership with citizenship, acknowledges the his-torical reality of African American experience up to and including the Great Migration and its concomitant raced and gendered effects while attempting to reconfigure what movement means.

HISTORY, GENDER, AND GENRE DURING
THE GREAT MIGRATION

Previous discussions of Hurston's work have questioned its relationship to history, particularly in the context of the Harlem Renaissance and the Great Migration, revealing gendered notions of movement for African Americans and assumptions about how those movements should be represented. More recent scholarship has shifted focus, highlighting the importance of the genre of the migration novel for this period but often locating Hurston's work on the margins of that category. Along with this awareness of genre, some schol-ars now are attending to transnational elements in Hurston's text by pointing to her anthropological engagement with Haiti and other African diasporic locales. My work builds on recent scholarship's understanding of *Their Eyes* as directly participating in the major debates and historical issues of its time by revealing how it engages with issues of movement and expands the migration novel genre by presenting an allegorical, gynocentric migration narrative in the South.

Hurston's interest in the African American cultural history that sur-rounded her was long a part of her scholarly process, but critiques of her work as ahistorical by her contemporaries were a real concern for Hurston. From the perspective of some of the African American male writers in Hurston's time, her subject matter marked her as avoiding the political because her writ-ing about the rural, mostly black South was nothing like "the black urban pro-test novel [which] was then in vogue."[12] Such criticisms connect masculinist concerns with political, progressive movement and feminist ones with regres-sive movement, and much of this criticism maintains this dismissive binary

12. Cronin, *Critical Essays on Zora Neale Hurston*, 9. Importantly, not all writers or critics viewed Hurston's work negatively; after all, she was one of the most well-known African Ameri-can women writers during the '30s and '40s. She aligned herself with some of the younger writers whom she termed the "Niggerati," such as Langston Hughes, Arna Bontemps, Countee Cullen, and Dorothy West (Boyd, *Wrapped in Rainbows,* 116). Additionally, this concern about Hurston's lack of political engagement has not completely disappeared in more recent criticism. Hazel Carby argues that the book's reemergence into popularity during the 1980s, when "one in four young black males are in prison, on probation, on parole or awaiting trial[, allows the book to act] as a mode of assurance that, really, the black folk are happy and healthy" (*Cultures in Babylon,* 182).

by separating the novel from its historical and cultural context.[13] For example, Richard Wright wrote in the 1930s that the novel "carries no theme, no message, no thought."[14] The lasting effects of these critiques can be seen even sixty years later, when Hazel Carby states, "Hurston's representation of the folk is not only a discursive displacement of the historical and cultural transformation of migration, but also a creation of a folk who are outside of history."[15] In fact, Hurston certainly did "dis-place" the centrality of the historical migration to the North, but, as I will argue, her book reflects her knowledge in the social sciences and the creative arts through her use of an allegorical literary form and a distinct attentiveness to her cultural moment, particularly in regard to the movements of African Americans in space and time.

More recent scholarship has delved into the topic of migration in African American literature and Hurston's role in that field. Lawrence Rodgers categorized the genre of the Great Migration narrative, but while discussing Hurston's work in this context as a "fascinating variant on the migration novel form," he focuses on the "fictional erasure" he sees her work performing, removing any migratory story.[16] As he adds:

> The story that Hurston composed [. . .] is decidedly not about migration. By completely ignoring the presence of the North at a time when its effect on African-American life in the South loomed ever-larger, Hurston's novel represents an almost willful desire to negate the existence of the movement that had propelled her into the middle of Harlem culture more than a decade earlier.[17]

He sees Hurston's sense of space as purely "mythic."[18] Even Susan Willis, who sees some of the historical elements of Hurston's work, chastises Hurston for "offer[ing] a utopian betrayal of history's dialectic [. . . that] chooses not to depict the Northern migration of black people."[19] By contrast, scholars such as Farah Jasmine Griffin and Robert Stepto more directly consider Hurston's work as an African American migration narrative in their thoughtful and foundational research on the genre. Griffin's own explanation of the genre,

---

13. See Cronin's substantial collection of reviews on Hurston's work in *Critical Essays on Zora Neale Hurston,* which includes analysis by Richard Wright and Otis Ferguson. Moreover, that collection also includes an overview of Hurston criticism (9–12). See also Gates and Appiah's *Zora Neale Hurston* for a review by Alain Locke.

14. Wright, "Between Laughter and Tears," 75.

15. Carby, *Cultures in Babylon,* 172.

16. Rodgers, *Canaan Bound,* 94.

17. Ibid., 92.

18. Ibid.

19. Willis, *Signifying,* 48.

however, limits the significance of *Their Eyes* because of its counter-migration: "Most often, migration narratives portray the movement of a major character or the text itself from a provincial (not necessarily rural) Southern or Mid-western site (home of the ancestor) to a more cosmopolitan, metropolitan area."[20] Other Hurston scholars are investigating alternative kinds of migra-tion, from the regional to the transnational, with some specifically looking at "African traditional beliefs and practices that enslaved people amalgamated in Haiti and brought to the North American mainland."[21] My research builds on this previous scholarship, especially the careful reading of Rachel Blau DuPlessis, by continuing to think about Hurston's relationship to her move-ment and her time, both within and without U.S. boundaries, while broaden-ing the definition of the migration narrative to emphasize how her work is engaged with historical developments.

I wish to connect this research on Hurston's relationship to the culture of the black diaspora to the historical analysis her novel is providing because Hurston does investigate the potential of migration for women and for Afri-can Americans in the midst of the twentieth century—but that migration is into the South. As historical journalist Nicholas Lemann notes, "in 1940, 77 per cent [*sic*] of black Americans still lived in the South—49 per cent in the rural South."[22] To turn her attention away from Northern migration was not, therefore, a turn at all, but an awareness that the new stories of Northern urbanity did not encompass the entire African American experience or even the majority one. Hurston, unlike her vocal critics, was interested in the story and possibilities of a return to the South—or at least to its culture—for those who left and those who stayed. Her views on the Great Migration become clear precisely in her reversal of its direction and goals. Instead of viewing the urbanized North as the only location for discussions about African Ameri-can experience, *Their Eyes* shows mythic *and* historical presentations of the rural South; furthermore, Janie's physical and allegorical journeys through it connect her with black culture and people. Stepto has pointed to the impor-tance of such travel for the "symbolic geography" of the novel in which there are expeditions of "immersion" into the South and "ascent" into the North to find a place for internal transformation.[23] I extend this idea to argue not

20. Griffin, "*Who Set You Flowin'?*," 3.

21. Jennings, *Zora Neale Hurston*, 19. While early works such as Ellease Southerland's "The Influence of Voodoo on the Fiction of Zora Neale Hurston" point to Hurston's knowledge of black culture that she had studied in Louisiana as well as in the Caribbean, much has been studied on this topic recently, including Bone, "The (Extended) South of Black Folk," which considers the movement both within the South as well as from the Caribbean, and the recent Jennings collection mentioned at the start of the note.

22. Lemann, *The Promised Land*, 6.

23. Stepto, *From Behind the Veil*, 166–67.

simply for a symbolic geography but for a consistent allegory that describes an individual's travel while telling a story about African American history and the survival of African American culture, moving from the lack of self-hood and community occasioned by slavery to the systemic oppression of sharecropping and eventually to the foundation of black communities.[24] This allegorical journey reveals the novel's possible real and imagined solutions of self-possession that can be created via narrative and cultural knowledge to overcome precarious citizenship.

SIGNIFYING THROUGH ALLEGORY: MOVEMENT IN THE AFRICAN DIASPORIC TRADITION

Angus Fletcher in his seminal book on allegory states that the classical representation of this mode "involves the use of 'continued' or stretched-out metaphors, whose developed analogies inspire in turn a continuous commentary following the same stretching process."[25] Of course, Fletcher himself complicates this idea with many allegorical texts that depart from this definition, but for my purposes this general conception of allegory will help us to understand the larger shape of *Their Eyes*. By organizing the narrative as an allegory that draws upon the Western biblical tradition, African American oral traditions, and Caribbean narrative traditions, Hurston creates an alternative form to "express the racial spirit," as James Weldon Johnson put it, that works on the level of the character and on the level of the novel's structure.[26] As exhibited

24. This balance between the individual and the community can be seen in Hurston's own concerns as well about issues of segregation and racial pride. In a 1943 letter to Countee Cullen, she states, "Now as to segregation, I have no viewpoint on the subject particularly, other than a fierce desire for human justice. The rest is up to the individual" (Carla Kaplan, *Zora Neale Hurston*, 480–81).

25. Afterword to the 2012 edition of Fletcher, *Allegory*, 381–82.

26. Although most scholars have been uninterested in allegorical readings of Hurston's canon, some have noticed her use of allegorical elements. Blyden Jackson sees in her novel *Moses, Man of the Mountain*, "a story about black America, not because Hurston anywhere says that it is, but because Hurston's folklore everywhere happily transports Hurston's readers to a position from which every Jew in Goshen is converted into an American Negro and every Egyptian in Old Pharaoh's Egypt into a white in the America where Hurston's folk Negroes live" (introduction, xv–xvi). Jackson, however, misses that *Their Eyes* utilizes the same structure, saying instead that in this work folklore is "mere contribution to the atmosphere of [the] tale" (xv). Carla Kaplan in *The Erotics of Talk* recognizes sections of *Their Eyes* as allegorical, but Susan Willis has most fully explored the symbolic structure of the novel when she states that the novel "works through three historically produced economic modes" (*Signifying*, 46). Even Willis's allegorical analysis, though, is limited because her primary concern is how African American women authors use language subversively rather than how the allegorical elements of the novel are tied to the historical and migratory awareness of the text.

by Janie's movement into the South, the novel offers a counter-narrative to the Great Migration of masculinized urbanization and shows the importance of both an awareness of history and imagination on the part of the character and in the shaping of the story itself.[27]

Recognizing this counter-migration allows us to see the larger historical movements that Janie's experience allegorizes. All of her major life events reflect a symbolic progression through space and time. This progression is one often mentioned by scholars of allegory. For instance, though talking about the well-known allegory of Dante's *Inferno,* Jeremy Tambling is also effectively describing the structure of *Their Eyes*: "Life as a journey means that a temporal process is being explained as a movement from place to place."[28] The literal journey follows Janie Crawford, a woman born in West Florida shortly after the end of Reconstruction to a mother who was raped, the mother herself being the product of sex between an enslaved woman and her master.[29] Janie's migration from the home space begins when her grandmother marries her off, hoping that her life will be better than that of her forebears. In the course of the novel Janie travels deeper into Florida because of each of her three marriages until, after her last husband's death, she finally returns to Eatonville, the town she helped to build, to her own property and self-possession. Along the way, however, Janie has been subjected to the various forms of governmentality and precarious citizenship found in the novel's allegorical history of Afri-

---

27. In *Allegory in America,* Deborah Madsen comments that twentieth-century American allegory has often been used "as a fundamental expression of dissidence" (4) and gives specific examples of how it can be used as "counter-history" (3). Also, of course not every male text during this period took this northern journey, as Jean Toomer's *Cane* will serve as an example, but it was a common discourse that gained much attention then as now.

28. Tambling, *Allegory,* 3.

29. Nanny speaks of her sexual experiences with her master with terms that show they were against her will. For instance, he *"made me* let down mah hair" (17; italics added). More telling than what could be construed as a more superficial control of her body is her statement, "Ah didn't want to be used for a work-ox and brood-sow and ah didn't want mah daughter used dat way neither. It sho wasn't mah will for things to happen lak they did" (16). While she's covering a lot of time when talking about what wasn't her "will," part of what is included in opposition to that will is her being used as a "brood-sow"—as a breeder for her master. Although she states her will, as an enslaved woman, she is put into a double bind from others' perceptions, where the owner sees her as unable to be raped since she is property and thus always willing to do the bidding of the master, but he also sees her as unable to desire since she has no ability to consent to the interaction. Saidiya Hartman sets out this idea and elaborates, "The opportunity for nonconsent is required to establish consent, for consent is meaningless if refusal is not an option" (*Scenes of Subjection,* 111). Additionally, the fact that Nanny's mistress calls her back "yaller" (18) implies that Nanny's experience with her white master is not the first generation of such interactions for this family.

can American experience.[30] With her first husband, Logan Killicks, who lives just down the road from her childhood home, we see Janie symbolically linked to the agricultural space and lifestyle of sharecropping that too closely resembles slavery. Her subsequent movements continue this pattern. Her marriage to Jody Starks takes her south to help to develop the town space of Eatonville, moving her forward in time to question whether W. E. B. Du Bois's concept of the "Talented Tenth," the idea that elite blacks are needed to help to lift up the rest of the community, reinscribes white hegemonic power onto the African American community. Later, with her last husband, Tea Cake, Janie moves even further south to the Everglades, a swampland in the southern tip of Florida built upon migratory labor. There she attempts to connect to the "folk" to form a more egalitarian community. Countering the Northern migration into industry, the novel presents the possibility that southern migration leads to a fuller "immersion," as Stepto puts it, in folk culture and a space for self-determination. As Janie states, "You got tuh *go* there tuh *know* there" (192).[31] Migrating south—not north—leads Janie deeper and deeper into the spaces that tie her to African American culture. Janie's movement through space connects her internal journey to her external journey and thus allegorically reflects the oppression within African American history while also imagining alternative ways to use that history to find new spaces—a Thirdspace—of personal empowerment and, by extension, empowerment for African Americans.

This Thirdspace idea of combining the historical and the creative also functions on a structural level in the novel, as is evident in Hurston's use of allegory. Hurston's application of allegory integrates elements of Christian hermeneutical practices of "speaking that is other than open"[32] with African American and Caribbean elements of storytelling, making it "double-voiced," as scholar of African American literature Henry Louis Gates, Jr. labels such a

---

30. Edward M. Pavlić comments on Hurston's movement south as an inversion of sorts—what he calls an "absorption" ("'Papa Legba,'" 118), but his focus is on defining this work structurally in relationship to the modernist novel and Stepto's idea about the need for northern movement into awareness (119).

31. Zora Neale Hurston, *Their Eyes Were Watching God* (1937; repr., New York: HarperCollins, 2006). All citations are from this edition.

32. This is a loose translation of the "inversion" of allegory's split between words and meaning that "encod[es] our speech" (Fletcher, *Allegory,* 3). Fletcher states,

> The whole point of allegory is that it does not *need* to be read exegetically; it often has a literal level that makes good enough sense all by itself. But somehow this literal surface suggests a peculiar doubleness of intention, and while it can, as it were, get along without interpretation, it becomes much richer and more interesting if given interpretation. [. . .] What counts in our discussion is a structure that lends itself to a secondary reading, or rather, one that becomes stronger when given a secondary meaning as well as a primary meaning. (*Allegory,* 7)

combination of literary antecedents, with "modes of figuration lifted from the black vernacular tradition."[33] For example, Hurston's use of black vernacular ties her to the history of African American culture.[34] As Gates explains, "It is in the vernacular that, since slavery, the black person has encoded private yet communal cultural rituals."[35] In *Their Eyes*, African American linguistic practice also includes the storytelling style of "signifying," a word typically used in oral folklore to explain a trickster figure's use of verbal wit or (often veiled) insults to defeat a stronger power.[36] Gates defines it more generally as "the figurative difference between the literal and the metaphorical, between surface and latent meaning," which "presupposes an 'encoded' intention to say one thing but to mean quite another."[37] For linguistic anthropologist Claudia Mitchell-Kernan, this indirection of language defines signifying; it also shows how the metaphoric can then be extended to the level of allegory.[38]

At the same time, Hurston's text participates in a Caribbean or black diasporic tradition that is often linked to allegorical modes of writing. While Fredric Jameson once described "third-world literature" as being "necessarily allegorical" in reductive, nationalist terms, later scholars such as Roberto Strongman have modified this sweeping view, finding that "far from being a simplistic genre pronouncing literature from the area as elementary, allegory functions as a powerful anticolonial discursive mechanism exposing the need for personal and collective self-determination in the Caribbean."[39] Hurston's experience in the Caribbean, specifically in Haiti and Jamaica, in the 1930s also places her writing in the tradition that Sheri-Marie Harrison labels as the "first wave of West Indian writing," which extended from the 1930s to the

---

33. Gates, *The Signifying Monkey*, xxiii. Gates borrows the term "double-voiced" from Bahktin's discussion about specific words that should be understood on more than one semantic level (*Signifying Monkey*, 50). He also specifically names Hurston as using this trait: "This double voice unreconciled—a verbal analogue of [Hurston's] double experiences as a woman in a male-dominated world and as a black person in a nonblack world—strikes me as her second great achievement" ("A Negro Way of Saying," 3).

34. Some of Hurston's contemporaries were concerned that the black vernacular distanced a writer from politics and instead engaged with black minstrelsy. See James Weldon Johnson's preface (xxxix–xli) for the argument against the use of the black vernacular.

35. Gates, *The Signifying Monkey*, xix.

36. Although Gate's punctuates the term as "signifyin(g)" to highlight the orality that often drops the final "g" and its separation from the more general term of "signification" through capitalization (*Signifying Monkey*, 45), I employ its more common spelling since I am pulling together definitions from various sources.

37. Gates, *The Signifying Monkey*, 82. Hurston would agree, elaborating that African Americans' "interpretation of the English language is in terms of pictures. One act described in terms of another. Hence the rich metaphor and simile" ("Characteristics," 79).

38. Mitchell-Kernan, "Signifying, Loud-Talking and Marking," 310, 314–15.

39. Jameson, "Third-World Literature," 69; Strongman, "A Caribbean Response," n.p.

1960s.[40] As Sandra Pouchet Paquet explains, this type of diasporic allegory provides not just "self-inquiry [. . .] and self-evaluation" but also "cultural assessment," so that "the autobiographical self as subject is transformed into cultural archetype."[41] In this way, Hurston's choice of allegory for her novel embraces a sophisticated tool that developed in response to governmentalities of bare life and slavery and that extends beyond the boundaries of the United States.

Hurston's hybrid use of allegory in its European and black diasporic modes is itself a kind of Thirdspace, creating new possibilities from the interactions among cultures. *Their Eyes* employs it to challenge Western, specifically U.S., notions of law, citizenship, and ownership. As a writer interested in religious narratives, which a glance at her titles *Moses, Man on the Mountain*, and *Jonah's Gourd Vine* instantly reveals, it was logical for Hurston to employ allegory, a form used to interpret the Old and New Testaments. When Janie is expelled from her yard and the pear tree, for instance, on one level she simply is repeating the European biblical story about being expelled from Eden; however, on another level Hurston is challenging the Western tradition by reframing it through a major topic in black vernacular storytelling—undermining the master's asserted power of ownership over the slave—since Janie, a woman, is expelled from an Eden for seeking carnal knowledge and control of her own body, and in the process gains free will.[42] Hurston also uses the Western conception of allegorical peregrination—the notion that the pilgrimage functions as an allegory of human life, and the fall from grace in Eden marks humans as an exiled and diasporic people—to explore the limitations of black citizenship in the United States and the creation of community in the South. Following in the path of Dante and John Bunyan's Christian, Hurston's Janie takes on the role of the traveler, but her voyage forces an adjustment of the gendered and raced protagonist.[43] A black woman takes the literal and symbolic journey in Hurston's narrative; the novel's alternative ideology begins with a powerful shift in representative body and voice.

---

40. Harrison, *Jamaica's Difficult Subjects*, 7.

41. Paquet, "West Indian Autobiography," 359.

42. These common folktales include "Ole Massa" stories and the symbolic trickster animal stories, where the smaller animal often outwits a seemingly more powerful animal. See Hurston's own work in *Mules and Men* for some of these tales.

43. Griffin discusses other African American women in literature who were also "walkers" during this time period created by authors such as Ann Petry, Marita Bonner, and Gwendolyn Brooks, but even where the gender is shifted, the location of these examples still focused on the "urban landscapes" (*Toward an Intellectual History of Black Women*, 143), making Hurston's attention to the South of particular interest.

Hurston's mixing of Christian and African diasporic allegorical techniques allows her narrative to remain true to African Americans' painful past while expressing hope for the future that preserves rather than severs ties with the majority of black experience. In *Their Eyes* she demonstrates this new allegorical method and her interest in movement by bookending Janie's tale with two key images that reflect the interconnectedness of both space and time.

Mikhail Bakhtin's term "chronotope" is useful in understanding Hurston's method. A chronotope is a "unit of analysis for studying texts according to the ratio and nature of the temporal and spatial categories" to better understand "the cultural system from which they spring."[44] Consider, for example, how Hurston begins *Their Eyes* with the image of a ship in generalized, abstract language: "Ships at a distance have every man's wish on board. For some they come in with the tide. For others they sail on the horizon, never out of sight, never landing until the Watcher turns his eyes away in resignation, his dreams mocked to death by Time" (1). Functioning as a chronotope because the object both takes up space and moves through space over time, this ship, which is tied to unrealized hopes and dreams, evokes the ship image within the African diasporic tradition that is also laden with death and despair.[45] As Paul Gilroy explains in *The Black Atlantic*, this most famous of chronotopes, "refer[s] us back to the middle passage, to the half-remembered micro-politics of the slave trade and its relationship to both industrialization and modernization."[46] By invoking the image of a ship as the book's first idea, Hurston locates her work as engaging with the history of slavery and the slave trade, and announces migration as a central, if not the central, concern in *Their Eyes*.

Even though Hurston employs this chronotope that demonstrates the significance of African diasporic history to her narrative, she does not wish to remain within this space of violence and oppression or of white-defined and white-controlled migration. According to Hurston's use of the symbolic slave ship, "the life of men" (1) stays forever with that image, their dreams "mocked to death" (1).[47] Her response, however, is not to get stuck waiting for that ship

---

44. Bakhtin, *The Dialogic Imagination*, 425–26.

45. She used the phrase "slave ships in shoes" to talk about the results of poverty on some individuals (Carla Kaplan, *Zora Neale Hurston*, 17).

46. Gilroy, *The Black Atlantic*, 17.

47. As Tiffany Ruby Patterson says of Hurston's representation of African American experiences and those of her critics:

> Hurston's eyes were watching those atrocities, but her eyes were open to other aspects of the lives of southern black folk as well. Unlike her detractors, who preferred to view black people in relation to whites, Hurston sought first and foremost to study black people on their own terms. Although she recognized oppression as a daily fact of African American life, Hurston's literary and ethnographic work

to arrive, because for women "the dream is the truth and they act and do things accordingly" (1). Rather than watching the hopeless images of "industrialization and modernization," Hurston and the female protagonist of her text remember the past but also actively move into a new and different present and future through space and time—themselves taking on a chronotopic role that eventually reaches the horizon.[48]

Instead of *dwelling* in the place of oppression—and there are still key moments when whites arrive to threaten and harm her characters as symbols of the government at large—Hurston fights oppression by writing about the positive and negative elements of black life as defined by black people themselves. By engaging with the possibilities within the African American community, she attempts not to focus exclusively on the death that she sees tied to the return to the idea of the slave ship and the oppressive governmentality it signifies. She acknowledges and presents the history of slavery. Through these kinds of symbolic moments, she reveals the external forces that created an enslaved, bare life and continue to create precarious lives, yet she wants to free blacks from the death of the slave ships by also talking about the potential within the African American community and the power of the mind to imagine beyond that past into the possibilities of the future.

Hurston transforms the chronotope of the slave ship into something positive through her repetition of the image of the horizon, the image that ultimately concludes Janie's journey. Indeed, with the word "horizon" appearing in her opening sentences, its repetition throughout the text reveals it as an alternative chronotope.[49] The horizon, like the slave ship, breaks down traditional boundaries: as the place where the land or sea meets the sky, it is itself always moving based on a viewer's location.[50] Additionally, it contains a tem-

---

focused more on what black people were doing for themselves than on what their oppressors and tormentors were doing to them. Her contrarian gaze moved black people to the center of inquiry, establishing them as subjects, a place reserved for white people in the dominant race-relations paradigm in African American history and thought. (*Zora Neale Hurston*, 6)

48. Hurston herself stated, "I do not belong to the sobbing school of Negrohood who hold that nature somehow has given them a low-down dirty deal and whose feelings are all but about it. [. . .] No, I do not weep at the world—I am too busy sharpening my oyster knife" ("How It Feels," 115).

49. In the original holograph that I was able to see at the Beinecke Library at Yale University, the first lines of the novel were crossed out and rewritten with edits on the front side of the first page as well as on its reverse. Even so, the words "ships" and "horizon" remain throughout this process, revealing them to be key words as Hurston developed her overall idea.

50. This focus on the horizon also points to her interest in how black culture extended beyond national boundaries. Additionally, this curiosity about the horizon appears in her autobiographical novel *Dust Tracks on a Road*: "The most interesting thing that I saw was the hori-

poral element, often referred to in the text, in that its spatial location marks the passage of time—the setting and rising of the sun and the potential of that passage of time.

Thus, unlike the predetermined meaning of the slave ship that is rigidly self-contained, the positive or negative possibilities of the horizon are expansive and shift according to the individual's viewpoint. Each person's position in time and space affects how the horizon is seen. Janie, and by extension the reader, learns from the many perspectives on the horizon that she encounters, enabling her to find her own definition that stems from, but also expands beyond, those presented to her. The first mention of the horizon is associated with the ship in the opening lines of the novel, showing the direct connection between two elements: slave ships come from the horizon. But then, while Janie's horizon still includes the ships of slavery, her perspective also humanizes those who would have been on such vessels since she eventually realizes the journey of her life would be "to the horizons in search of *people*" (89). Unlike the men in the initial image of the novel, whose goal remains forever at a distance, Janie completes her goal: "Ah done been tuh de horizon and back and now Ah kin set heah in mah house and live by comparisons" (191). By the end of the Janie's journey, as I will explain, Hurston expands upon the chronotope of the horizon to emphasize the importance of being true to the oppression of history while also stressing how people might live with hope for the future and themselves by thinking about a new relationship to space and movement.[51] As Strongman explains regarding the history of European colonization,

> One of the ambitions of the state has always been to establish a certain "territory" as its referent [. . . .] But what is often overlooked is the way in which identity is location as well, one that finds its coordinates within the sphere of the nation. Critical theory interprets the subject's mapping of its community and nation as "Who am I?" when the more appropriate interpretation is: "Where am I?"[52]

In Hurston's narrative of Janie's movement as a means of defining her identity, the images of the (slave) ship and horizon are especially effectual because they exceed the boundaries of an isolated U.S. history, pointing elliptically to

zon. Every way I turned, it was there, and the same distance away. Our house then, was in the center of the world. It grew upon me that I ought to walk out to the horizon and see what the end of the world was like" (27).

51. It is not surprising that she wrote *Their Eyes* while in Haiti, where a successful slave rebellion took place. She was immersed in a location filled with the history of slavery but also filled with a community that threw off that yoke.

52. Strongman, "A Caribbean Response," n.p.

the triangle trade and the black experience in the Caribbean and thus unsettling dominant narratives of oppressive governmentalities through counterexamples such as Haiti, which rejected colonial control via its successful slave rebellion.

By beginning and ending the novel with the symbolic chronotopes of the slave ship and the horizon, respectively, Hurston indicates to the reader that Janie's physical journey will also explore African American history and movement allegorically. Janie's story starts with a prolepsis: "She had come back from burying the dead" (1). This is followed by the harsh judgment of the people watching her return to town. These first steps of the protagonist inform the reader that this story is about travel and the complexity of community. The narrative then re-embarks with Janie relaying her story to her friend Pheoby, starting with her as a teenager in the Edenic space outside her grandmother's house. This telling rewrites the entire history of Judeo-Christian theology, placing an African American teenager as Eve under a "blossoming pear tree" (10). In this version the snake who tempts this new "Eve" is a neighboring boy whom Janie kisses "across the gatepost" (13). Janie sits in Eden alone because, as the novel tells us, "the beginning of this was a woman" (1). Located "in the place of, taking the world-creating place of the Word of God," Janie/Eve precedes Adam.[53] Gynocentrically, this narrative starts at the very beginning of a recreated Judeo-Christian time and space. With the foreshadowing of the biblical story, the narrative prolepsis reveals that Janie will be cast out from Eden to wander on her own so as to control her own body and space, in contrast to what was possible for her grandmother and mother before her. By understanding Janie's counter-migratory journey as an allegory and in terms of Thirdspace, we are able to see that Hurston's novel revises Western tradition and uses African diasporic history productively for future empowerment.

UNFREE CITIZENSHIP: SHARECROPPING AND OPPRESSIVE OWNERSHIP

The farming system known as sharecropping seemed to offer economic independence to African Americans after the Civil War and the Thirteenth Amendment. In reality, however, sharecropping in several ways was simply an extension of slavery because of its combination of a lack of ownership with the exploitation of black labor. These elements produced a precarious existence in which black workers could not earn enough money to buy land, instead remaining continuously indebted to the landowners. Even politicians of the

---

53. DuPlessis, "Power," 90.

time, such as George W. Julian, chairman of the House Committee on Public Lands, saw that without a breaking up of the "land monopoly," the newly freed would be trapped in "a system of wages slavery . . . more galling than slavery itself."[54]

Their Eyes engages with the system of sharecropping and its connection to slavery in a complex, allegorical fashion. Previous scholars have been divided on the symbolism of Janie's first marriage to Logan Killicks and her work on his farm. DuPlessis states, "In fact, allegorically speaking, this marriage is an image of slavery," while Willis claims that Janie marries into the sharecropping system that followed the end of slavery.[55] I posit that Hurston represents both sharecropping and slavery because she, as well as many other scholars, saw sharecropping as a new form of slavery. Allegorically, Janie's marriage moves her forward into the historical economy of sharecropping that replaced the economy of slavery, but she will continue to be worked like those who came before her under slavery because, although the system shifted, the governmental treatment of African Americans did not.

The plot of this section can be read allegorically, as can the names of the characters. For Janie, Logan Killicks is a double weight around her neck since his last name means a stone used as an anchor and his first name is similar to logan stone, a stone that rocks with the slightest touch but cannot be dislodged with any force. Though Killicks is not the most obvious allegorical agent in Janie's life, he does embody abstract ideas.[56] The initial "weight" Janie feels is her lack of passion for him, putting her in the position of her mother and grandmother: "Ah wants to want him sometimes. Ah don't want him to do all de wantin'" (23). Janie wishes to claim her desire for herself since the history of slavery prevented its free articulation. Her grandmother, however, misconstrues Janie's view because she believes the sole goal of a woman must be to attain a "lawful husband same as Mis' Washburn [i.e., a white woman] or anybody else!" (22). She thinks marriage will free Janie, but without love there is little chance for equality between the partners. In this marriage the forced sexuality of slavery is reinscribed.

Although Killicks seems pliable as both a rocking stone and a stone in water may at first appear, his heavy weight holds Janie down and ties her to a past that she wishes to escape. This burden becomes obvious in his desire

---

54. Foner, *Reconstruction*, 68. Hurston's own family "rejected sharecropping as an improved version of unfree labor and looked for a place to create a self-determined life" (Lucy Anne Hurston, *Speak*, 6). Hurston was born into a family that worked on sharecropping cotton. Only after she was born did they move to Eatonville, where her father eventually became a reverend.

55. DuPlessis, "Power," 90; Willis, *Signifying*, 46.

56. Fletcher, *Allegory*, 26.

to work her in the field. DuPlessis comments, "It is significant that as she leaves the marriage, Janie was about to become Killicks's third mule and be put behind a plow."[57] He plans to return her to the field labor of slavery, where she and the mule she leads are both property used for labor. In this marriage, rather than gaining what her grandmother hopes, she takes on the role of "de mule uh de world" (14) that her grandmother wished she would have escaped. On the literal level, Killicks is a pathetic man who does not understand how to create a relationship with a wife, but allegorically, he stands as a landowner with sixty acres and a mule (he has more than was promised and retracted by the North at the end of the Civil War). Janie, by comparison, does not truly own the organ in her parlor, which was a high sign of Victorian womanhood, or the parlor it is in, or the land itself.[58] As a woman, she does not share in that ownership; she is just asked to share in the labor. Killicks promises his worker a portion of the fruits of the labor at the start—as was the case under sharecropping—but does not fulfill even that meager promise. Instead, like Southern blacks after the Civil War, Janie finds that little has changed through sharecropping, with her economic subordination maintained, her access to landownership limited, and her private life regulated.[59] Some of the dialogue also demonstrates that this new system functions as another rendition of slavery, with Killicks as the slave master unwilling to allow his slave her own independence; he precisely accuses her of being too "powerful independent around here" (30). The language escalates from there; for instance, Janie warns Killicks she might "run off" (30) from this life, using the terminology of fugitive slaves. Shortly thereafter, when she attempts to show her ability to rule her own body, he threatens, "Ah'll take holt uh dat ax and come in dere and kill yuh!" (31). Sharecropping too closely resembles slavery and the oppression created via this economic and legal system. Janie's experience with Killicks ties her to the culture and pain of the past; as she loses faith in the life Killicks can give her, "she beg[ins] to stand around the gate and expect things" (25), challenging the barriers around her by spending her time near a door that opens onto new spaces and possibilities away from the powers holding her back. She seizes her first chance to escape when Jody Starks arrives.

---

57. DuPlessis, "Power," 90.

58. Domosh and Seager, *Putting Women in Place*, 13. This use of the piano symbol will also be seen in chapter 2.

59. Reich, *A Working People*, 10, 17.

THE TALENTED TENTH: REPLICATING THE GOVERNMENTAL STRUCTURES OF THE PLANTATION

When Janie turns to Jody to flee her new enslavement, she escapes her current position by marrying him and moving to Eatonville. In Eatonville, which historically was Hurston's childhood home and one of the first all-black towns, the possibility for the escape from older forms of governmentality seems possible through self-governance, yet this promise fails through an elitism that replicates white hierarchical structures.[60] Based on the timeline for Janie's birth, it can be calculated that at this point in the text it is now the turn of the century. Therefore, while Jody epitomizes the "nascent black bourgeoisie," as Willis generally labels it, even more specifically in his actions and circumstances he represents the theories of W. E. B. Du Bois, which Hurston criticizes in the text and opposed in her life.[61]

In his approach to existence, Jody haughtily embodies the qualities of Du Bois's idea of the Talented Tenth. "The Negro race," Du Bois states in *The Negro Problem*, published in 1903, around the moment of Jody's arrival in the text, "like all other races, is going to be saved by its exceptional men," and these exceptional men are "the educated and intelligent of the Negro people that have led and elevated the mass."[62] Embracing the notion that the educated elite should lift the black masses, Jody positions himself as part of this upper echelon through his demonstration of his education and his ability to lead. Although his place of education is never stipulated, the novel states, "he was more literate than the rest [of the townspeople]" (47). He is also interested in helping "uplift" his community by bringing his money and education to Eatonville:

> He had always wanted to be a big voice, but de white folks had all de sayso where he come fro and everywhere else, exceptin' dis place dat colored folks was buildin' theirselves. Dat was right too. De man, dat built things oughta boss it. Let colored folks build things too if dey wants to crow over somethin'. (28)

Jody wants to help start this black community so it can run itself and have something of its own. Nevertheless, his travel to create "uplift" that might

60. Hurston herself wrote about Eatonville in her unpublished documents for the Federal Writers Project, "The Negro in Florida, 1528–1940," 120–21. Although she only briefly discusses it, she states its self-governance. Thanks to the National Humanities Center and Brooke Andrade specifically for helping me to access this document from the Florida State Archives.

61. Willis, *Signifying*, 47.

62. Du Bois, "The Talented Tenth," 33–34.

yield egalitarian self-ownership is undermined by Jody's own self-interest. His desire to be a "big voice" seems to outweigh his desire to help the black community to take ownership of their own work.[63] His "exceptional" education makes him believe he is superior to others, which they notice: "'Whut Ah don't lak 'bout de man is, he talks tuh unlettered folks wid books in his jaws,' Hicks complained. 'Showin' off his learnin'" (49).[64] He also uses his money to gain a position of authority. He buys land for the town and is promptly named as mayor, the person who "tells ya'll what to do" (35), Jody's own definition of the job.

In Hurston's novel, Jody is a satire of the Talented Tenth because of his pompous self-interest in power for himself instead of "lifting up" the rest of the black community. If anything, Jody is taking on an old, familiar position: when others hear him, they say he is acting like "a section foreman" (35) and that "you kin feel a switch in his hand when he's talkin' to yuh" (49). He even gets townspeople to build a drainage ditch for the road, causing the community to whisper about the issue directly in play here: "They had murmured hotly about slavery being over" (47). As DuPlessis notes, although Hurston may have stated elsewhere that slavery "occurred in the past and [was] of no particular concern to her," her writing demonstrates precisely how she acknowledges that past and the ways in which it remains within U.S. culture.[65]

Hurston argues through her characterization of Jody that the exceptional man runs the risk of reinscribing the hierarchy of slavery by substituting himself for the white master and sole arbiter of governmental authority, thereby undermining the will of those around him. Jody's attitude demonstrates his desire to take on the role of whites from the first time Janie sees him: "He was a seal-brown color but he acted like Mr. Washburn [i.e., a white man] or somebody like that to Janie" (27), and he was "kind of portly like rich white folks" (45). At first his demeanor suggests to Janie that he has lofty goals, but as time goes on, both she and the community see that he takes on the role of whites and does not share the authority he has gained.

The house that Jody has built for himself spatializes this reinstitutionalization of the slave system:

---

63. He also seems unaware of the irony that of course "colored folks" had long been building things and that he was setting out not to build something for himself but to have others do it for him.

64. While Hurston makes no direct comment on education here, focusing instead on the idea of being "elite," education is far from untouched by this book, starting with Janie's own inception through her mother's rape by a teacher. The educational system holds threats to blacks in its current state.

65. DuPlessis, "Power," 99n25.

It had two stories with porches, with banisters and such things. The rest of the town looked like servants' quarters surrounding the "big house." And different from everybody else in the town he put off moving in until it had been painted, in and out. And look at the way he painted it—a gloaty, sparkly white. The kind of promenading white that the houses of Bishop Whipple, W. B. Jackson and the Vanderpool's wore. (47)

Adding to this allegorical identification of Jody's home with a plantation house, this house is even painted like the homes of the prominent whites of the area, broadcasting Jody's desire for the power of whiteness in its color. Even his spittoon is an attempt at emulation: "[He] [s]aid it was a spittoon just like his used-to-be bossman used to have in his bank up there in Atlanta" (47); the gold-colored vase helps him take on the role of the white boss. Jody governs like a slave master but his righteousness about his black elite power comes from his enactment of Du Bois's theories. More dangerously, Jody's ownership of his house and of Janie does not critique dominant views linking landownership to citizenship or create a Thirdspace of egalitarian opportunity. Instead, Jody focuses on purchasing land, incorporating the town, getting a post office, and building a store so that he may economically and politically dominate his neighbors as mayor, replicating governmental structures previously imposed by whites.

Overall, Hurston rejects the "uplift" idea of the Talented Tenth that undermines the potential of anyone other than that top 10 percent. As scholars such as Jerome Thornton have shown, Hurston "urged that lower class African Americans had something better to offer."[66] In her own words, turning Du Bois's language against him, Hurston states, "Everybody is already resigned to the 'exceptional' Negro, and willing to be entertained by the 'quaint,'" but "the average, struggling, nonmorbid [sic] Negro is the best-kept secret in America."[67] She wants to look at not the exception but the rule.

Not only is the community hurt by Du Bois's theory under the rule of Jody, but so too is Janie. For her, Jody's desire to be the boss of his people also places her in a new servitude. Although she has the economic benefits that her grandmother intended for her, her husband is viewed as the owner of their property and home with "that new house of his" (47). He is the one who "walks in the way of power and property" (48), and he commands her interactions with the community. She is merely a display for Jody, with him requiring her to act in an elite manner that prohibits her from sitting on the porch with her neighbors. Jody "class[es] her off" (112), telling her to "look

66. Thornton, "The Paradoxical Journey," 743.
67. Hurston, "What White Publishers Won't Print," 121.

on herself as the bell-cow, the other women [as] the gang" (41). Then, when the townspeople ask her to make a speech, Jody says, "mah wife don't know nothin' 'bout no speech-makin.' Ah never married her for nothin' lak dat. She's uh woman and her place is in de home" (43). Even as the top black men lead the way, following Du Bois's idea, Janie is told that she cannot be part of the grand project. She has instead become Jody's ornament, the wife of an elite man "against the honor of whose womanhood no breath was ever raised."[68] Women are overlooked for their exceptionality except in their chastity. Like Du Bois, who was twenty-three years Hurston's senior, the much older Jody wants to assume a powerful and protective role over his young wife, a hierarchical positioning that demonstrates in Hurston's view the problem of Du Bois's theory for the African American community in general and for African American women specifically.

Janie resists this subjugation by trying to connect to and support her community through a literal engagement with black vernacular storytelling, which symbolically results in the destruction of Jody and the power structure he represents. Although her husband "has forbidden her to indulge" (54) in the conversations of the community, and in a type of signifying called the dozens where two people trade insults, she still learns how this kind of communication works by listening to the "big picture talkers [. . .] using a side of the world for a canvas" (54). As DuPlessis points out, "Janie's alienation from her marriage [with Jody] is marked by her growing identification with folk life, its contests and rituals, its pleasures and its narrative skills."[69] Eventually Janie manages to rise up on her own, even though Jody as an "uplifter" is ironically trying to keep her down. She defeats his silencing power over her by claiming her right to speak in the ways of the people. She devastates his "big voice" by using her voice and her knowledge of the dozens against him. He tries to humiliate her by saying that she looks old, and she tells him: "You big-bellies round here and put out a lot of brag, but 'tain't nothin' to it but yo' big voice. Humph! Talk' 'bout *me* lookin' old! When you pull down yo' britches, you look lak de change uh life" (79). By imagining him as *stark* naked, she strips away the layers of pretense derived from his view of his education, house, and attitude; she stakes her claim as one of the people. This striking blow deflates the idea that his position as the elite, as the one in the "rulin' chair" (87), gives him the right to control everyone else. Starks, aptly named as being hard and unyielding but powerful, leads to barrenness and desolation. Janie's defiance in effect "kills" him, and she then moves on to new spaces and interactions that

---

68. Du Bois, "The Talented Tenth," 44.
69. DuPlessis, *Writing beyond the Ending*, 156.

show how African American communities should work away from the forces of the white hierarchy.

After Jody's death, Janie finds that her real desire is expressed through travel and community: "She had been getting ready for her great journey to the horizons in search of *people*; it was important to all the world that she should find them and they find her" (89). Her journey becomes a reciprocal one focused on humanity and culture instead of this "back road after *things*" (89) that only creates hierarchies. She also acknowledges that she has been tied to the past of slavery—even with Jody—because instead of being treated as an individual with "a jewel down inside herself" (90), "she had been set in the market-place to sell" (90). She has been treated as an object to be bought and sold all her life, and she is determined to escape from that objectified and oppressed role. She quickly begins to bask in her new role: "Ah jus' loves dis freedom" (93). She sees her new life without Jody as a possible escape from yet another form of slavery. The ideas of Du Bois and their reinscription of the elitist white power dynamic do not contain the answers that Janie—or the black community—needs for full independence and citizenship.

Rereading moments in African American history through Hurston's allegorical migration narrative does not simply repeat or romanticize historical events; instead, the symbolic reconfiguration of evidence to show the problems and repetitions within that history allows Hurston and her reader to envision future possibilities for community and self that can lead to a Thirdspace that imagines autonomy. Just as sharecropping failed to replace slavery with a system that enabled full black autonomy and an escape from precarity, so too does the oppression of black people by other blacks merely replicate preexisting governmental structures without providing independence for the whole community.

EGALITARIAN OWNERSHIP AMONG THE FOLK

When a new man, Tea Cake, appears in Janie's life, he connects her to the folk and rural space and seems to be moving her away from the white power structure. Tea Cake's full name is Vergible Woods, and, like Virgil in Dante's *Inferno,* he helps guide Janie through the woods back to herself. The allusions to the *Inferno* continue throughout their experience. For instance, when he is away from her, it is like the nine circles of hell: "He did not return that night nor the next and so she plunged into the abyss and descended to the ninth darkness where light has never been" (108). By patterning Tea Cake after an emblematic example from a traditional allegory, the relevance of allegorical peregrination for *Their Eyes*'s structure is again stressed.

As with the previous example of Janie's expulsion from Eden, however, Hurston constructs Tea Cake by combining Western and African diasporic traditions, using the signifying allegory to revise expected narrative patterns. Tea Cake is more than a guide from classical literature, since he represents the African American culture Janie seeks. His name itself shows this doubling role: his formal name may tie him to classical literature, but his nickname, Tea Cake, refers to a Southern sugar cookie. In this figurative way, he is the sweetness of African American folk culture that Hurston sees as being rooted in the South. Tea Cake embodies the community that Janie seeks socially, and through him she more fully explores rural, Southern, black life, if only temporarily.

Tea Cake and Janie's relationship models the egalitarianism of the ideal African American community that escapes the white model of hierarchy, patriarchy, and subjugation. Unlike Jody, Tea Cake includes Janie in his game playing. When they first meet, he teaches her to play checkers: "Somebody wanted her to play. Somebody thought it natural for her to play" (96). He respects her and asks her to take part in the culture around her. He does not belittle her like Jody did; instead, he says, "You got good meat on yo' head" (96). Tea Cake helps her find a cultural center for herself, and the way they interact illustrates the potential for an equal relationship both in terms of heterosexual partnership and women's inclusion in cultural activities. Together they play games, fish, and cook, and they both get pleasure out of their interactions. She likes it when he brushes her hair, but he also likes doing it. Later when they are fleeing from the hurricane, they both help each other: "Tea Cake bore her up," and then "Janie held him up" (164). They support and include each other reciprocally; Janie needs her culture, and her culture needs her.

Hurston's allegory of women's full participation in black culture continues in Janie's linguistic connection to Tea Cake. Tea Cake stands as a representation of the importance of storytelling—of signifying—to the African American tradition in that he both tells stories and enables Janie to develop her own storytelling skills. When Janie first meets Tea Cake, he says hello to her "with a sly grin as if they had a good joke together. She was in favor of the story that was making him laugh before she even heard it" (94). Although there is no actual "story," Tea Cake is immediately connected to the idea of stories, an association furthered when he opens his mouth to request a match: "You got a lil piece uh fire over dere, lady?" (95). His metaphoric diction turns even a simple question into a signifying one about whether she is aware of her own potential—her own internal fire.

While showing her her own potential, Tea Cake teaches Janie new ways to use language. As they get to know each other, she says that Tea Cake "done taught me de maiden language all over" (115). This "maiden language" refers directly to her courtship but also recalls and corrects her teenage "expulsion from Eden" for her sexualized thoughts, returning her to a prelapsarian space while allowing for female sexual desire and an African American paradise. Tea Cake helps with this connection by getting her in touch with the figurative possibilities of language, as we see when she explains her relationship with Tea Cake to her friend Pheoby in a rhythmic and slant-rhyming couplet: "Some of dese mornin's and it won't be long, you gointuh wake up callin' me and Ah'll be gone" (115). This is the first time that Janie uses rhyme, revealing that Tea Cake has enabled her to recognize her own internal fire, thus preparing her for their literal marriage, which signifies her long-sought-after connection to the black community.[70]

Although this marriage between the individual and the imagined folk community is realized in their union, as DuPlessis has commented, Janie's link to a lived community only begins to be realized when they move to the Florida Everglades to work as migrant agricultural laborers, a common practice at the time.[71] This movement to the Everglades, the center of the state's agricultural zone as well as a center for black culture, shows both Janie's progression in learning about her community now that she is no longer restrained from doing so and the continued oppression experienced by that community with her awareness of the governmental precarity of such work and such spaces.

MIGRANT LABOR AND THE SHIFTING ROLE OF MOVEMENT: LIVING ON THE MUCK

Hurston focuses on this migrant community in Florida to symbolize the very thing it is—a contemporary phase of black labor often overlooked by those focused on the urbanization caused by the Great Migration. This economic migration began in the United States shortly after the start of World War I, and from the teens through the '30s over one-and-a-half-million African Americans moved from the South to the North.[72] Their reasons varied from

---

70. Various critics such as DuPlessis have remarked on this connection: "Through Tea Cake, Janie becomes one with the black folk community; indeed, marrying Tea Cake is a way of marrying that community" (*Writing beyond the Ending*, 157).

71. DuPlessis, *Writing beyond the Ending*, 157.

72. Lemann, *The Promised Land*, 6. Historian Carole Marks explains that this kind of movement—what she called a labor migration—differs from other migrations that are more traditionally about moving to the frontier: "Labor migrations represent a modern form of population movement in which workers, in search of employment, are encouraged to move from

seeking work on the railroad, fleeing cotton land destroyed by the boll wee-
vil, taking advantage of labor shortages caused by the slowing of immigration
during World War I, and hoping to earn higher wages and more freedom.[73]
The out-migration from the South was not as swift as migrations enforced by
a major natural disaster or government decree. Rather, the economic migration lasted for multiple decades. It changed the racial and cultural makeup of
the country and affected economic possibilities, resulting in "nearly one-tenth
of the African-American population of the United States [. . .] mov[ing] from
the South to the North."[74]

African Americans began to move in massive numbers starting in this
period, but the Great Migration did not just lead to the North. Historian Cindy
Hahamovitch states, "By the 1920s African Americans outnumbered all other
ethnic groups in the East's migrant population."[75] Although some migrated to
the North permanently, others were trapped in a cyclical pattern once urban
jobs became scarcer, requiring their return to the South for seasonal work.
These migrants, who also included significant numbers of immigrating blacks
from the Bahamas—further broadening the idea of the Great Migration to
include a transnational pattern of migration—became part of the growing
population of the "'permanent transient,' the migrant farmworker who had
no sharecrop arrangement to return to, no state of residence, and no home to
speak of."[76] The migrants moving south regressed even further than sharecrop-

---

less developed peripheries to more developed cores" (*Farewell*, 4). In this case, the South is the
peripheral society with abundant workers and the North is the core with a need for workers.

73. Marks, *Farewell*, 2–3. Others have underscored the reasons that extended beyond economic motives, stressing the agency of these migrants. Farah Jasmine Griffin argues that additional reasons are made clear in the black artwork of the time, showing that the move north
would take away their "blues" in their various guises, whether caused by the violence of the
South, Jim Crow, or a woman—basically migration would remove the "psychological state of
someone who is exploited, abused, dominated, and dispossessed," and they chose to flee that
oppression (Griffin, "*Who Set You Flowin'?*" 19).

74. Marks, "Great Migration," n.p.

75. Hahamovitch, *The Fruits of Their Labor*, 114.

76. Ibid., 114–15. On the Bahaman migrant labor, see Raymond A. Mohl, "Black Immigrants" and Howard Johnson, "Bahamian Labor Migration to Florida." In general, it is worth
noting, as Mohl points out, that the National Origins Act of 1924 that was used to limit nonwhite immigration did not affect Bahamian immigration to Florida in the long term because
the Bahamas was considered under Britain's quota, and Britain never filled its annual 65,000
emigrant quota to the United States. The idea of temporary migration also grew with six-
month work permits ("Black Immigrants," 292). This continued until the negotiation of the
guest worker program in the 1940s that included Mexico as well as the British West Indies.
These immigrants could work in the United States but without the hope of citizenship and with
the threat of being sent back if they did anything that would be seen as breaking their contract. See Hahamovitch, "Slavery's Stale Soil," 246, 251. This program will be discussed further
in chapter 4 because "the fact that guestworkers couldn't build up a permanent, legal, settler

ping because they did not own anything—not the land, not a portion of the crops. Their drudgery may have been paid, but the working conditions were too similar to slavery's lack of citizenship rights to ignore. A key difference in this broader view of the Great Migration, however, is the role of movement, the restriction of which was a sign of dependency under slavery. Rather than movement representing greater freedom after World War I, the results of such movement to northern cities often offered only an illusory freedom because of the labor conditions and limitations on housing and citizenship there. In the South, by contrast, the constancy of movement in the migrant laborers' lives meant that the older link between a lack of citizenship and a lack of move-ment changed while the lack of landownership remained constant. Hurston's text calls attention to this shift, which diminishes the rights of those unable to remain stationary, via the plight of African American migrant workers in the South who have few rights during their daily labor and even fewer when their economic displacement becomes an environmental displacement under a state of emergency. While the United Nations' codification of the categories of the refugee and the internally displaced person was still many years away, Hurston's depiction of the September 16–17, 1928, Okeechobee Hurricane and its destruction and displacement of the black migrant community shows how the United States gave little attention to the rights and protections of inter-national workers and of its own citizens because of their race. Without the greater awareness of past displacements afforded by treatments such as Hur-ston's, we will fail to see their connections to ideologies of ownership as well as imagined solutions to them.

Hurston, who may have coined the oxymoronic term "permanent tran-sients" herself—in my view a likely possibility given her engagement with migratory discourse and since I am unaware of any earlier usage in con-temporary writing—applied it to the labor force in *Their Eyes*. Janie and Tea Cake watch as these migrants arrive in the Everglades. The initial description of these migrants illustrates their need as they come from all directions for work—the migration is not unidirectional, nor even contained to only those originally from the United States:

> Some came limping in with their shoes and sore feet from walking. It's hard trying to follow your shoe instead of your shoe following you. They came in wagons from way up in Georgia and they came in truck loads from east,

---

population meant they couldn't wield the rights of subjects or citizens in their own defense" (Hahamovitch, "Slavery's Stale Soil," 255). This statement about the status of Bahaman laborers under this later program shows ways that citizenship and power were withheld from people of color long after this moment in time.

west, north and south. Permanent transients with no attachments and tired looking men with their families and dogs in flivvers. All night, all day, hurrying in to pick beans. Skillets, beds, patched up spare inner tubes all hanging and dangling from the ancient cars on the outside and hopeful humanity, herded and hovered on the inside, chugging on to the muck. People ugly from ignorance and broken from being poor. (131)

Out of their desperate search for work comes a positive sense of community, but because it is precarious as well as rooted in shared hardship and oppression, it is far from ideal. We see their "sore feet" and their exhaustion so that when Hurston says that "the jooks clanged and clamored" (131), we understand their use of entertainment as a release from their pain, not an erasure of it.[77]

This segment addresses the role of the rural South in the history of the 1920s and the precarity of African Americans who occupy temporary, overcrowded spaces that they do not own. Janie and Tea Cake's house may be "full of people every night" (133), but crowded quarters are also part of quotidian existence on the muck. Tea Cake warns Janie: "Two weeks from now, it'll be so many folks heah dey won't be lookin' fuh rooms, dey'll be jus' looking fuh somewhere tuh sleep. [. . .] Yuh can't live on de muck 'thout yuh take uh bath every day. Do dat muck'll itch yuh lak ants" (129). Historians explain that the area is called the muck because of the rich, dark soil found there, but much of this soil was only exposed to the air and the plow at the turn of the twentieth century when canals were dug to drain the swampland and part of Lake Okeechobee.[78] In this respect, the development of the land shows the large-scale environmental effects prompted by capitalist governmentalities that seek increasing profits and power while diminishing the rights and opportunities

---

77. Hurston shows her awareness of life in Florida for blacks, including farm laborers and their means to entertainment, from singing to jook joints and gambling. However, she states, "There is little provision for diversion for this underprivileged class" ("The Negro in Florida," 79).

78. Kleinberg, *Black Cloud,* 5 and Mykle, *Killer 'Cane,* 18. Thinking back to how Hurston and Du Bois were at odds in their philosophies, Gates gives a nice example about how they use the space of the swamp distinctly:

> The trope of the swamp, furthermore, in *Their Eyes* signifies exactly the opposite of what it does in Du Bois's *Quest for the Silver Fleece.* Whereas the swamp in Du Bois's text figures an uncontrolled chaos that must be plowed under and controlled, for Hurston the swamp is the trope of the freedom of erotic love, the antithesis of the bourgeois life and order that her protagonist flees but to which Du Bois's protagonists aspire. Whereas Du Bois's characters gain economic security by plowing up and cultivating cotton in the swamp, Janie flees the bourgeois life that Du Bois's characters realize, precisely by abandoning traditional values for the uncertainties and the potential chaos of the uncultivated, untamed swamp, where love and death linger side by side. Du Bois's shadowy figure who seems to dwell in the swamp, we recall, is oddly enough named Zora. (*Signifying Monkey,* 193)

for raced, poor workers to own anything and to remain stationary. While the land provided economic independence for landowners, for the migrant workers who labored in the fields, "the rich black earth cling[s] to bodies and bit[es] the skin like ants" (131). The black earth, like their black labor, has been manipulated by capitalism into a force that is destructive to them and is productive for someone else. Hurston may use descriptive language, but the text still reveals the ways in which space and movement are used to continue the disempowered position of migrant labor in the South.

While this economic migration marks a general shift in the value of movement from freedom to oppression, it is also true that the places migrants occupy often trap them when catastrophe strikes, since then rapid movement becomes necessary in an environmental migration but is exceedingly difficult for the poor. Hurston accurately recounts a great devastation to the temporary location of these migrants. In a direct historical allusion, she recounts the hurricane that hit Lake Okeechobee and breached the dike, sending a wall of water that enveloped the entire area and left the forty-mile region from Belle Glade to West Palm Beach separated by water for days.[79] An estimated 2,500 to 3,000 people were killed. This second-deadliest hurricane in the United States killed almost fifty percent of the area's population, including many undocumented workers who lived near the levees with no means of escape.[80] Historian Robert Mykle notes that at the time of the hurricane

few gave any consideration as to what the black migrant workers would do. They had nowhere to go and no cars to carry them to safety, they could not

---

79. Mykle, *Killer 'Cane*, 205.

80. Ibid., 213. The deadliest hurricane was in 1900, which killed an estimated 8,000 people in Galveston, Texas (Blake et al., "The Deadliest," 7). While numbers fluctuate between organizations, the death totals for Hurricane Katrina, which swept the Gulf Coast in 2005, directly compare with the U.S. totals for the 1928 hurricane, with the death toll range from just under 2,000 to just under 3,000 (Knabb, Rhome, and Brown, "Tropical Cyclone Report," 11, and Louisiana Department of Health and Hospitals, "Hurricane Katrina"). Only two years before Katrina, while marking the 75th anniversary of the 1928 hurricane, the National Hurricane Center adjusted its numbers for the San Felipe/Okeechobee Hurricane to 2,500 but stated that the numbers could have been as high as 3,000 (Klinkenberg, "Unmarked but Not Unmourned" and Blake et al., "The Deadliest," 7). This recent discussion of the hurricane, however, did not prepare the country for Katrina, a storm reminiscent in many ways of the 1928 hurricane. Even the newly adjusted casualty numbers underestimate the overall impact of this storm, since deaths in Puerto Rico, Guadaloupe, and other parts of the Caribbean are not included in the number listed above. The possible number of deaths could have easily reached over 4,000 (Rappaport and Fernandez-Partagas, "The Deadliest Atlantic," appendix 1). Beyond the scope of hurricanes, the 1928 storm is the third deadliest of all natural disasters in U.S. history, with only the San Francisco earthquake and subsequent fires in 1906 surpassing it, with current estimates at 3,000 deaths (Hansen and Condon, *Denial of Disaster*, 160). These data show the historical import of this event and the surprising lack of attention given to it.

travel on the barges, and they had no relatives in high and dry places. They would have to take their chances in their flimsy shacks built of scrap wood and tarpaper, most no stronger than poorly built coffins.[81]

Three quarters of the dead were black, and, as Kleinberg reports, "the hurricane may have also accounted for the most deaths of black people in a single day in U.S. history."[82] Mykle's wording is telling because if blacks did not survive in the housing that was built like a coffin, they would not receive coffins for their burials, although whites did—a piece of the record that Hurston also reported in her novel.[83] In West Palm Beach, 674 unidentified black bodies were buried without ceremony and only received an official marker in 2000.[84] In this state of emergency, surviving blacks were then forced into work gangs on the basis of old vagrancy laws to handle and bury the dead.[85] In Hurston's fiction, Janie and Tea Cake observe this death and destruction wreaked on the African American community, and then Tea Cake is forced into such a work gang by two white men carrying rifles. The way that movement functions for migrant laborers shows the precarity of their ordinary existence, while the storm shows their inability to control their movement when necessary during the disaster; both of these states are shaped by the governmental racism against blacks, who are neither given a means for escape when they are alive nor treated with respect when they are dead, which would be expected for internally displaced people.

Hurston's focus on the harsh conditions for blacks is then paralleled by the positive energy she gives those living in this situation. Although Tea Cake represents this vision of culture, he and Janie live in the realized world of the migrant worker, which is far from that imagined version of community. Here the real and imagined do not fully open up a new spatial option of Thirdspace, but instead, at this point in the narrative, highlight the disparity between them.

Tea Cake helps others overcome some of the hardships in the lived space of the muck by using his imaginative skills of storytelling, but he does more than tell stories. He becomes the story by taking on the role of a trickster figure, a disruptive literary character who turns situations on their head.[86] A key example is when he upends Mrs. Turner's restaurant. On the individual level, she threatens Tea Cake because she wants to set her brother up with Janie,

---

81. Mykle, *Killer 'Cane*, 118.

82. Ibid., 211; Kleinberg, *Black Cloud*, xiv.

83. Klinkenberg, "Unmarked but not Unmourned" and Mykle, *Killer 'Cane*, 209.

84. Mykle, *Killer 'Cane*, 211 and Klinkenberg, "Unmarked but not Unmourned."

85. Mykle, *Killer 'Cane*, 209.

86. Blyden Jackson generally acknowledges, "In his very special and very important way, Teacake [*sic*] in *Their Eyes Were Watching God* was a folk figure" (introduction, xv), but he does not explain that role any further.

but her real threat is to the community because her goal with this pairing is to "lighten up de race" (140). She believes, "If it wuzn't for so many black folks it wouldn't be no race problem" (141). To protect the community, Tea Cake emerges as a trickster, pretending to help Mrs. Turner turn drunks out of her restaurant when he is really adding to the chaos and confusion: "Mrs. Turner saw with dismay that Tea Cake's taking them out was worse than letting them stay in" (151). He upsets the authority figure at hand and creates a carnivalesque atmosphere.

Eventually, Tea Cake becomes associated with the African diasporic trickster, Big John the Conqueror—sometimes called High John—whom Hurston brought to the general public's attention in various pieces of writing both anthropological and fictional, showing Hurston's interest not just in African American culture, but in how that culture extends beyond national boundaries because of the forced migration of the middle passage that brought this narrative figure to the United States from Africa.[87] The reverence with which African Americans held Big John is directly named in conversation in *Their Eyes*:

> "He was uh man wid salt in him. He could give uh flavor to *anything*."
> "Yeah, but he was uh man dat wuz more'n man. 'Tain't no mo' lak him. He wouldn't dig potatoes, and he wouldn't rake hay: he wouldn't take a whipping, and he wouldn't run away." (66–67)

Hurston adds to this explanation in her anthropological work, defining him in *Mules and Men* as "the wish fulfillment hero of the race. The one who, nevertheless, or in spite of laughter, usually defeats Ole Massa, God, and the Devil. Even when Massa seems to have him in a hopeless dilemma he wins out by a trick."[88] Hurston also explains this African character's mythical origins and purpose:

> High John de Conquer came to be a man, and a mighty man at that. But he was not a natural man in the beginning. First off, he was a whisper, a will to hope, a wish to find something worthy of laughter and song. Then the whisper put on flesh. His footsteps sounded across the world in a low but

---

87. Varro E. Tyler marks Hurston as the "definitive" source of this narrative ("The Elusive History," 165). Carolyn Morrow Long also notes that Hurston herself is the one to tie the folk stories of Old John to John the Conqueror. She adds that the possible connections extend beyond the borders of the United States to "Yoruba/Dahomean deities brought to the Americas with the African slaves. The most likely candidate is Shangó, the spirit of thunder and lightning, fire, and passion, who is also irresistible to women. Other possibilities are Ogún, the spirit of warfare and iron implements, or Eleguá, the divine trickster" ("John the Conqueror," 51).

88. Hurston, *Mules and Men*, 247.

musical rhythm as if the world he walked on was a singing-drum. [. . .] High
John de Conquer was a man in full, and had come to live and work on the
plantations, and all the slave folks knew him in the flesh.[89]

Big John helps those in need by giving them hope and laughter as a way to
survive and occasionally overcome their situation. As an abstraction of "hope"
that "put on flesh," Big John represents the mix of allegorical traditions, both
African and Christian, upon which Hurston draws for her novel. As a plantation figure, though, Big John must transform as African American experience
and culture do, protecting the slave first on the middle passage and then on
the plantation.[90] Here, he returns through Tea Cake, who takes on Big John's
attributes, to help Janie find her own sense of freedom. Right from their first
meeting, when Janie seems to already know Tea Cake, he assumes a mystical
role since everything he says makes her laugh. He frees her from the "slavery"
of running Jody's shop and shares with her the positive elements of black culture. He gives her hope.

Tea Cake becomes Big John not just for Janie, though, but, once they move
to the muck, for all of those around them, both African American and immigrants from the Caribbean. Right before the hurricane, on the muck, a crowd
at Tea Cake and Janie's house discusses the figure, saying that he "had done
everything big on earth, then went up tuh heben without dying atall. Went up
there picking a guitar and got all de angels doing the ring-shout round and
round de throne" (157), which is followed by the statement, "That brought
them back to Tea Cake" (157). John the Conqueror's guitar playing reminds
them of Tea Cake's playing. By uniting Big John and Tea Cake (even in the
length of their names), Hurston connects Tea Cake to the stories and the culture of blacks to show how they help migrant workers maintain their hope
even as they live in the present-day "slavery" of migrant agriculture.

The hurricane disrupts the fragile hope that the muck community will
ever be able to arrive as a fully utopian space—one shaped without the hierarchical structures of landownership—that is free from the external forces
of governmentality. Once the storm begins, Janie says, "Ole Massa is doin'
His work now. Us oughta keep quiet" (159). The oppression the workers feel
becomes a force of nature. As the hurricane destroys the community, it also
leads to Tea Cake's descent. Janie loses him and her connection to the area
because "the muck meant Tea Cake and Tea Cake was not there. So it was
just a great expanse of black mud" (191). After the hurricane, the community
is lost, and animosity appears. Symbolically, the arrival of the storm signals

89. Hurston, *The Sanctified Church*, 69.
90. Ibid., 69–70.

the dissolution of the black community that is caused by external power-ful forces, and this loop of the Great Migration contains those on the move who are now not just economic migrants but also environmental migrants.

THE HARLEM RENAISSANCE: URBAN PROTEST AND ITS DISCONTENTS

The final portion of the novel expresses Hurston's ambivalence toward the nature and definition of black community as opposed to its culture. The present moment of the novel, which details Janie's continuing migration, lines up with the early years of the Harlem Renaissance, thus influencing how Hurston envisions the possibility of community building because of her own difficult relationship with her fellow writers.[91] Therefore, while Tea Cake initially represented for Hurston the black community Janie seeks, following the hurricane both he and the lived community of the muck become a weight on Janie. Tea Cake becomes an image of the violence Hurston sees penned by Richard Wright and some of the older members of the Harlem Renaissance, but in spirit he is able to maintain his role as the African American folk hero Big John. Because the Everglades community also turns against Janie after Tea Cake's death, and the Eatonville community, where she finally returns, still judges her, Hurston's text argues that an imagined, inclusive African American community has yet to be realized and that full citizenship will not come through the violence and hatred espoused by much urban protest writing of the 1930s. Even so, Hurston's own imagined solution remains limited because it is tied to the ownership ideology of white governmentality.

As Janie and Tea Cake flee from the storm and the ensuing flood, Tea Cake is bitten by a rabid dog and quickly becomes violent and vengeful. This initial incident occurs just outside of Palm Beach, "the city of refuge" (166). With the muck destroyed and their move to this white-run city, Tea Cake is beaten down by the oppression he experiences under whites who put him to work separating white and black bodies to be buried; here their position as migrants shifts again from environmental migrants to political migrants because of how they are being controlled by the governmentality of vagrancy laws used against blacks to restrict their movement. This loss of black auton-omy leads metaphorically to Tea Cake's sickness. If he had been able to stay away from Palm Beach, it seems that the violence that ensues may have been avoided. This urban migration also indicates that Tea Cake is infected not just by rabies but by the accepted literary representation of black men in white-

---

91. Carla Kaplan, *The Erotics of Talk*, 108.

dominated space. Tea Cake's "madness," Hurston seems to be saying, embodies the violence often found in urban protest fiction such as Wright's.

The story Wright published a year before *Their Eyes'* release, "Big Boy Leaves Home," displays his focus on violence between whites and blacks. Big Boy is a defenseless child sought for a lynching because he was caught swimming naked by a white woman. The story shows how trapped he is by the racism of the community that would want to kill him for being a playful kid in the water. He hides from his attackers in the woods, but they are very near to finding him. As he waits in fear, he considers wringing their necks in order to survive, but what he actually ends up killing are a snake and then a dog that gets his scent:

> Then, he never exactly knew how—he never knew whether he had lunged or the dog had lunged—they were together, rolling in the water. The green eyes were beneath him, between his legs. Dognails bit into his arms. [. . .] With strength flowing from fear, he closed his fingers, pushing his full weight on the dog's throat. The dog heaved again, and lay still . . . Big Boy heard the sound of his own breathing filling the hole, and heard shouts and footsteps above him going past.[92]

We feel the boy's desperation, but since Hurston is more interested in showing the autonomous spaces of blackness with little interference from whites, she resists the politics of Wright's vision and rewrites it. Big Boy's violent killing of a dog prefigures Tea Cake's own killing of the rabid dog that he "seized [. . .] by the neck" (166) and wrestled to death in the water.[93] Although killing the dog in both cases is a reasonable response to the attack, Hurston wishes to focus on representations of compassion instead of violence stemming from hatred.

Her repeated rejection of the idea of hatred in both her fiction and her criticism reveals the connections she sees between these representations. When she reviewed *Uncle Tom's Children,* which included a republished version of this story, she makes her differing perspective clear in similar terms:

> This is a book about hatreds. Mr. Wright serves notice by his title that he speaks of a people in revolt, and his stories are so grim that the Dismal Swamp of race hatred must be where they live. Not one act of understanding and sympathy comes to pass in the entire work.[94]

---

92. Wright, "Big Boy," 156.
93. Ibid., 166.
94. Hurston, "Stories," 9.

Whether one agrees more strongly with Hurston's or Wright's view, Hurston's work is significant in that it addresses the literal swamp of the muck and reveals her outlook on the devastating results of hostility in her rewriting of Wright's dog attack. In *Their Eyes*, Janie mentions animosity as residing in the dog's eyes of "pure hate," showing that "he didn't aim tuh jus' bite [her. . . .] He aimed tuh kill [her] stone dead" (167). Tea Cake responds with similar language, saying, "Ah didn't mean tuh take his hate neither. He had to die uh me one. Mah switch blade said it wuz him" (167). Here the language of hatred creates a slippage because, while Tea Cake means that he planned to stand up against this enemy, what happens is that Tea Cake does "take his hate" by taking it into himself, becoming violent. Once in the hostile environment, Tea Cake, just like the boy in Wright's story, does not seem to have much choice in making his initial attack, but Hurston's text shows how Tea Cake's violence only leads to more violence and death. After the attack, Tea Cake shifts from Hurston's representation of African American folk culture to Wright's representation of the oppressed African American. For Hurston, the presence of this type of representation forces her, through Janie, to expunge it by killing Tea Cake. Janie shoots him in self-defense as he approaches her in a rabies-induced rage with his own gun. Hurston wants to rid literature of the violent black male and the image of the South as "a dismal, hopeless section ruled by brutish hatred and nothing else" that allows little space for positive images of growth.[95] Therefore, Janie does not kill her representation of community; she destroys what Hurston sees as the warped view of African American culture represented in other literature of the Harlem and Chicago Renaissance.

After Tea Cake dies, the people from the Everglades turn against Janie. They, like Tea Cake, the book tells us, have been "infected" with those types of views from the Harlem Renaissance. The migrant community wrongly gossips about Janie, saying, "He worked like a dog for her and nearly killed himself saving her in the storm, then soon as he got a little fever from the water, she had took up with another man. [. . .] Hanging was too good" (186). Janie has not run off with another man and disavowed Tea Cake for Mrs. Turner's lighter-skinned brother, as the community claims, nor has Hurston disavowed the black community and wed herself to minstrelsy, as Wright claims. Hurston continues to write even with the loud opposition of her critics, perhaps continuing to hope for the resolution that Janie receives. For Janie, the community eventually apologizes to her, but by then she has decided to return to Eatonville.

---

95. Ibid., 10.

On returning to Eatonville, Janie knows that it too is not the community she has sought. The town itself now metonymically represents the bourgeois ideology of her second husband and Du Bois. While in the courtroom, she witnesses the spread of the views of the Harlem Renaissance; with her return to Eatonville, she travels back "North" to where she first experienced the root of those ideas when she was married to Jody. Even so, she tries to spread some of the folk culture that she has learned by becoming a storyteller herself, but she doubts whether her story will be heard, just as Hurston doubts if other African American writers will listen to her. The community may fight against Janie, but she wants to remind them how to listen to the stories as she has. In her friend Pheoby she finally gets a listener. She tells Pheoby, "You can tell 'em what Ah say if you wants to. Dat's just de same as me 'cause mah tongue is in mah friend's mouf" (6), but as the novel ends it is left unresolved as to what Pheoby will do with the story she has been told.[96] Janie and Hurston know that the community is going to question them, but even though they present a tone of indifference, they still speak/write. The problem with Janie's solution is that it relies upon an assumption of ownership and autonomy similar to that of the white governmental structures upon which Eatonville was founded.

A UTOPIAN THIRDSPACE OF OWNERSHIP AND SELF-POSSESSION

In the end, Janie is finally "freed" to know herself. This freedom is demonstrated in two key ways. First, Tea Cake's death parallels Big John the Conqueror's return to Africa when slavery ends.[97] Big John, and by extension Tea Cake, is no longer needed the way he once was, "but he left his power here, [. . .] and he can be summoned at any time."[98] The last paragraph of the novel shows a second example of Janie's newfound freedom; she brings together her ownership of her house in Eatonville and the power of Tea Cake:

> Then Tea Cake came prancing around her where she was and the song of the sigh flew out of the window and lit in the top of the pine trees. Tea Cake,

---

96. Although Carla Kaplan refers to Pheoby as an "ideal listener" in *The Erotics of Talk*, how ideal their friendship is remains questionable because her relationship with Pheoby is just as complicated as her relationship with the community at large. Though Janie tells her story to Pheoby, there are moments when she withholds things from her friend. At one point, "Janie acted glad to see her" (112) but was not. At another point, "she pretended to Pheoby" that she liked a man in Sanford, and because of that Pheoby is later unaware that Janie is interested in Tea Cake.

97. Hurston, *The Sanctified Church*, 71.

98. Ibid., 72.

with the sun for a shawl. Of course he wasn't dead. He could never be dead until she herself had finished feeling and thinking. The kiss of his memory made pictures of love and light against the wall. Here was peace. (193)

This materialization of Tea Cake inside her home reveals that she has created a new space for herself—a Thirdspace that combines the real and imagined. Tea Cake remains with her, showing that his death is not a death—just like for Big John the Conqueror who "went up tuh heben without dying atall" (157). He has not left her, and the culture he represents that ties her to the black diaspora remains accessible to Janie. Tea Cake gives Janie hope along the way, just as Big John gave hope to those who were enslaved. Now that she is freed, he continues to symbolically give her solace.

Janie views space anew within her home but also with the world as a whole. Having returned from her journey to the horizon, she now "pull[s] in her horizon like a great fish-net. Pull[s] it from around the waist of the world and drape[s] it over her shoulder. So much of life in its meshes! She call[s] in her soul to come and see" (193). She bends space and time in a new way, illustrating the possibilities of a chronotope that displaces (without erasing) the slave ship. The horizon does not choke Janie as her grandmother's horizon did, since she can now wrap herself in her experiences of the world and her new knowledge of African American culture from the Edenic space of her childhood, to enslaved sharecropping at her first husband's home, to elitist empowerment of Jody's Eatonville, to the migrant communal hardship on the muck, and then to a new Eatonville where she finally acquires self-possession and landownership.[99] This utopian Thirdspace, however, remains limited not only because of Janie's isolation from her neighbors but also because her empowerment is achieved through her reclamation of property; such a Thirdspace does not imagine solutions for internally displaced persons without their own home and without the same level of privilege.

By following her movement through these external spaces, it is possible to track both Janie's internal journey and her troubled relationship with her various communities—her process to an imagined spatialization that escapes the precarity imposed by society and that incorporates the shifting relationship between labor and land in African American history into a narrative

---

99. Janie's grandmother Nanny takes the possibilities of the horizon and transforms them into the horrors contained by a lynching rope:

> Here Nanny had taken the biggest thing God ever made, the horizon—for no matter how far a person can go the horizon is still way beyond you—and pinched it in to such a little bit of a thing that she could tie it about her granddaughter's neck tight enough to choke her. (89)

of personal and social development that acknowledges oppression without being defined by it. She finds culture but not community, just like Hurston herself. In contrast to some previous assessments of Hurston's work, this novel presents a consistent allegorical structure that moves through the history of African American experiences via Janie's relationships with the men she marries, the communities she encounters, and the spaces in which she resides. Hurston's desire to focus African American literature on African American culture in the southern United States in the larger context of trans-Atlantic experiences was shaped by her response to migratory patterns and the role of women in the early twentieth century, and it adjusts our standard notion that the northern progression of the Great Migration and urbanization are the only way to view this moment in African American history. Instead, Hurston's text presents a counter-narrative to American exceptionalism and freedom through movement that reveals the increasingly refined governmental controls disenfranchising African Americans. Finally, as a piece of literature, the novel shows the potential outside of historical narratives for individuals and communities to search for a Thirdspace that can combine real and imagined elements to try to find something new outside of the existing power structure.

CHAPTER 2

The Environmental Displacement of the Dust Bowl

From the Yeoman Myth to Collective Respect and Babb's *Whose Names Are Unknown*

PART OF the last chapter showed how an economic displacement could become an environmental displacement with migrant labor in the South being moved again by the disastrous effects of the 1928 Okeechobee Hurricane, as stated in the historical record and in Zora Neale Hurston's novel *Their Eyes Were Watching God*. This chapter also follows an environmental displacement but one that prompted an economic displacement. Taken together, these events broaden our understanding of the varied causes of internal migration while showing the effects of ideological and governmental forces on seemingly natural disasters. Both remind us of the ways in which citizenship rights are denied at various points in U.S. history as well as how the category of internally displaced person needs to be rethought to include the ethical imperative of the refugee.

On Sunday, April 12, 1935, a date that would be called Black Sunday, a dust storm of unprecedented size enveloped the U.S. plains. Historian Timothy Egan describes that day:

> People looked northwest and saw a raggedly-topped formation on the move, covering the horizon. The air crackled with electricity. *Snap. Snap. Snap.* Birds screeched and dashed for cover. As the black wall approached, car radios clicked off, overwhelmed by the static. Ignitions shorted out. Waves of sand, like ocean water rising over a ship's prow, swept over the roads. Cars went into ditches. A train derailed.[1]

---

1. Egan, *The Worst Hard Time*, 7.

The dust storm inundated a north-to-south stretch from North Dakota to Texas and a few days later even deposited dust onto the East Coast and into the Atlantic Ocean.[2] It was the most memorable in a long line of such storms during the 1930s that covered the "Dust Bowl" region.[3] The dust and wind combined with drought to create a natural catastrophe of the vastest proportions known in U.S. history, and this environmental disaster accompanied the economic disaster of the Great Depression. Communities whose mainstay was farming saw the earth and people's means of living being swept out from under their feet, so much so that it triggered an environmental migration of 250,000 people from the region by the decade's end, mostly to the West.[4]

The historical reality of U.S. migrant workers on the West Coast during the Depression included a dominant population of whites, but this racial breakdown was not and is not typical. As Douglas Wixson affirms,

> For generations, non-native-born workers—Mexican, Filipino, Asian—have planted, pruned, and harvested California's farmlands and orchards. For a relatively brief time, however, from about 1935 to the early years of World War II, dispossessed Anglo-Americans, mainly from the Great Plains, accomplished the main field labor in California's fertile valleys. [. . .] It was considered intolerable [. . .] that Anglos should experience conditions viewed as normal for immigrants and blacks.[5]

During the Dust Bowl migration, it was whites in the center of the country who were the main racial group on the move, though they joined a variety of people of color who had long been working in migrant labor. Therefore, this migration is significant for several reasons: The inclusion of a large number of white people brought to the forefront the connection of citizenship and race to movement that previously had been used to disenfranchise other racial groups. Further, the Dust Bowl migration, which is often given an exceptional status, needs to be put in dialogue with other migrations that are mainly of nonwhite peoples because it was neither unprecedented nor dissimilar from other displacements. Additionally, in the short term, the Dust Bowl migration shows the strength of the governmental logic that links citizenship to whiteness and American-ness while denying the claims of all migrant workers

---

2. Ibid., 228.

3. Reporter Robert Geiger coined the term "Dust Bowl" in an article about this very storm ("If It Rains . . .").

4. Egan, *The Worst Hard Time*, 10 and 9. For more on environmental migrations, or, as he labels them, "ecomigrations," see Wood's "Ecomigration."

5. Wixson, introduction, xvi.

regardless of race, since California laws, corporations, and local communities created new categories—turning U.S. white people into nonwhite, immigrant "Okies"—rather than acknowledge their rights and citizenship. In other words, the Dust Bowl migration brought to the national consciousness the plight of migrant workers in a way that exposes the ideological contradictions regarding and lack of care for internally displaced peoples that is typically concealed by racism. Only by attending to the mixed racial character of the actual migrant laborers as well as the ways in which the category of whiteness was changed during this extended state of migratory "emergency" in California can we see how exploitation is based on long-standing notions of landownership and their relationship to class and race.[6] I will consider these configurations of landownership, citizenship, and power through a theoretical framework that calls upon concepts of governmentality, bare life, and precarity discussed by Giorgio Agamben, Judith Butler, and Alexander Weheliye.[7] Applying such terms to moments of migration reveals the need to retheorize the concept of the internally displaced person so as to demand protections from the state and ensure equality for all citizens.

While the first chapter showed how landownership and rights were shaped by the foundation of slavery that led to limited citizenship for African Americans, this chapter approaches the same issues of landownership and rights for white settlers by tracing the nineteenth-century settlement of the Great Plains and the subsequent disaster of the Dust Bowl migration back to Jeffersonian ideals, which are themselves responses to the spatializations of slavery. Drawing on the version of space and ownership found in Henry Nash Smith's view of the mythic yeoman, an independent farmer who cultivates his own land, I argue that the Dust Bowl migration exposes a specific incarnation of the "white settler society myth," the idea that white Europeans came to a "blank slate" (in this case what would become the United States) and "developed" it without the aid of other people, including slaves, women, and laborers of various races.[8] The myths of possession of the yeoman and of the white settler society equate power and success with landownership and self-possession. This ideal is framed through an imagined individual who moves where there is economic opportunity to cultivate and possess the land and

---

6. To read more about the migrant labor in the Southwest from a nonwhite-centered viewpoint, see Carlos Bulosan's *America Is in the Heart* (first published in 1946) and Chris Vials's analysis of this text in *Realism for the Masses*, 110–48. Michael Denning states that Bulosan's novel includes characters based on Sanora Babb and her sister, since they knew each other (Denning, *The Cultural Front*, 519n33).

7. See the "Theorizing Migration and Citizenship" section of the introduction for a fuller overview of these theories.

8. Razack, *Race, Space, and the Law*, 3.

himself. The farmers who settle in the plains accept the governmental myth about their ability to access both the land and the power which that landownership promises. They believe in the values the myths represent of independence and autonomy in relation to a foundational movement to claim a legal territory. In its Depression-era manifestation, however, the mythic yeoman no longer opposes the plantation slave system, as Smith states was the case in the nineteenth century. Rather, this figure in the twentieth century, who is still both white and male, now opposes the capitalist incorporation of farming on the West Coast.

Sanora Babb, a young, white woman who had grown up in the plains, was working with the Farm Security Administration in the 1930s to help displaced farmers in California while at the same time writing a story about their plight, *Whose Names Are Unknown.*[9] This novel, set during the Depression, follows the Dunne family's fight to hold onto their land until adversities force them to leave Oklahoma and move to California, where they are faced with the problems of homelessness and an incorporated farming system. Although Babb's opening chapters were accepted by Random House Press, John Steinbeck's *The Grapes of Wrath* (1939) was released before her book was published, cornering the market. Thus, *Whose Names,* a novel written by a woman with firsthand knowledge of her subject, unlike Steinbeck, was not published until 2004.

Babb's newly available novel presents historically specific issues about white farmers during the Depression, the gender and racial politics of their homes and workspaces, and far-reaching environmental and economic change on the plains and in California. My investigation of the historical Dust Bowl migration and its fictional telling in Babb's novel begins with a consideration of the relationship of land to ownership and citizenship as shaped by governmentality and its associated myths. Many Americans were motivated to move to the middle of the country because of governmental advertisements and policies that offered more opportunity for those who could farm their own land. Their arrival, of course, displaced Indigenous people already on the land, who were erased from the promises of available territory. Furthermore, the farming practices encouraged by the government destabilized the land, affecting farmers' abilities to economically sustain themselves and their property. This environmental and economic disaster resulted in their loss of landownership and their displacement to the West. As internally displaced persons, however, they were now subject to a precarious life as migrant labor. The farming system turned farmers into laborers on the move precisely to prevent them from being autonomous and able to possess land. Corporate farm owners, local officials, state representatives, and even the federal government developed

---

9. Woo, "Sanora Babb, 98."

or contributed to new migrant laws, restrictive corporate farming practices, and harsh domestic spaces that dispossessed the migrants and brought into question their "American-ness." All of these entities held a capitalistic view of ownership that fought against any attempts to unionize and desired to keep property and its economic benefit in the hands of the few.

Babb's *Whose Names* is valuable because it reveals how the claims of the farmers in the Dust Bowl region are "unsettled" as the land, in its ecological and legal properties, shifts beneath their feet. The book exposes the empty promise of the yeoman myth while also depicting the characters' response to the atomizing effects of capitalism that led to precarity; this utopian, Thirdspace solution, helped along by the federal housing camps and their own unionization, extends the farmers' ideas of collective respect to the land, animals, and neighbors beyond just the white community to one united across race and gender in the aims of social justice.[10] In contrast to the first chapter, where I demonstrate how Hurston's novel addresses precarious citizenship for African Americans through individual home ownership, Babb's novel more fully imagines a community connected through class. Ultimately, though, *Whose Names* cannot sustain its notion of inclusive community. At first, an idealized vision is possible because the farming corporations view their employees as interchangeable units of labor, no matter their race or gender, and ironically this bare life status bereft of rights and protection enables workers of various backgrounds to occupy shared spaces of employment. This breaking down of boundaries between individuals allows workers to conceive of a cooperative space among themselves. The fulfillment of this cooperation is unattainable, though, because finally the legal system, racism, and internalized gender discrimination prevent boundary crossings when the workers attempt to rise above the lowest economic level. The new farm system that separates farmers from a connection to the land and animals also inhibits a progressive environment among people. In the end, Babb's text concedes to only expanding the Thirdspace of empowerment to include white women at the periphery of the white male political space, while people of color are left behind, literally and figuratively remaining imprisoned.

HISTORY OF THE YEOMAN

In the previous chapter, I pointed to landownership's connection to citizenship as a foundational element brought by European colonists that was then expanded not only to disempower those who did not have the wealth to own the land but also as a means to disenfranchise along racial lines and to keep

---

10. See Soja, *Thirdspace* and Bhabha, "Third Space."

power in the hands of the few. Slavery and blackness were set against land-ownership and citizenship from the start of North American colonization. While many early colonists relied upon this binary for restrictive purposes based on class and race, later some U.S. politicians attempted to use this ideology as a path to class egalitarianism that eventually also included blacks.

The yeoman myth played a large but shifting role in constructing space and movement in the United States. In the late eighteenth century, scholar Thomas Cooper, describing to the English the prospects for an emigrant, embraces the yeoman myth: "In America a farmer is a land-owner, paying no rent, no tythes, and few taxes, equal in rank to any other rank in the state, having a voice in the appointment of his legislators and a fair chance, if he deserve it, of becoming one himself."[11] The glorified yeoman represents the possibility of a white egalitarian society where power is gained through the hard work of the individual, not through birthright. The most famous proponent of the yeoman's possibilities was Thomas Jefferson, who presented the white farmer as an American image in opposition to the laborer of Europe. However, as 1940s Americanist Chester Eisinger stresses, in this "Jeffersonian myth," land was still strongly connected to economic power. The yeoman not only worked the earth but owned it, with the land itself facilitating his social status and wealth.[12] In theory, all could share in the bounty of the land through its ownership. In fact, however, the space was finite and with it the power; by putting so much stress on the lone individual, a strong community could not emerge to address problems that extended beyond the capabilities of one person.

The yeoman's location in the heart of the country was crucial. Benjamin Franklin stated that the "body of our nation" consisted of "the industrious frugal farmers inhabiting the interior part of these American States," and he believed the country's focus should not be on the seaports when "the great business of the continent is agriculture. For one artizan [sic] or merchant, I suppose, we have at least 100 farmers, by far the greatest part cultivators of their own fertile lands."[13] This shift of focus to the interior did not just reimagine the economic structure of the United States. It also reimagined the land itself, previously known as the Great American Desert, a label that described the region as "inappropriate for cultivation and uninhabitable by a people dependent on agriculture."[14] In an early form of "rebranding," that space was now presented as a place desirable to settle, attracting immigrants and eastern

11. Cooper, *Some Information Respecting America*, 72–73.
12. Eisinger, "The Freehold Concept," 42.
13. Franklin, *Autobiography and Other Writings*, 347 and 344.
14. Lookingbill, *Dust Bowl, USA*, 9–10.

citizens to new economic opportunities as part of the government's advertising this yeoman myth.

By the middle of the nineteenth century, when the government debated granting small homesteads to farmers who would cultivate and live on land in the plains, spatial ideology remained a central factor. As historian James Shortridge states, "The region became America's middle ground, literally and figuratively between the urbanized East and the western wilderness," making the plains an appropriate place to mediate the argument about America's future economic principles.[15] Attempting to maintain a pastoral ideal while accommodating the perceived progress of industrialization, these politicians spatialized a distinction between the bucolic and the technological, but this endeavor to have both the machine and the garden, as Leo Marx labels these disparate perspectives, in the long run reduced this "middle ground" to long-established colonial views of landownership and power in order to populate the area.[16] Added to this view, however, was an antislavery hope articulated by Rep. George W. Julian of Indiana that under this plan

> poor white laborers of the South, as well as of the North, will flock to our territories; labor will become common and respectable; our democratic theory of equality will be realized; closely associated communities will be established; whilst education, so impossible to the masses where slavery and land monopoly prevail, will be accessible to the people through their common schools; and thus physical and moral causes will combine in excluding slavery forever from the soil.[17]

National and personal economics would unite to create a prosperous, egalitarian country and community.

As Julian's words emphasize, the yeoman ideology countered the plantation slave system. If a farmer cultivated his own land, he was not using slaves for that work. "Slavery only thrives on extensive estates," Julian stated in 1851. "In a country cut up into small farms, occupied by as many independent proprietors who live by their own toil, it would be impossible—there would be no room for it."[18] This argument, which explicitly acknowledges and inverts the colonial view that prevented blacks from acquiring citizenship rights, held that slaves cannot work land to the fullest because, without civil rights, payment for their labor, and landownership, they cannot love their country.

---

15. Shortridge, "The Emergence of 'Middle West,'" 214.
16. Marx, *The Machine in the Garden,* 354.
17. Julian, 31 Cong., 2 Sess.
18. Ibid.

Conversely, independent farmers—white or black, though the overwhelming majority were white, as was the popular image of the yeoman—would not only work the land to the greatest avail, but they would also fight for the country because "the man who loves his home will love his country."[19] Slavery hurts the individual, the land, and the country, Julian argued, and a yeoman society would right those wrongs. But as this imagined yeoman society was realized, the same mythology of the rugged individual removed any sense of shared responsibility for others as well as of the communal nature of work and home.

By endeavoring to bring the yeoman to the plains, the government created a new role for the internal United States and its inhabitants. The homesteads served to erase the association of this space with a desert and instead focused the nation on using the region to alter the country's economic system, to expand the area's white population, and to pacify and rejuvenate the populace of the white underclass by promoting a move to the center of the country. All of these changes were quickly turning the middle of the country into the symbolically "most American part of America."[20] Conveniently, as this myth was propagated, it described the new settler as a rugged, white individual, erasing the association of that land with its Indigenous inhabitants. Uncovering that erasure through Babb's novel will give us a better sense of the significance of migration and space in American culture in general, and of a key transitional moment in the logic of mid-century capitalism and its spatialization.

CIMARRON COUNTY, OKLAHOMA

In Sanora Babb's novel, two of the oldest characters had engaged in this governmentally supported migration to the center of the country by journeying to Oklahoma to homestead most likely in the 1890s, shortly after the Organic Act of 1890 made the panhandle region part of the newly formed Oklahoma territory.[21] As Old Sandy explains, "Me and your father-in-law there [old man

---

19. Ibid. Homesteading itself was not exclusively a white male enterprise. African Americans (as well as white women and immigrants) were among the homesteaders, especially after the Civil War. Even so, the figure of the yeoman, like most prototypical "American" ideals promoted by the dominant culture, was conceptualized in racial terms as a white man. For information on the Exodus of 1879, when a large group of African Americans moved westward, see Neil Irvin Painter's *Exodusters*.

20. Shortridge, "The Emergence of 'Middle West,'" 216.

21. Lowitt, *American Outback*, 15. The complicated history of the unusual panhandle-shaped area of Oklahoma is worth noting, if briefly. In 1836, Texas revolted from Mexico and, in 1845, became part of the union. This inclusion after the Missouri Compromise created a complicated No Man's Land, however, since no new slave territory could extend above the 36.5 line of latitude. Consequently, the Oklahoma panhandle could not be claimed by Texas, creat-

Dunne], we've knowed each other a heap of years. Me and him is old nesters. We proved up goviment claims side by side in the early days" (52).[22] These claims remained small, first at 160 acres and then doubling to 320, in order to ensure that one pair of hands would both own and cultivate the land, unlike plantation farms.

Old man Dunne and Old Sandy represent the new Anglo wanderers who believed the advertising that this territory was a new "Promised Land."[23] This form of governmentality promoted the idea that America developed and strengthened itself by "continually beginning over again on the frontier," what Frederick Jackson Turner explained as the "frontier hypothesis."[24] Because of these new inhabitants, the grassland, previously grazed by buffalo when Indians still controlled the area and then by cattle, was soon overwhelmed with farmers; they were told that new methods of "dry farming" could be utilized in this area that did not receive the twenty inches of rain necessary for conventional farming. They also hoped that the "rain follows the plow," the pseudo-scientific viewpoint believed by many, which stated that "by the repeated processes of sowing and planting with diligence the desert line is driven back [. . .] so that in reality there is no desert anywhere except by man's permission or neglect."[25] Although the farmers did their best to be diligent in order to prove these disingenuous governmental tactics true, eventually, instead of rain and ongoing progress, drought and dust arrived, and with it the Depression.[26] In other words, by encouraging internal migration to the Great American Desert through racial displacements and land claims, the United States' large-scale governmentality would eventually result in environmental and economic catastrophe.

The white world that Babb presents in Cimarron County, Oklahoma, involves an erasure of the thousands of Native Americans who were relocated to the state and whose land rights were repeatedly ignored via U.S. assertions of Manifest Destiny, as discussed in my introduction's look at the Cherokee

---

ing the strange "panhandle" that continues to exist today, "35 miles wide and 210 miles long" (Egan, *The Worst Hard Time*, 34).

22. Sanora Babb, *Whose Names Are Unknown* (Norman: Oklahoma University Press, 2004). All citations are from this edition.

23. Lookingbill, *Dust Bowl, USA*, 11.

24. Turner, *The Frontier in American History*, 2.

25. Wilber, *The Great Valleys and Prairies*, 69.

26. While some, like the Dunne family, did migrate after experiencing dust storms, many more moved because of the drought (without dust) and the economic depression that accompanied it. Most were from Oklahoma, Texas, Arkansas, and Missouri (Gregory, *American Exodus*, xiv, 11).

on the Trail of Tears.[27] In fact, the white families' claims exist only through breaking the Medicine Lodge Treaty of 1867, which had given this area to the "Five Civilized Tribes" of the Cherokee, Chickasaw, Choctaw, Muscogee (Creek), and Seminole, unsettling these tribes yet again. Yet Native Americans are barely mentioned in the text, even as white ranchers and farmers fight over who rightfully "possesses" the land (6).[28] It is therefore significant that while "the government placed the geographic heart of the dust-lashed land" in Cimarron County, making it a symbolically appropriate location for the novel, Babb's story originally took place in southwestern Kansas and southeastern Colorado, both areas also within the hardest-hit parts of the Dust Bowl.[29] According to Lawrence Rodgers, author of the book's foreword, the location was changed to Oklahoma when the University of Oklahoma Press accepted the text.[30] This movement just a few miles east may seem inconsequential, but it alters our insight into the initial racial picture. The white world that Babb portrays is more true to Colorado than Oklahoma at the time, since U.S. military campaigns against Indians between 1863 and 1865 led to the forced removal of the Comanche, Arapaho, Kiowa, and Cheyenne from the Colorado area to Oklahoma.[31] That is, the Oklahoma area that Babb names in the book had a significant number of Indigenous people that would have been difficult for anyone, including her, not to see.

27. In the Medicine Lodge Treaty of 1867, the United States limited the hunting terrain for the Comanche and other tribes to the area south of the Arkansas River—much of modern-day Oklahoma (Egan, *The Worst Hard Time*, 17). The treaty was supposed to guarantee at least this area, but instead it marked the space that would continue to be constricted around the Indigenous peoples.

28. The Comanche lost the Red River War of 1874–75, and then the United States systematically destroyed the buffalo. "'For the sake of a lasting peace,' General Sheridan told the Texas Legislature in 1875, the Anglos should 'kill, skin and sell until the buffaloes are exterminated. Then your prairie can be covered with speckled cattle and the festive cowboy . . . forerunner of an advanced civilization'" (Egan, *The Worst Hard Time*, 19). In just a few years the last bison had been killed, and in 1907 this region became the 46th state: Oklahoma, another U.S. conquest.

29. Egan, *The Worst Hard Time*, 153.

30. Lawrence R. Rodgers, e-mail message to the author, October 16, 2008. Although happenstance pushes the story to Oklahoma, the geographic names in the text reflect the Mexican and Native American foundations of the area. "Oklahoma" is the combination of two Choctaw words meaning "red people" (Egan, *The Worst Hard Time*, 35), and the country of "Cimarron" is "a Mexican hybrid word, descended from the Apache who spent many nights in these same buffalo wallows. It means 'wanderer'" (Egan, *The Worst Hard Time*, 15) (as the characters themselves wander).

31. In addition to the Indians' absence from the novel, other people of color are also excluded in these opening pages, including Mexican "immigrants." These inhabitants remained in the vicinity since the panhandle of Texas had not long before been part of Mexico. Additionally, no African Americans appear in the text, although many African Americans had traveled west to become cowboys or migrant workers themselves. For more information, see J. LeSeur, *Not All Okies Are White.*

Moreover, this omission should be analyzed based on the author's own priorities. Her later memoir, *An Owl on Every Post* (1970), follows much of the same action in this novel but keeps it in its original location of Colorado. In the memoir, Babb mentions Oklahoma as the place of her early childhood, and with that association she mentions "the white man's unjust treatment of the Indian."[32] She also writes extensively about spending much of her childhood with people in an Indian community who welcomed her, only answering to her Indian name, Cheyenne. As she states in her memoir, when an adult teases her about her connection to Native American culture, she responds: "I was dead serious about my Indian family and he was not."[33] Even outside her texts, Babb showed an investment in the Indian community. When she died, she asked that funds be sent in her memory to support the American Indian College Fund.[34]

This dedication to Native American issues suggests that her text, though not directly confronting the issue, questions the United States' proprietary view of the land. Old man Dunne recalls the old days by stating, "If there was no need for a man one place he could go another. New land to claim—why, I had two horses and a spring wagon and I rode like Blitzen into the Cherokee Strip and didn't get any land, but I just went someplace else" (100). Readers should not take this reminiscence as nostalgia. Instead, Dunne conveys a perspective that the U.S. landscape is free for the taking even as he acknowledges that others inhabit the space through labels such as the "Cherokee Strip." These words expose the white settler society myth, which ignores Indians' claim to this land—the fact that the land is not a *terra nullius* or "virgin land" before the settlers' arrival. As Dunne continues, his words more directly reveal the problems in U.S. attitudes: "In those days we just went somewhere and started building a town" (100). But now there is "no more new land, no more free gold out west" (101), he says, pointing to Turner's idea that the frontier is now technically closed. "Danged if I know what we'll do when we 'Mericans run out of west to move on to. [. . .] Guess we'll go to sea" (102). Old man Dunne's conclusion points to the novel's skepticism about the project as a whole; Manifest Destiny disrespects those already on the land and the land itself by treating it as limitless. Therefore, the novel may be focused on a white community that created itself through government claims, but Babb, even as she respects her characters, quietly asks us to consider the appropriateness of even the early moves of these white settlers, showing how the myths that bring these white settlers dispossess many and call into question the notion of possession itself.

32. Babb, *An Owl on Every Post*, 65.
33. Ibid., 22.
34. Woo, "Sanora Babb, 98."

FLAWS IN THE YEOMAN MYTH

Because the fictional characters in Babb's novel correspond to the historical circumstances of many migrants and farmers in the heartland, the novel
allows us to see how within this white community, people distinguish their
identities based on space and movement, particularly as it relates to heritage
and gender.[35] These differentiations even early in the novel reveal some of the
ways that the myths of possession are flawed. The white characters, though
they are supposed to represent a new, permanent farming culture, have all
recently moved to Oklahoma, and every main character was born elsewhere.
Among the characters of *Whose Names* are many of these displaced peoples.
For instance, Mrs. Starwood comes from generations of internal U.S. movement. Her parents moved from Ohio, and she and her family traveled from
Missouri because they mortgaged their farm when the Depression hit and
now need to rent land (50). The Brownells came with some saved money, but
they too are the first generation hoping for a better life on the plains (18) even
as they yearn for the simple things they have left behind, much as Julia Dunne
wishes for "fruit like we had back home" (70). Despite the fact that the yeoman myth presents an idea of an enduring settlement, these characters have
long been on the move, showing that the myth misrepresents the nature of
success under such a farming system.

These specific families made internal migrations to get to Oklahoma, but
the novel also emphasizes that they are the descendants of Europeans who had
journeyed to the United States. Many had been convinced by the propaganda
that they should "flee [. . .] exhausted land for prairies untouched."[36] Therefore,
in the Oklahoma community they mark their generational transience by labeling each other with their family's country of emigration, often in a joking way
or to speak about their heritage. For instance, Milt Dunne's grandparents, the
old man's parents, were Welsh and Irish on his father's side and Irish/English
and Spanish on his mother's (58–59). Although two generations back, this tie
to the family's now optional ethnicity remains a part of how these characters
identify themselves. Some of the identification, admittedly, takes on more stereotypical qualities: "Where do you suppose she gets that Dutchman's blood?"
(28), Milt asks when his younger daughter saves her candy. Mostly, however,
these stereotypes are delivered in a lighthearted manner that the characters
themselves invoke. Mrs. Starwood turns to Frieda Brennerman, "'You Germans sure are cleaner'n anybody,' she said, and the girl laughed. 'And stubborn
too'" (123). Mrs. Starwood states a generalization about Germans that is often

---

35. Egan, *The Worst Hard Time*, 60–72.
36. Ibid., 57.

used to undermine, but she says it with appreciation of Frieda, not with anger or hatred. Even the young lovers in the novel, Max and Anna, refer to each other based on ethnic stereotypes. Max mentions Anna's "old German discipline" (105), and then she scoffs at his "old English muddling" (105). The "old" countries give them roots. At the same time, Max proudly proclaims that he may be "half Irish" but is vitally "all American" (105). The characters invoke their heritage in order to create a history for themselves, but they still want to claim this "new" American culture in order to demonstrate their connection to this space and their full citizenship.

The characters also differentiate themselves based on the spatial, gendered relations of separate spheres that limit the women's access to the benefits espoused by the yeoman myth. Women control the house, cooking, cleaning, gardening, and entertainment while men run the fields, but although the women control their own spaces, they are trapped within them.[37] In the case of the Dunnes, their small dugout keeps Julia Dunne in a cramped, underground space all day to complete her duties.[38] The novel, like the historical record, emphasizes that women were not seen as part of the yeoman myth: both the concept and the label are exclusively male. Women were often made "invisible in representations of the frontier," even though they were essential workers to this farming society, something which this novel points out by having wom-

---

37. Woman as culture bearer was a common distinction. One way that women entertained and cultured the family was by playing the piano. As Domosh and Seager note, "even the crudely built farmhouses on the western frontier contained elements that would have resonated with middle-class urban Victorian women. Parlor organs, for example, were often hauled long distances and installed as the primary object of pride in sod houses on the Nebraska frontier" (13). Egan also points to this historical phenomenon (*The Worst Hard Time*, 14). Julia Dunne's piano is her pride, but because of financial burdens, the family eventually sells off that token of dignity, entertainment, and self-identification. Julia also reports that she built a small garden to expand her domain, but drought ruined it—a miniature equivalent to the men's fields. Additionally, although Anna Brennerman holds a position as a schoolteacher, the widespread marriage ban during the period makes it likely that she will be forced to resign upon her marriage See Cooke, Cardwell, and Dark, "Local Residents and Married Women as Teachers," 236. The journal of Mary Knackstedt Dyck confirms the historical veracity (Riney-Kehrberg, *Waiting on the Bounty*, 17).

38. Pamela Riney-Kehrberg notes, "Daughters aside, most of the Dycks' visitors were men. The mobility afforded by the automobile was more easily enjoyed by males, who were generally unfettered by the constant round of repetitive daily chores that tied the area's women to the farmhouse" (*Waiting on the Bounty*, 16). Mobility is, however, not always desirable. As Domosh and Seager state, "the spatial boundedness of women is not only—and not always—a constraint. Just as mobility is not inherently a path to power, so immobility is not always a disadvantage" (*Putting Women in Place*, 120). Later these characters will yearn to be in the domestic space of their sod homes.

en's daily activities—cooking, cleaning, interacting with neighbors, as well as bearing and caring for children—be such a dominant part of the story.[39]

While Babb's white community formulates its identity based on a sense of constant movement, stemming from recent internal migration as well as its ancestors' immigration to the United States, within the group, the key category that separates workers is gender, creating varying levels of opportunity and access for different inhabitants. Babb's distinctions show the failures of the myths of possession because they do not take into account the lived experiences that transpire under the cover of these fictions.

COMMUNITY INTERACTIONS AND COLLECTIVE RESPECT

With a community built upon recent and generational migration, the farmers in *Whose Names* work to develop a strong support system based on social interactions. They visit each other for entertainment and give assistance, such as helping to dig wells and harvest crops. They even offer food when they do not have enough for themselves. This form of communal bonding stands in stark contrast to the individualistic and atomistic mentality of the yeoman myth, pointing to the incongruity between these ideas of movement for individual ownership and movement for community togetherness and showing how, even as the characters believe in the myth at this point, they are still trying to engage with each other using what I am calling "collective respect." This idea of community is based on the acceptance of differences between people, giving assistance to others who need it, and treating others as valuable, whether they be other people, animals, or the land itself. Some kindnesses are part of the farmers' quotidian existence, but support expands even further when situations are dire. Although Mrs. Brownell, a neighbor, offers to have Julia stay at her house when it is time for her to have a baby (19), it is after Julia loses the baby that the community demonstrates its full potential. Various women come to the house to cook, clean, and take care of the children (49). The women spend most of their time indoors with Julia, echoing the traditional spheres of their daily lives, while the men talk to Milt or the old man out in the field. The social support of these neighbors shows a willingness to aid others for the well-being of the entire community.

Although the farmers want to prove their self-sufficiency, their actions belie their complete belief in the individualistic notions of the yeoman myth through their compassion that extends to the treatment of animals and the land; the farmers respect the animals that work the land just as they respect

---

39. Domosh and Seager, *Putting Women in Place,* 162.

each other. They even think of them like friends and call them by name (12, 24, 37, 63). When the dust gets bad, old man Dunne sets up a breathing contraption for the family, but then he stays in the barn, spraying the air with water to help the animals' breathing. Making the connection between themselves and the animals, the farmers consider that the animals "are frightened by death same as we are, poor things" and grieve for them when they die because "the animals are like persons to us" (92). At the same time, they maintain a pragmatic eye, recognizing that the loss of an animal costs them its use. When the cow dies, the Dunnes mourn both the animal and the fact that "the kids won't have milk now" (92). In general, though, old man Dunne sums up the feelings of his neighbors: "I'd rather go hungry myself than the horses, they can't say much" (117). This community makes sure to protect those who cannot speak for themselves.[40]

The farming families also value the land and nature in general. They are not boastful or intentionally harmful to the world around them because they know even ecology and meteorology have to be on their side in order for them to survive. Rain, a sought-after element, brings joy with its arrival. When it comes, Milt Dunne and the old man "listen [. . .] happily to the even thudding on the roof" (8). The weather affects not only the harvests but also relationships; for Max, he needs the beneficial snow in order for him "to get married on [his] wheat crop" (64). The weather alters lives in many ways, so they think of the climate as an essential part of themselves. The old man's journal expresses this link: "He named the day and the year of natural disturbances the way another man names the events of his life" (90). It is this environmental connection that stands in stark contrast to the governmental notions of settlement that limited land solely to an economic source of production that can be mastered and which would result in the ecological disaster of the Dust Bowl.

All of these instances demonstrate the connection between the self and the environment, anticipating an ecocritical ideal not to be theorized as such until decades after Babb wrote her text—that identity and place are interrelated—but more importantly showing how the characters resist basic elements of the myths that they more generally embrace. The farmers not only better understand themselves through their association to nature but also realize that they are able to empathize with those not directly like themselves—in this case, animals and inanimate objects in nature. This recasting of the pathetic fallacy rejects the idea that the yeoman should have individual mastery over nature through possession and instead points to a responsibility toward all liv-

---

40. Vials discusses similar tactics of showing the positive relationship between a farmer and his animals in *America Is in the Heart* and other agrarian novels (*Realism for the Masses*, 141).

ing things—a collective respect.[41] This egalitarian bond between each person's life and the environment resurfaces throughout Babb's writing. As a character in her own memoir, the young Babb states, "We were not separate from all of nature; we were not looking on, we were a part."[42] Seeing oneself as a piece of the universe underlines much of what happens to the characters in *Whose Names*. When the characters see the ties among self, place, and social relations, they enhance the community, but that society is fractured when some replace respect and responsibility with hierarchies and greed.

Some of the wealthier individuals do not ascribe to collective respect. The key representative is Mrs. Brennerman, who is unwilling to think about the betterment of the community even on the human level. Because she does not want to share her dinner with Julia Dunne and her girls (a rare occasion when only women are traveling and socializing), she asks them to leave in the midst of an impending storm. This expulsion leads to Julia's giving birth to a stillborn child. Although women in the text yearn for companionship, Babb shows that class overwhelms gender. Mrs. Brennerman's failings confirm that a democratic society as presented by the yeoman myth does not fully exist; those who "have" are precisely the ones who do not share.[43] Erin Royston Battat's recent discussion of Babb's novel highlights the stress within the community during the drought, reading this conflict in terms of an opposition between producers and parasites, between groups such as farmers and bankers.[44] I would add that this distinction reveals a deeper opposition between two forms of ethical behavior, namely collective action and individual selfishness, and that this split is the basis for class distinctions within the community.

This class separation becomes accentuated when the banks follow Mrs. Brennerman's viewpoint—appropriately, since her husband works as a banker. When the economy worsens, the banks demand payment regardless. They hide behind the claim, "It's simply business" (112). The rest of the community, however, is not based upon a business model of survival. Instead, farmers expect businesses to function with humanity, realizing the circular logic of repossess-

---

41. Evernden, "Beyond Ecology," 101.

42. Babb, *An Owl on Every Post*, 85.

43. Some, however, who could prosper by ignoring the needs of others do not. Flanery, the owner of the grocery store, allows the farmers to shop on credit (while customers who could afford to pay full price haggle). The doctor in town gives his services in trade or for free to those who cannot afford it. Because of their actions, the doctor has been left by his wife and lives in the back of his office, while the store owner eventually descends into such despair and debt that he kills himself. These two men could have individually fared better if they thought only of themselves, yet because of their willingness to throw their lot in with their neighbors, they are esteemed members of the community.

44. Battat, *Ain't Got No Home*, 51.

ing someone's farming equipment when a dry year occurs. As Mrs. Starwood notes when she confronts the bank's overdue notices, "All I know how to do is work and if I can't pay back that little mortgage on our things you'll stop me from working" (112). The banks take away the very things that would allow the farmers to pay back the banks, and then they take away the land itself.

These farmers espouse an egalitarian society from the way they think of animals and land to their treatment of each other. Yet, although the yeoman myth posits a society without class limitations, in middle America people and organizations with more money finally do exert power over those they see as beneath them. As the environment makes farming more difficult, the farmers begin to adjust their sense of identity. Their tie to their ancestral countries becomes less of a factor than money. As Max states, "Funny how we talk about our roots when our people have been here for generations." Anna responds, "We're not really divided according to our nationalities, but by how much or how little money we have" (105). Ancestry does not, in fact, distinguish them; instead class separates people in this supposedly classless society. To return to Rep. Julian's words, this practice does not result in "our democratic theory of equality" being "realized," in part because of a flawed understanding about the relationship of territorial possessions and the nature of the land itself.

THE EFFECTS OF THE DEPRESSION AND THE DUST

In both historical reality and in Babb's fictional representation, economic and environmental displacements are intertwined. Such an understanding underscores the harm done by governmental ideologies that cause environmental catastrophes through a misrepresentation of human beings' relationship to the earth and the natural world. The onset of the Depression heightened the cyclical effects of an already falling market for crops, which had been declining throughout the 1920s, showing how the capitalistic and imperialistic logic of limitless expansion ignores the finite space of the country and the damage to the farmers and the land they work. As the price of wheat plummeted, farmers, believing in their government's promise that they could tame the earth, plowed more and more land to try to make the same amount of money, even though each turning of the land weakens its long-term viability. Scholars have often connected this disregard for the land to the dust storms that began appearing with great regularity.[45] As more land was plowed, more dust was available to be swept into the air in the windy clime of the central states.

45. For examples, see Timothy Egan's *The Worst Hard Times*, James N. Gregory's *American Exodus*, and Pare Lorentz's documentary *The Plow That Broke the Plains*.

These storms continued the vicious cycle by inhibiting social interactions; as the land eroded, so too did the community. It was not Adam Smith's invisible hand of the economy alone that destroyed them but what Babb describes as the "smell of dust [. . .] strong in their noses now, slapping their senses like a thick fat hand" (77). By harming the land, the economic pain the farmers feel becomes palpable.

In Babb's novel, although the farmers attempt to maintain their ideas of communal responsibility for all living things, the incompatibility of collective respect with the ideology of individual gain espoused by banks and corporations begins to become apparent and, indeed, to shape the farmers themselves. As the farmers overwork the land in order to make it profitable, their respect for others also begins to wane. Even those who do not let a lack of money stop them from helping their neighbors find themselves in circumstances that begin to remove them from the benefits of community. As the Depression and the drought wear on, kindness breaks down: Milt gets angry at his family; Julia gets angry at the old man; then the two girls, Lonnie and Myra, fight with each other. All express their pent-up anxieties. The interactions between neighbors could be stronger if things were not so bad, the old man explains: "Since the depression [sic] it 'pears to me the same troubles bothering us are the ones bothering everybody else in the world. Everybody has to keep his nose so close to the grindstone he can't know his neighbor or anybody else" (72). The long-term frustration and additional work caused by the economic downturn diminish the benevolence between neighbors.

The farmers also misdirect their frustration onto the land. Therefore, the farmers not only sometimes disrespect their neighbor, but they also disrespect the land. In Babb's memoir, her grandfather, who closely resembles old man Dunne, observes, "Man is the only one out of kilter. [. . .] And the chances are he has it in him to get back when he finds out he's a part of nature and not its lord and master. Right here, now, if we plow up all this grassland and kill off all the wild animals, there'll be a hard price to pay."[46] The farmers' view of the interconnectedness of all living things breaks down when individual economic concerns overwhelm a holistic view of the collective good.

The nearly surreal experience of the dust storms captures the dissolution of the farmer's egalitarian relationship with nature through the literal movement of the land into their farms, houses, and bodies, showing how the loss of collective respect harms both the environment and humanity. When the storms begin, the people are startled by them, even though their plowing is the direct cause. They cannot understand the change to their environment through their own experiences and so must compare their space to other

---

46. Babb, *An Owl on Every Post*, 151.

things that have been read and seen: "It looks like the desert you read about in books, desolation itself" (90), and "the dust could be seen lying in gentle waves, like pictures of desert sand they saw on calendars" (87). Ironically only able to understand the region of the country formerly known as the Great American Desert through pictures of deserts from elsewhere, they reveal the totalizing acceptance of the governmental myths that has repackaged this region as farmable while obscuring the fact that this nonarable land was not suitable for crop expansion. While the farmers do not understand the cause, they do, however, recognize it on the literal level as the movement of earth. Milt says, explaining an approaching storm, "It looks like Canada raised up and flew this way" (78). He also recognizes that with the movement of this land goes his livelihood:

> He knew it was not his own loose field soil that was often picked up by the regular winds. This was a rich, organic loam, torn from its bed because it was without root and moisture to hold it. If no rain came and the wind kept on, this same precious layer of his own field would rise and follow the great dark clouds to other land. (87)

As the land literally erodes, fleeing and smothering as it destroys the farmers' wheat, symbolically the ground continues to shift beneath them. The government had told those who moved here that they would be able to make a life for themselves on these plains. If, however, the land itself is not permanent, how can the farmer himself avoid transience?

Once the dust arrives, this "evil monster" (77) not only alters humans' routines and threatens the wheat, but it also invades their homes: "Look how it's sifting in around the windows" (79), "sifting in from places that had kept out even the wind" (86). Because of this ongoing invasion, "Old man Dunne nailed gunnysacks over the windows outside" (86), but eventually they have to strengthen the barrier and board up the windows (88, 90). They physically try to separate themselves from the outside world, but the boundaries continue to be permeable: "Think someone's farm is in our house, maybe our own" (91). The spaces of the field and the home are no longer personally theirs—the boundaries have been eroded, revealing both that possession is not permanent and that the problems of the community, the economy, and the environment have become unsettled, seeping into everyone's lives.

The intrusion does not stop with the assault on material space; Babb again anticipates the formal arguments of ecocriticism by showing that when the land is harmed so too are individuals. The dust repeatedly invades their bodies: "He felt it in his throat like fur and had to cough" (79), and "she felt the dust in her clothes and on her skin, in her mouth and nose, on everything she touched" (86). The farmers have to cover themselves and make masks, but, just like the house, their bodies remain permeable (89). Because of the disturbed earth, people die from blindness, from dust pneumonia, and from losing their way in the storms. Even for those who do not die, Julia hypothesizes that "the effects of the dust will be showing up on a lot of people later" (94). The power of the environment over the well-being of the farmers refutes the image of the lordly master who is superior and distinct from his possessions.

Instead, as these storms develop, the environment controls the actions of the community. Because of the dust, neighbors isolate themselves in their homes. The children also have to stay home from school during storms. The physical limitations are reflected in a new phrase, "when the dust clears," that anticipates the communal connections but, because of the perpetual presence of dust, keeps these wishes from being fulfilled. For instance, Julia states, "When it clears up, I'll make her a nice cake" (95). This "when" quickly dissolves into "hope," such as "Hope the dust clears a little so I can go over and help Mrs. Starwood" (95). Finally, it becomes an accepted opposition and excuse: "I mean to write him but this dust has got me so I just do what I have to" (106). The partitions that block windows and bodies emblematize the barriers between farmers, their social support, and their previous positive relationship with their environment.

Historically, women journaled about their experiences during the storms. Mary Knackstedt Dyck, for example, composed short entries that reveal the cyclical patterns of chores and the weather, including Dyck's often mentioned "terrific duster[s]."[47] These journals make women's lives on farms visible because they are a "glimpse into life *inside* the farm house."[48] They also demonstrate, however, the claustrophobia caused by this space. In Babb's account, the limits to their world are taken to the extreme when the dust forces them to "nail a cover over the door when we were inside" (94). They are trapped alive inside their own coffins.[49] Once the dust storms start, an entire chapter of the novel is written as journal entries by Julia. The adjustment in mode and point of view to the solitary diary creates a sense of isolation, with just one

---

47. Riney-Kehrberg, *Waiting on the Bounty,* examples 78, 122, 283. Battat comments that Sanora's fictional diaries are slightly modified versions of her mother Jennie Babb's diary entries. The edits show how the environmental crisis impacts Julia's home as well as Milt's crops: "Her fictional rendering of the 'push' factors in the dust bowl migration [*sic*] thus balances the masculine implications of an agricultural bust with the domestic image of a home besieged by dust" (*Ain't Got No Home,* 56).

48. Riney-Kehrberg, *Waiting on the Bounty,* xii; italics added.

49. This natural disaster, just like the earlier natural occurrences, is treated as a part of their identities, and Julia notes this by recording the dust storms like the old man recorded previous disasters.

voice speaking about the events—it is anti-communal. The annalistic style that lacks narrative continuity also shows the repetition and disjointedness of living in such seclusion. Here we see that the farmers' attempts to become the yeoman of myth confine them. They own their homes, but those homes suffocate them.

Even as the novel aligns landownership with a symbolic death, the characters attempt to bring their society back to life by extending their help to others in ways that the storms now mandate. They leave the house's external light on so that people lost in the storm may find their way, even though it raises their electricity bill (91). Some strangers stop, wanting something to drink, and although they "looked liked bandits with noses and mouths tied up, faces and hair dirty, and clothes covered" (91), the Dunnes provide for them and then later "hope those people get where they are going safely" (91). They still care for others, but now the people are strangers with hidden faces; they may try to help their community, but they can no longer "know" it.

Their environment pushes them toward an individualistic approach represented in the myths of possession, but the farmers continue to fight for a more collective sense of identity. One new way they attempt to connect to the outside world is by listening to the radio, an item that many people during this period considered their most valuable commodity, because it allows them to recognize "we are not the only ones to suffer. It is just terrible for everyone" (93).[50] The radio broadcast is a way of relating to others that at the same time highlights their physical separation (91, 93). They are searching for new, egalitarian ways to interact with society that transcend space, but they are starting to see that their pursuit might require them to give up their land and move elsewhere.

The farmers take a last stand for their community, recognizing that the individual cannot succeed alone. For instance, at Mr. Starwood's funeral all of the men talk about what they need to do to survive, and their general conclusion is to make "the best kind of life for ever'body" (100) by "stick[ing] together" (98). While the farmers are not unionized, they are strong as a community. They lack a means to fight the banks and to stabilize the prices they receive for their crop, but they maintain respect for each other. When the grocer feels so alone that he kills himself, he still thinks of his neighbors and burns all of the books that list the farmers' debts (115). Even in death neighbors look out for each other. On various levels, these characters understand the importance of communal support and do not need to be taught this lesson.

---

50. Lewis, "'A Godlike Presence,'" 29.

Finally, though, the dust points to the cracks in the yeoman myth that already existed, the inequality between classes and the imprudent use of the land on which it is based. In the end of the novel's first section, the characters find that they need to build a new community somewhere else; they begin "feeling utterly desolate" (130) in the space that is supposed to be their home. Wisely, as they leave, they continue to realize that the ideal of a lone individual is not the way to make a move, even on the simplest level: "If we stick together we can eat cheaper" (127). The yeoman ideal has shattered in Oklahoma. They continue to believe, though, that it can be found somewhere else, so they still cling to the myth of "get[ting] me a little orchard someday" (129).

The Dunnes join with Mrs. Starwood and her family and even take in Frieda Brennerman, the kind, unmarried daughter of their unkind neighbor, when they move as a group. "They went out together and alone, like animals moving with their backs to the storm, moving to shelter they knew was nowhere, yet they could no longer stand still in their stricken lives" (120). They become transient because "the whole plain seemed unpeopled and deserted" (128). This deserted aspect, in both senses of the word, causes their flight.

This economic and environmental disaster of the Dust Bowl would prompt the movement of a third of the region's population—one of the largest internal migrations in U.S. history.[51] Following the logic of expansion, white Americans were impelled to move to the center of the country and then to move again to the West Coast in search of fulfilling the promised ideology of the yeoman myth, which equated landownership with prosperity. The behavior and conditions of the farmers prior to their migration to the West helps to reveal the full extent of the bare life they inhabit once they arrive at the factory fields.

PRECARIOUS INTERNAL MIGRATION IN CALIFORNIA: THE "FACTORIES IN THE FIELDS"

When the Dust Bowl farmers moved west, they became migrant laborers, trapped in a cycle of movement without a permanent home or the chance for landownership. Identified as homeless, they were subject to local laws, restrictions, and other violent tactics designed to mark them as laboring bodies without citizenship rights. The corporate farming system and the government

---

51. Of course, many did not flee. Although a staggering third of the population left, the remainder stayed within the confines of the Dust Bowl, moving at most a few hundred miles, surviving through such extreme situations as having to eat tumbleweed. See Timothy Egan's *The Worst Hard Time*, which vividly describes the experiences of those who stayed even as their community and their crops withered around them.

produced a precarious, bare life that reduced or eliminated their voting, housing, health, and education rights while concentrating power in the hands of the wealthy. Though the Fourteenth Amendment after the end of slavery supposedly guaranteed equal citizenship rights for all, the Dust Bowl migrants in California reveal the persistence of such systems of disenfranchisement as well as their alignment with the forces of capitalism, which transformed human beings, in this case predominantly Anglo-Americans, into merchandise.

The cycle of migrant labor enables the government and corporations to more easily see migrant laborers as inhabiting a bare life that allows them to be excluded from citizenship and encourages the local government and corporations to keep them moving. This idea is paralleled in *Whose Names* through the erasure of the arduous trip that the Dunnes and their companions make from Oklahoma to California. Instead, the novel skips entirely over this journey and jumps, via its section markers, from "Part I: Oklahoma Panhandle" to "Part II: California." While some may see this omission as undermining the story's interest in migratory experiences, I stress that in the past the family was constantly at risk of being forced to move, and in this new section they *are* constantly on the move. Movement remains their defining characteristic. By skipping the expected discussion of their longest migration, the novel highlights the many smaller migrations and the overall precarity that dominates their existence.

The family's lack of stability focuses them on pragmatic concerns and complaints. Because this section starts *in medias res,* they already have aching backs and suntan lines from picking cotton in the fields. We hear the children asking, "Why are we moving again?" (134), instead of the traditional "Are we there yet?" for there is no specific, final "there" as a destination. While the children bemoan being on the road, Milt fears that they will fail to be able to move, running out of gas before they find work and money.[52] All these signs serve as reminders that this journey is not an adventure; it is frightening. Its goal is survival.

Travel is not always freedom; as Domosh and Seager point out and as has been shown by the migrant laborers' experiences on the East Coast in chapter 1, sometimes it is its own punishment.[53] These characters, as Samira Kawash explains, like other homeless people, "are forced into motion not because they are going somewhere, but because they have nowhere to go."[54] Even so, Babb shows that they still hope to fulfill the yeoman myth, but they start to doubt their ability to take part in the plenty they see around them even as they drive by it or labor in it:

52. This concern about the need for movement will be expanded upon in chapter 4.
53. Domosh and Seager, *Putting Women in Place,* 120.
54. Kawash, "The Homeless Body," 327.

The Dunnes and the Starwoods moved on. [. . .] They moved on, past the date-palm ranches in the desert—then going higher into the green country again, through almond groves, apricot lands, orange and lemon trees, they took long breaths of the high air heavy, intoxicating, fragrant with blossoms. Here were the tall trees, the Spanish names on signs, the tenderness and gentleness of spring.

A few miles on were the cherry trees, ripe and waiting. (160–61)

They see the abundance they had been promised, the land itself and the food to feed their hunger, yet their enforced movement keeps it out of reach—as indicated by the repetition of "they moved on" and the distance from the more immediate senses of touch or taste. Even the cherries that are waiting to be touched by their harvesting hands ultimately cannot satisfy because they will be immediately relinquished to the owners. The workers can only observe the bounty instead of partaking of it; they begin to see themselves as part of a failed myth. Babb shows the characters' changing perspective as they begin to see they are abandoned for the new system of incorporation that keeps them "moving on."

The U.S. government's ostensible, political goal of having farmers practice the yeoman myth in subsistence homesteading was to turn the country away from the plantation slavery system. Now that the United States was decades removed from slavery, the forces of capitalism produced a new farming system more focused on large profits, in which ownership remains the ultimate goal, but the access to ownership is limited to a few. Possession continues to create a struggle that empowers some while disempowering many others, but now the old white settlers are the ones being disempowered through displacement. Additionally, on these new farms, run like factories, the once independent farmers are bound into an unending cycle of migratory labor, continuing their unsettled status and withdrawing any real chance at land possession. No longer are they being told that their movement will gain them a settlement. Instead, farmers work in a system of unequal labor relations that seeks to dispossess them: they own no land, receive no benefits, hold no job security, move seasonally, lack a permanent place to live, and perform the repetitive task of picking. These policies of enforced itinerancy by the corporations and the state legislators constitute a governmentality of precarity and dispossession that differs in type and scale from the U.S. governmentality of encouraging settlement in middle America. These migrant laborers have become part of the new "factories in the field," which, as writer Carey McWilliams explains, are "large feudal empires" where "farming has been replaced by industrialized agriculture [and] the farm by the farm factory."[55] Within this economic sys-

---

55. McWilliams, *Factories in the Field*, 6–7.

tem, human beings in many ways can still be owned because they are not paid enough to allow for any independence from their employer—the "farmer-industrialist," as Babb calls the owner in her notes.[56] Economics and a process of dehumanization—or, more accurately, the stripping down of the citizenship rights that had previously constructed the farmers' personhood and American-ness to a kind of bare life—form the basis of this inequality. After one conceives of another human as merely a body that can provide labor, all that is necessary, as Milt himself states, is "money, enough to hire another man" (168). This new system adapts some of the dehumanizing elements of the plantation system to new forms of mechanization and organization to enhance the dominance of the owners and the demoralization of the workers through taking away their rights, their autonomy, and their landownership potential, all in ways that are deemed legal in the post-slavery era.[57]

The large-scale farming system was able to be established so readily in California because of its distinct history from more eastern states. Those reasons extend from a history before the land was part of the United States because under Mexican rule, colonialism supported large tracts of land that were then usurped by Anglo newcomers.[58] With these larger parcels intact, it was more difficult to establish and maintain the Jeffersonian ideal for smaller farms. Instead this region established a "monopolistic pattern of landownership" for the California agricultural system.[59] The nineteenth-century, large-scale, "bonanza" wheat farms showed the desired tradition and model—slavery— with owners asking if black slave labor could be brought in from the South.[60] Though this importation did not occur, over time farm owners recruited various people from abroad and from within with the same intentions of having "powerlessness" as a key element of the workforce, thereby marking the labor system in California as far removed from the yeoman egalitarian ideal.[61]

Although the businesses resemble the old plantation system in size and worker dependence on the employer, the farms that the Dunnes find in California are part of the new system of incorporation, what cultural scholar Alan Trachtenberg defines as "a changed, more tightly structured society with new hierarchies of control, and also changed conceptions of that society, of Amer-

---

56. Babb and Babb, *On the Dirty Plate Trail*, 55.

57. In this new system, gendered locations are diminished, as was true in chattel slavery. Migrant women work alongside their husbands for needed money and have no home to maintain. Here is an equality of the least: the workers are seen not as people but as units of labor, with gender mentioned only to compare women's and men's capacity for output.

58. Daniel, *Bitter Harvest*, 18.

59. Ibid., 19.

60. Ibid., 24.

61. Ibid., 68.

ica itself."[62] This absorption of farms into mass conglomerations nullifies the yeoman's self-sufficiency. He is now a laborer, tied not to one plantation, but to the whole system at large.[63] The farmer must move seasonally, at best, in order to keep working and thereby feed his family and himself. Additionally, this labeling of the farmer as farmer is itself suspect, since "farming" now consists of the repetitive task of picking, similar to assembly-line specialization. This industrial view of farming has reshaped the yeoman from an independent farmer to a cog in the machinery: a migrant field worker living under precarious conditions—something I discuss further in chapters 1 and 4.

These laborers may hope against hope that land possession is still possible, but the corporations and the state "dispossess" these workers into homelessness. From the large corporations' capitalistic perspective, profits are the goal. Keeping workers subservient is a means to those ends. In the novel, bosses beat up the workers, hold them on any "convenient charge," make them pay for mandatory work needs like sacks, and force them to buy their goods at the more expensive company store.[64] This show of power against workers corresponds to general historical instances, such as the frequent strikes throughout the 1930s when workers were beaten and arrested on the authority of owners threatening their bodies and their civil rights; the findings of the La Follette Civil Liberties Committee at the end of the decade confirmed these violations.[65] All of these actions regulate the masses, and they fit within the standard explanations of the violence perpetrated against the homeless to control and contain them.[66] Symbolically, Babb's characters are separated from that place of safety that one thinks of as "home," forced from place to place with only temporary housing available to them in California. Having given up their land in Oklahoma and not being able to afford land in California, the migrant workers must respond to the question of "Home address?" with "We haven't got one anymore" (145). Once in California, wherever they go they are marked as homeless.

Historically there were more obstacles for the migrants than are portrayed in Babb's novel. Some of these barriers help to elucidate how local govern-

---

62. Trachtenberg, *The Incorporation of America and Society in the Gilded Age*, 3–4.

63. Of course, enslaved people were also bound to the system at large, but migrant workers fully experience that tie when they move from harvest to harvest.

64. Another possible exertion of power is even more sinister. After the migrants eat in the orchards, "for some reason or another, none of the women got with child" (163). This possible inference of insecticides on the fruit suggests that serious health risks exist (something I will discuss at more length in chapter 4).

65. See Daniel, *Bitter Harvest*, 151 and 160 as well as Auerbach's chapter 8, "The Committee and the Farm Factories," in *Labor and Liberty*, 177–218.

66. Kawash, "The Homeless Body," 330.

mental policies that connected movement and lack of citizenship operated in direct opposition to the federal government's Fourteenth Amendment, which offered equal rights protection to blacks after slavery. At stake were the issues of citizenship rights, freedom of movement, and poverty. In 1936, California created a border patrol commonly called the "Bum Blockade" that stopped "indigents" at the state line, arresting them and anyone who helped them to move or simply preventing the migrants from entering. While these local actions were eventually deemed unconstitutional by the Supreme Court case *Edwards v. California,* this decision was not made until 1941.[67] Until that time, the local government employed extreme, biopolitical measures to diminish the migrants into a state of bare life that undermines their lawful citizenship.

Although the actions of the state and the federal governments were distinct, it is worth noting that California's policies were found to be unconstitutional because they violated the Commerce Clause in Article I, Section 8 of the Constitution. In other words, the Supreme Court decision in favor of the migrants justified their legal entry into California by labeling the migrants as "commerce." Startling as this reduction of human beings to merchandise may seem, there were at least concerns on the Court about this choice of precedent and logic. For instance, Justice Douglas in his concurring opinion stated, "I am of the opinion that the right of persons to move freely from State to State occupies a more protected position in our constitutional system than does the movement of cattle, fruit, steel and coal across state lines."[68] Once he acknowledges how these individuals have been doubly dehumanized, first by California's prohibition of their entry and second by the highest court in the land labeling them as commerce, Douglas proceeds to argue for the freedom of movement based on citizenship: "The right to move freely from State to State is an incident of *national* citizenship protected by the privileges and immunities clause of the Fourteenth Amendment against state interference."[69] Stating that freedom of movement is a fundamental right of all citizens, Douglas draws on the Fourteenth Amendment to show how in this instance, class distinctions, rather than racial ones, are being used as a means to disenfranchise. As he puts it, California's policy

---

67. Although the court case only occurred in 1941, the blockade stopped years earlier because of the cost. Interestingly, California had been warned about the prohibitive costs by Florida, who had also tried such a tactic. Thus, this approach is another small example of how agricultural workers are being treated similarly in different geographic locations (Leader, *Los Angeles and the Great Depression,* 217).

68. *Edwards v. California.*

69. Ibid.

would also introduce a caste system utterly incompatible with the spirit of our system of government. It would permit those who were stigmatized by a State as indigents, paupers, or vagabonds to be relegated to an inferior class of citizenship. It would prevent a citizen because he was poor from seeking new horizons in other States.[70]

Douglas points to the inherent contradictions in a nation that has created the Fourteenth Amendment and the California Border Patrol. This contradiction extends even to the Court's decision supposedly protecting those migrants, which reduces them to chattel. In general, this case, with its inability to fully defend personhood, demonstrates the connections among landownership, mobility, and issues of identity such as race and class that would continue to be utilized in other ways in local governmental acts against the migrants.

Several of these local governmental acts represented in Babb's novel return to this problem of vagrancy via the spaces the migrants can inhabit. Because Babb's characters do not have a home, the corporations' overarching control mechanism is the management of housing and with it space and movement. The "free rent" in a wooden shack they give workers requires that the residents pick a minimum of 900 pounds of cotton a day, which means that the Dunne family, Frieda, and the Starwoods must live together. Still, they require residents to pay $6 each month for lights, no matter what their usage (174). When the season ends, or whenever the workers cause any problems, they are evicted; and even when they are housed, someone else dictates how they can use their "private" space. Agamben's concept of bare life is applicable here because the migrants are reduced to labor without rights and become classified as vagrants. At the same time, the space of the owners' housing camps reflects this basic structure by eliminating any privacy or ownership.[71] Additionally, local legislation that further reduces housing options quickly passes, supported by the corporate farms. That is, not only do companies exert control but also the surrounding community wants to "efface their presence altogether."[72] In *Whose Names* this occurs under the guise of protection, a common response to the homeless:

> Before the crop season, on the basis of stricter health rules, an ordinance had been conveniently and quickly passed prohibiting all squatter camps in the county. This meant that most families must live in private camps on the

70. Ibid.

71. Agamben, *Homo Sacer*, 88.

72. Kawash, "The Homeless Body," 330.

owners' places. It meant there was no place to go except the public road, and moving on the road called for gas. (192)

Vagrancy laws keep the migrants moving since sleeping by the side of the road is also not tolerated. They are forced to move precisely to exhibit their disempowered status.

Although the farmers attempt to fight for their housing rights, specific manipulations of the housing locations and hiring lists of the corporations keep them moving, something a sheriff himself admitted to the La Follette Committee as the goal to create "complete surveillance over every fruit worker in the district."[73] This registration could also stop laborers from being able to fight back through voting rights, as Babb demonstrates in a passage worth citing at length:

> The men who selected the small plot were careful to find sunken ground on the level valley floor, which would fill with water as soon as the winter rains began. This was just a precaution, a kind of suggestion that nature would make. Of course, there were other means of preserving the migratories as such. One of the most effective was a particular system of bookkeeping, ordained to keep migratory workers from registering and voting. All members of an organization of big farmers kept a record of their workers' car license numbers and the date they entered into the state. When a worker had been in a county for six months, by law, he could register. If convenient for the crop at hand, the worker was let out just before that time. As he moved on asking for work from other farmers, their records showed he should be on his way to another county. Unless he was fortunate enough to get work from a small independent farmer who had no such record or no reason for keeping one, he found the county an unwelcoming place. (200)

Babb takes these details regarding manipulative record keeping and housing almost directly from her field notes about historical working conditions.[74] With homeless status comes a loss of rights; people who lack permanent roots in an area are reduced to a bare life where they are seen as outsiders, not deserving of the same treatment as others. In this case, many Californians felt the "burden" of the new members of their state and, therefore, as if responding to a state of emergency, limited public services, such as hospital support, which Babb noted in the novel and in her journalistic writing (142, 144).[75]

---

73. Auerbach, *Labor and Liberty,* 188.
74. Babb and Babb, *On the Dirty Plate Trail,* 84.
75. See Babb, "Farmers without Farms."

Even though these migrants are technically citizens, they feel ostracized. The state sees them as invaders, a drain on the established community, both financially and socially. Significantly, this elimination of rights stems from the overarching myths of possession. If landownership leads to empowerment, then the loss of land (and by extension a home) quickly leads to disempowerment, as represented here through a loss of rights. Historian Douglas Wixson explains, "[Dust Bowl migrants] were a declassed homeless people, their rights as American citizens ignored and violated; an uprooted folk for whom the American creed of work and success had failed."[76] Or, as I might state it, they were a people for whom the instantiation of the yeoman myth had turned to dispossession. The myth was revealed as something no longer to be sought, since it had disintegrated to dust like their land in Oklahoma.

Without a place to call their own, the characters begin to feel separated from the larger society, and this isolation leads to a withdrawal into the self that inhibits community even among the migrants themselves: "They had come to think of the rest of the world as the outside, because they had lost all the things that connected them to other people" (201). This sense of exclusion is common among the homeless, since, as Kawash notes, "who belongs to the public, who has access to public space, and who has the right to decide what uses of space are within the public interest" ironically excludes those who are forced to live only in "public."[77] This paradoxical situation occurs because "to be without a home is to be without that domain of the private into which the public subject is supposed to be able to withdraw."[78] Always exposed, the migrants discover that others no longer see them as a part of their community. Still, the migrants themselves need to believe they are necessary members of society; as the characters recognize, "not to be needed is to be isolated, displaced and dried up, a dead root" (201). They feel shame about their housing options, so they avoid each other, making even their temporary housing spaces "quiet and [. . .] unlived in" (199). They also feel separated from each other because the companies pay spies to live among them to uncover any unionization plans. These literal invaders cause "a great silence in the fields" (202), creating distrust between neighbors and a general atmosphere of anxiety.

Being stripped of home, community, and voice, workers have only the labor potential of their bodies, revealing the full dehumanizing results of dispossession: "All they had to sell now was their labor—this was all they had to withhold" (202). Each one feels the fear of becoming a "shadow of a man"

---

76. Babb and Babb, *On the Dirty Plate Trail*, 22.

77. Kawash, "The Homeless Body," 320.

78. Ibid., 325.

because, as Kawash states, "the homeless do not appear as individuals with distinctive identities."[79] With this lack of acknowledged personhood and citizenship comes the realization that the yeoman myth is empty, so that by the end of the book, "their dreams thudded down like the over-ripe pears they had walked on, too long waiting on the stem" (222). They see the prosperity of the country around them, but they have learned that they are not allowed to take part in it or in any myth of possession.

This destruction of the myth partly results from the fact that the frontier is now closed.[80] The corporate owners represent a new vision that excludes the yeoman. From their view, since they possess the land, they control all of the space: the expansive fields and the migrants' housing. The owners even complain that the federal housing camps, which I will turn to shortly, are paid for by their taxes, so they think they own that land, too (205). Above all, the owners' physical absence from most of the text demonstrates that true power is disembodied.[81] Their omnipresent absence gives them a godlike, immaterial status in opposition to the physicality of their workers. Even in the one scene where we overhear the owners, there are no descriptions of the men, just quotations of their dominating voices.

From this new economic standpoint, power continues to be shown through permanence and ownership, and weakness through the inability to remain static, but significantly the difference is an abandonment of care for the individual citizen and community building through a combination of various governmental and corporate forces, including increasing mechanization of farming, legal strictures, and the exploitative power of capitalism. This loss reduces the supposedly democratic and equal owners of the yeoman myth to dispossessed, homeless, and isolated physical bodies—to bare life—recognized simply for labor. The owners' power is stamped on the landscape through the name posts on the land and buildings they own. The workers are the ones who must move and exert themselves; they are the ones who are embodied. From this ideological position, there is no freedom of movement; everything is already owned, so you stay where you "belong," or you remain perpetually, precariously on the road.

---

79. Ibid., 324.

80. Turner, *The Frontier in American History*, 1.

81. Lonnie and Myra play at this kind of power with a bug, shaking leaves and putting obstacles in its path. The girls see themselves as "giants," but they are *unseen* giants who harm the bug's progress without his understanding how, just like the corporations. The girls also come up with a response to such acts of aggressive power: "If he would tell all the bugs what we've done to him, they could hurt us" (177). They see the value in community.

DEFINING AMERICAN-NESS THROUGH CLASS, PLACE, AND RACE

In addition to being disenfranchised and rendered precarious by their homeless status, the migrant workers in California are also racialized in a way that serves to justify their exclusion from American-ness and an unqualified whiteness. Greeted with the slur "Okies" as soon as they arrived, these internally displaced people, rather than receiving aid and protection, are subject to anti-migrant attitudes that mark them as "foreign" and as racial others. Babb's exploration of this discrimination in her novel, however, leads to a unifying desire for social justice because "Okie" cuts across gendered and racial lines, allowing the novel to imagine a Thirdspace out of the temporary housing camp. Based on a collective mentality united by class, this Thirdspace is born beyond the boundaries of traditional ownership and domesticity. Even so, it fails to achieve its full utopian potential of a labor struggle that overthrows the myths of possession because the workers are not fully integrated, holding out only the promise of social justice without incorporating an ethic of care for all internally displaced persons.

Historically, many Californians during the Depression felt that they had been strapped with too many of the migrants and the costs associated with poorer inhabitants, so their fears became quickly tied to anti-migrant attitudes.[82] These fears manifested in the construction of the slur "Okie," which in history and in the novel marks the migrant workers as spatial outliers. They do not belong to California. Although this slur locates them as Oklahomans and therefore citizens of the United States, the language of deportation is still associated with these words, calling their citizenship into question. Egan states that historically, workers experienced "strangers staring at [them] like just another piece of Okie trash, saying [they] should be deported. Deported? Where?"[83] These insults of deportation parallel those leveled at the Mexican migrant workers and Asian workers, since Babb writes in her field notes that the migrant farmers are called "Oklahoma coolies," adapting the slur used against Asian laborers.[84] James Gregory agrees that "white, old-stock American natives, Protestant Americans, rural Americans, heartlanders [. . .] were now bearing the brunt of prejudices traditionally addressed to 'foreigners.'"[85] The white characters' geographic alienation and economic oppression tie them

---

82. Gregory, *American Exodus*, 80–81.
83. Egan, *The Worst Hard Time*, 157.
84. Babb and Babb, *On the Dirty Plate Trail*, 89.
85. Gregory, *American Exodus*, 102.

to other marginalized groups seen as "un-American," uniting them in diminished access to the rights of citizenship.

The fact that the new migrants were white, however, brought attention to the problems in California, since much of America saw these migrants as unfairly unable to fulfill the American dream in a way that was not expected (or desired) by racist whites for nonwhite Americans. Writers capitalized on "the empathetic value of white skin."[86] Therefore, while the connection between the white migrants and other groups is repeatedly made, the whites still had advantages based on race. For instance, during this time period Mexicans were deported en masse from California with Mexican Americans sometimes deported along with the undocumented, while Anglo-American migrants were never subjected to such measures.[87]

Babb's novel explores and contests these racializing slurs through an examination of the myths of possession and the idea of collective respect in this new migrant community. In this space where corporations own everything and new land cannot be bought, the farmers need to adjust their view of what constitutes an "American" identity. In Oklahoma their ancestry and class defined them; in California they find that the spatial histories still matter but in ways they do not expect. The migrant workers quickly stop making references to their own ancestral roots once in California, as they see the owners doing, but, for them, without the money and the land necessary to "transcend" their origins, they are not escaping their link to another land. Instead, their tie to Oklahoma replaces their older geographic connections, and being from Oklahoma takes on meanings of nation, class, race, and citizenship that diminish these characters in the eyes of the powerful while opening up new possibilities for connections, even across gender and race, that expand further than the putatively white community in Oklahoma.

The corporate farm owners symbolize the "successful" method for identity formation in California, and Milt thinks specifically about the European names he notices on some corporate buildings: "Did any one of these men ever walk among the vines, picking the grapes with his own hands, remembering when he came to America a worker?" (168). The unseen owners, who have risen to become the names on the building, no longer connect themselves to their immigrant pasts. Their ethnicity may remain in their names but presumably not in their thoughts or actions, which focus only on money. From this view, to be truly prosperous, any embodied past needs to be shed. These owners do not need to remember coming to America, because "American-ness"

86. Ibid., 81.
87. See Balderrama and Rodríguez's *Decade of Betrayal*.

and with it the rights of citizenship are now marked as belonging to those with wealth and property as well as coming through the construction of a nonim-migrant past that claims an unmarked whiteness.

For the farmers, their embodiment and their past is fully seen by others. Not only do state inhabitants make remarks against their new neighbors, but company owners also clearly voice their feelings: "There's a class of people made for that kind of work the world over. Put them up and they'll be back down again" (205). While they are disparaged with these claims of inferior-ity, as well as continued reverberations of the spatializing slur of "Okie," the migrants see themselves as unified in this negative treatment. They start to re-form as a community because they are not welcomed by California. But the question they begin to ask is about their own standing in society because what they learn is "an okie [sic] is me. Someone different. Someone not as good" (164). They begin to doubt their equality because of their position as internally displaced people.

The term "Okie" also affects gender roles precisely because of its lack of gender specificity. Both men and women are equal targets of this slur since they are no longer perceived as having separate spheres but are instead inter-changeable in and out of the fields. As one camp manager tells them, in answer to Milt's protest that Julie was not strong enough to pick cotton: "To live in the cabin, you gotta average nine hundred pounds a day. Women usually always pick with the men" (172). The individual no longer matters; all that matters is the weight of cotton, fruits, or vegetables harvested each day, with gender only acknowledged in terms of relative productivity. This new view, which erases gender distinctions in an equal-opportunity oppression, also opens up new possibilities within the migrant group for the equal inclusion of women in their response to this subjugation.

The migrants' right to citizenship is called into question not just by a per-ceived foreignness but also by segregation and physical threats, which classify them as inferior nonwhites who must be kept separate. In *Whose Names*, this process starts with separate school systems: "They don't like their kids mix-ing" (171). Babb refers to this as Jim-Crowism, paralleling these attitudes to racial segregation.[88] The migrants also hear rumors about sterilization: "Yow, they want to fix us like horses. Just good for work" (171). In addition to the dehumanization revealed in the animal comparison,[89] compulsory steriliza-

---

88. Babb and Babb, *On the Dirty Plate Trail*, 99.

89. The prevalence of dehumanization is pointed out when a judge sentences a man for stealing junkyard radiators in order to buy food for his mother. He said, "It was the first time he had thought of these okies [sic] as human beings" (213), but he still put the man in jail for 11 years. This incident comes from Babb's field notes (she often pulls from her observations).

tion was supported during the time under a eugenics agenda that advocated it "as a means of eliminating the 'unfit' sectors of the population," including African Americans, which reveals the racist intentions that connect oppressed groups.[90] A quotation from a California physician about the white migrants makes this tie explicit: "There is such a thing as a breed of people. These people have lived separate for too long, and they are like a different race."[91] Such attitudes and actions toward the farmers elide the geographic with the racial, marking the migrants as just another portion of the "wrong" type of people and revealing that not even the kindness of collective respect that the farmers had given to their animals in Oklahoma is bestowed on them.

The connections among place, class, and race mutually reinforce the disempowerment of the farmworkers. This interaction is overtly stated by a "stooge" who speaks for the corporations: "'Get out of the way, okies [sic], or we'll give you some.' The men did not move. 'Git outa the way, you white niggers!'" (154). The migrant farmers are viewed on the same level as blacks, in a slippage from a geographic slur to a racial one—with both place and race equaling class and general inferiority.[92] All of this occurs in a lynching-type incident targeting an "Okie" who is a rumored unionizer. The slur becomes an attempt to keep this man and the community from changing their status. The term "Okie," then, is a crucial concatenation because it condenses movement, race, gender, and citizenship into one delegitimizing insult. It works as a spatializing term that marks the migrant workers as outsiders to California, as a racializing term that casts them as an inferior group only fit for manual labor, as a gender-neutral word that reduces individuals to their productivity, and as a synonym for "foreigner" (in opposition to American-ness) that makes the workers into possible targets for legal action and deportation. In other words, "Okie" is significant because it transforms white bodies and U.S. citizens into perceived racial others that can be exploited and threatened in the same way that various racial groups had experienced for years.

Moreover, her notes include this statement from another state official: "We ought to damn [sic] all the rivers in the state and drive them into them" (Babb and Babb, *On the Dirty Plate Trail*, 67, 65). The prejudice had expanded to threats of lynching.

90. Davis, *Women, Race, and Class*, 215.

91. Wasco field notes qtd. in Gregory, *American Exodus*, 101.

92. In the novel, this racialization begins with the dust storms that are referred to in various colors, from black and brown to yellow. When the residents' faces are covered by this discoloring dust, they are tied to the working past of African Americans and of Mexicans and Asian immigrants and separated from the "clean," white, dominant class. This association of dirt and darkness continues in California. The children consider why they are called Okies so hatefully, "when they washed their feet at night, bending low over the small pans, seeing the toes come up clean through the brown water" (164). Dirt's correlation with nonwhiteness is a relationship they see, even though their racialization is one that can "wash off."

Though the white owners equate the Okies with other racialized groups to disempower them, the conditions they create inadvertently allow the transplanted farmers to slowly begin to see their shared plight with these other groups. At first the racism of the owners causes the workers to develop their own prejudices against their competition, the "fast-working, and nimble-fingered Filipinos, the resident hard-working Japanese and Mexican" who could better "endure" the hot working conditions (160). These essentializing attributes as well as others related to stature, lack of ambition, and stoicism were historically stated by farm owners to the legislature when they were seeking workers as well as by the white migrants themselves.[93] With the realization of their common plight, however, the migrants start to adjust their bigotry. For instance, Milt begins to recognize how "poor Mexicans" are subject to the same corrupt working practices as he is, and "reckon[s] they work for nothing for the same reason we do": survival (180).

The racial diversity of the working conditions in the fields also leads to moments of potential interaction that break down prejudices and the corporately imposed hierarchies of difference. Milt demonstrates an unintended consequence of the corporate governmentality that reduces all racial groups to labor when he begins talking to a black worker, Garrison, in the cotton rows. His confusion as to how to broach the societal expectations about race is apparent, but so is his general respect for this other man:

> Milt waited automatically to hear the "suh" and when it did not come, he was relieved. He had been wondering how he would say it, tell him not to. *We're both picking cotton for the same hand-to-mouth wages. I'm no better'n he is; he's no worse.* The memory of being called a white nigger in Imperial Valley lay in his mind unforgotten, sore, like an exposed nerve. Milt looked at him. Garrison looked back, his eyes straight, and there was no difference. (185)

By recognizing the humanity in the man who picks alongside of him, Milt attempts to break down the expected racial barriers that ordinarily would not allow him to acknowledge Garrison as his equal. Quickly, Garrison becomes someone whom he esteems: "Somehow he wanted this man's respect, and suddenly he was not ashamed to acknowledge it to himself" (187). In part, the slurs leveled at Milt that negatively associate him with another racial group enable him to positively bond with a man who also does not deserve slurs. Others' hatred and shared working spaces facilitate the development of a tentative multicultural community.

---

93. Daniel, *Bitter Harvest*, 63–64.

Once the workers in the novel start to unionize, racial diversity is exemplified not merely in the workers but in the leadership.[94] Historically, this cooperation of races did not happen to such an extent. It would have been helpful, though, for unionization since, as Wixson states, the dispossessed Anglo farmers did not have experience in this area, but the "Hispanic farmworkers [. . .] were familiar with collective labor activities; it was central to the Mexican Revolution."[95] Babb's work imagines how multiracial interaction would help to develop social connections and to strengthen the political fight for empowerment.

Racism is, of course, not fully eliminated from this text through simple interactions. For instance, after the appearance of a white organizer named John Lacy, "a short, stocky Filipino" is introduced but not named as Pedro until after a caricature-esque description. Even as Milt overcompensates with statements about Pedro's neatness (194), which imply that the world expects him to be dirty, it is obvious that equal treatment of all of the characters is not achieved. In contradistinction to the limited views of American-ness promoted by the owners and framed through the derisive term "Okie," however, the novel does assert the need for gender-inclusive, multiracial community building and respect in order for people to gain strength in this new economic system that seeks to deprive some of its own citizens.

COMMUNITY BUILDING: A THIRDSPACE TOWARD SOCIAL JUSTICE

The value of considering fictional narratives about internal migration alongside the historical contexts is their ability to point to real and imagined uses of space that can change how we tell such histories and deal with displaced people in the future. Babb's novel in particular presents the space of the camp and the workers' precarious life there as the matrix out of which a utopian labor collectivity could be formed. This Thirdspace seeks social justice but ultimately falters on racial and gender distinctions.

Although the owners and the laws seek to diminish and divide the migrant laborers, community does begin to re-form in *Whose Names*. The

---

94. Phoebe, Garrison's wife, is not fully described, but since the laws at the time still prohibited marriage between races, it can be assumed that Phoebe is herself black. In that case, at this first union meeting Phoebe represents a second black person at the meeting, and the only woman of any race. Of course, Babb herself married interracially during the time when this anti-miscegenation law was still in force, to Chinese American cinematographer James Wong Howe, so this raced position does remain unclear.

95. Babb and Babb, *On the Dirty Plate Trail*, 16.

farmworkers, including men, women, and children, embrace a collective respect that recognizes the humanity in everyone across racial and gender lines, and with the support of one segment of government, they all work to provide for each other. The children show their interest in helping the community in ways that demonstrate their understanding of collective respect. Even the youngest, Tessie Starwood, helps out by proposing to steal alfalfa from a nearby field when their food supply has run out. Although she is told not to do it, the child goes ahead with her plan anyway and greatly aids everyone when they are starving (139, 149). Tessie sees a need, and she acts upon it, undermining ideas of individual ownership along the way. In the end, the children are building their own union to quit school because they are hungry and demand food (210). They fight for their rights as they watch the adults around them stand up for themselves.

Women are also a key part of the struggle in California, as they literally take up the fight to help the suspected union organizer, showing that unification is also an erasure of the separate gendered spheres that they had practiced in Oklahoma. The farming women scratch and tear at the attackers. In this moment, women unify across some class levels as an owner's wife also gets involved: "Patton's wife came through the crowd, screaming and crying and threw herself on the big man, scratching his face and pounding him with her fists. A diamond ring cut into his cheek before he could push her off" (154). Since Patton only owns a small business, this scene shows the collaboration of the downtrodden and the middle class, but it is a purposeful statement, as Mrs. Patton's money, her diamond, makes a deep slice into the enemy. Significantly, though, in opposition to their unification stands the woman who accompanies the attackers, "the powdered woman," (154) who runs from the conflict. Representative of the upper class in her silk dress and makeup, she keeps herself at a distance while her husband and other representatives of the upper class instigate the fight. Her makeup, however, shows her not only as distinct but as "made up": "One of the woman's tilted eyebrows had got rubbed off in the scuffle and she had a peculiar questioning look," and "[a] smear of lipstick marked her thin, youthless mouth" (154, 153).[96] As the other women break gender lines in the masculine activity of fighting, this woman stands out as false in her separateness. She remains gendered in a way that highlights the change in these migrant women.

In addition to the powerful voices and actions of men, children, and women, newly discovered support in the form of housing supplied by the federal government also helps the migrants to recreate community. The Fed-

---

96. Her powder also acts racially to separate by showing her intentions to appear whiter than those who work in the sun.

eral Emergency Migratory Camp, a minimal response to the ethic of care required for the displaced, keeps the characters out of the company camps and off the roads—in contrast to the designs of the state and local ordinances. The accommodations are very basic because of the limited allocations, but the workers can get floors for their tents to keep out the rainwater, have access to bathroom and washing facilities, and most importantly, perhaps, can surround themselves with positive support instead of the animosity of the owners. Woody, the man who runs the camp, cannot give them much, but kindness begins to spread again in this new space. The migrants have found an alternative to the myth of possession. Here the individualistic model of landownership is replaced by a collective respect model of society that is supported, although in a limited fashion, by positive government action.

In the camp, the migrants return to the idea of helping one's neighbor that they practiced in Oklahoma but without the incompatibility of also maintaining the myths of possession. Julia gives Tessie potato scraps when she sees her hunger, and then, as stated, the child gets her some alfalfa to eat when she cannot get out of bed. Everyone in camp, including Woody, helps a pregnant woman. They gather newspapers and scraps, and even use their precious gas to get milk for the baby (143).[97] This assistance often falls outside expected gendered roles, with women gathering food and men birthing babies. This new community helps each person based on necessity.

Additionally, one thing the government camp allows for is the space beyond necessity that exists for fun. Pleasure unites neighbors and helps them move past mere survival. Migrants play music in the camps,[98] and children play games such as "Run Sheep Run" (146, 152). Enjoying life with group pleasure and games invigorates workers, a benefit of grounded, communal space. With this newfound support and energy, migrants come together politically. Pamphlets about legal rights are slipped under their doors, and they start to recognize that a group is helpful in this situation as well: "We can get where we're going better together" (218). Unionization symbolizes a new type of community combining necessity and enjoyment.

In the final scene, Milt leads some of the men into his tent, the precarious, bare life space of this temporary camp. Surprisingly, in this space they find community and joy. As one man states, "Gee, it's a good feeling to be

---

97. Even so, the baby does not survive, becoming one of the statistics Babb notes in her journalism: in the San Joaquin Valley, in 1937, the death rate of births is "over two and a half times as great" as the national average ("Farmers without Farms," 17).

98. Sanora and her sister Dorothy Babb, who spent some time at the camps as well, saw the importance of music in the camp. Dorothy even took photographs of some of the musicians. See Babb and Babb, *On the Dirty Plate Trail*, 32.

together. It's sure good to feel the love of one another" (221). Part of this feeling of contentment is based on everyone joining financially. They collect money to move together to the next work site, with everyone sharing gas and food. Significantly, part of the way the money is raised is through the sale of a trailer. The one person who owns an individual "home" sells it for the greater good. They still have not found a solution to their constant movement, but the answer to group welfare lies in shared stewardship, the text says. Babb rewrites and resolves the conflict by positioning it into a socialist register: from each according to ability, to each and all according to need.

Not all of the union members are with them in this final scene because they are still being held in jail. Specifically, nonwhite members of the group and the female leadership are jailed (215).[99] This absence may point to the preferential treatment that the local government grants to whites, but it also points to a fundamental problem within the reestablished community. Even as the characters come together, the space returns to a white, male-dominated sphere; as the novel concludes, the key metaphor states that they need to "stand together as one man" (222). When the men come into the Dunnes' tent, Julia is able to join the circle, and Mrs. Starwood and Frieda also join them, but they are add-ons instead of primary members. The new group attempts to expand who is part of it, but in the end, that community does not yet include nonwhites, and it opens only a small space for white women.[100]

The political action they take in this scene continues to show the limits of their current group dynamics even as it articulates a utopian Thirdspace outside the confines of the individual home—using, as it were, the bare life of the federal camp to work toward collective justice. The characters write a letter to one of the women in jail, who is white, on the back of an eviction notice from a company camp sent "To John Doe and Jane Doe, whose true names are unknown" (220). The signing of this letter can be explained through social geographer Edward Soja's description of Thirdspace, which addresses the necessity of both real and imagined elements for the creation of new spaces.[101] The letter's salutation is a legal phrase that allows for expulsion of inhabitants without the need to know or acknowledge who is being dispossessed. The migrants all sign the letter as Jane and John Does to reclaim this nominal anonymity and imagine a power through this group demarcation. That is,

99. Even if the African American members had not been in prison, they still might not be present in this scene because federal housing was segregated (185).

100. Battat suggests that "in a unique twist to the conventional proletarian novel, her characters not only gain class consciousness at the end but a new gender consciousness as well" (*Ain't Got No Home*, 50), but while I see a change in the characters, as she does, they possess class consciousness from the beginning, and only realize in California how gender and race are related without fully implementing the consequences of that realization.

101. See Soja, *Thirdspace*.

by reversing the abstract, anonymous legal discourse as an act of resistance, the migrant laborers embrace the bare life space of their precarious existence and employ it to construct a collective identity of "Does." Even this symbolic gesture, though, exhibits the boundaries of this newly imagined union. Men and women are acknowledged through the distinct gendered names, but only an Anglo racial element is represented in the legalistic names. The sole use of the novel's titular phrase points to Babb's awareness of the ways in which the generic nature of legalized corporate discourse evacuates personal identity even as the workers' appropriation of it still leaves the multiracial element of their society unrealized. In other words, the workers' pooling of their resources in a shared working and living environment addresses the "real" element of Thirdspace in a pragmatic bid for collective justice, and their claiming of the anonymous name of "Doe" shows an "imagined," symbolic rejection of the myths of possession based on individual ownership. By claiming the terminology of naming already available, though, their imagined element does not reconstitute the idea of citizenship and American-ness because they do not consider who is left behind, and thus a more inclusive Thirdspace is not reached.

Babb's novel underscores that people should act ethically and enact protections for others, especially for the displaced, migrant workers, and those deemed "foreign," to create an egalitarian and enlarged sense of community. While Janie in Hurston's *Their Eyes Were Watching God* was only able to achieve a Thirdspace by herself in her own home without a full connection to her black community, the migrants in Babb's novel find a productive Thirdspace based on class, but in part due to the tactics of the owners and the local government, leave some out of the discussion. Nonetheless, the implications of Babb's conclusion still point to a communal Thirdspace based on shared ownership and equal citizenship across racial and gender lines without its being fully realized.

In *The Lay of the Land,* Annette Kolodny demonstrates that the United States' "pastoral impulse" led masculine texts over the centuries to represent the "land-as-woman," and she calls for others to analyze women's texts to see if they have avoided this limited metaphor.[102] By showing the yeoman who plows the virgin land as ultimately unrealizable and harmful, Babb's text presents an example of the alternative feminist discourse that Kolodny desired. Babb's belief in the land as belonging to all humanity—male, female, and all races and ages—in an ethic of mutual respect, reveals how we might have to change to save the land and ourselves. Or, as Babb states about her own experiences growing up,

---

102. Kolodny, *The Lay of the Land,* 146.

Long before I read that everything in the universe is connected, that all life is One, I knew it intuitively when I was seven years old. This was an awareness, not a discovery. It gave me a mystical sense of being in the universe, related, belonging, as transient as a flower but just as welcome. It gave me freedom from the need for specific beliefs and dogmas. It gave me tolerance. Perhaps it was the bigness of the plains and the sky that stretched my thoughts. *¿Quien sabe?* It is important to have mysteries. They urge us to seek and change and grow.[103]

Babb recognized her own transience in the world, but she also knew that with that impermanence comes the need to respect the people and space around you and stand up collectively for justice, as even her use of Spanish and her Native American connections show. She wrote *Whose Names Are Unknown*, finally, in the hope that others would perceive that principle as well. Overall, this chapter shows the potential of group action and political response in the face of governmental and corporate forces to control who has access to the land and power while still indicating the limits of the Dust Bowl migrants' use of the imagined aspects of Thirdspace. The environmental migration prompted by the settlement and plowing of the Great American Desert was in fact caused by a long-standing governmentality equating landownership with citizenship. This same ideology also recategorized white Americans as nonwhite, immigrant "Okies," thereby exposing how precarious citizenship is a construction that has certain structural similarities across several migrations and racial groups. The next chapter will show another group living in California who are denied access to citizenship rights, but they have almost no agency as the government forces them at the start of World War II from their homes in a migration back into the heart of America.

---

103. Babb, *An Owl on Every Post,* 219.

CHAPTER 3

The Wartime Displacement of Japanese American Incarceration

Disorientation and Otsuka's
When the Emperor Was Divine

IN THE 1930s, Anglo-Americans from the U.S. interior were moving to the West Coast and joined the migrant farmers already there, including those of Japanese descent, who by 1940 were producing about "40 percent of the California vegetable acreage."[1] The people of Japanese descent on the West Coast, however, were about to be sent into that same U.S. interior for the duration of World War II—but for them, the recently renamed Promised Land would regain its earlier title of desert. This movement was not induced, as in the previous examples of the economic and environmental migrations of the Great Migration and the Dust Bowl, but instead was a fully forced, mandatory displacement of people of Japanese ancestry, whether citizens born in the United States or first-generation immigrants who could not become citizens no matter how long they lived here. This forced movement of over 110,000 people from their homes to concentration camps in the U.S. interior remains of constitutional relevance today and is not the isolated, resolved "mistake" champions of U.S. democratic capitalism would like it to be.[2] By setting the wartime incarceration of people of Japanese descent alongside the migrations already discussed, we can see through this overtly political and constitutional displacement how internal displacements throughout the early twentieth century

---

1. Thompson, "The Agricultural Aspects of the Evacuation of Enemy Aliens."
2. Simpson, "Internment."

continue to depend on concepts of citizenship and landownership as well as racializing discourses in determining who can move where.

As with the white settlers who moved to the Great American Desert under the yeoman myth, the transnational experience of Japanese immigrants also was shaped by a larger pioneering story of economic improvement through landownership and farming. As Eiichiro Azuma argues, "Under the spell of bilateral intellectual traditions justifying colonialism, Issei [i.e., first-generation Japanese in the United States] historians discursively hijacked the American frontier as their own without disturbing its rhetorical foundations of conquest."[3] Such storytelling "led to an elaborate scheme of progressive history, tracing the trajectory of Japanese Americans from migrant laborers to sharecropper and from tenant farmers to idealized land-owning farmers," which would ultimately result in their reimagining themselves into "mainstream Americans."[4] Their quest for landownership, however, was not viewed by that mainstream America as a shared adoption of the yeoman myth but rather as a conquest of white territory. In other words, as Japanese agricultural landownership grew, so too did anti-Japanese sentiment.[5] Japanese immigrants, like their new government, created romanticized narratives that idealized landownership, but as time passed they watched that land be taken away from them, first through laws such as the Alien Land Law and later through World War II incarceration.

In the prewar period, legal decisions extending up to the Supreme Court displayed that the logic interrelating citizenship, landownership, and loyalty to the country was not an issue exclusive to black-and-white power dynamics. In *Terrace v. Thompson* (1923), the Court upheld the Alien Land Law, a California law that denied Japanese immigrants the right to own land. The Court's decision held: "It is obvious that one who is not a citizen and cannot become one lacks an interest in, and the power to effectually work for the welfare of, the State, and, so lacking, the State may rightfully deny him the right to own and lease real estate within its boundaries."[6] Here the Court uses the fact of noncitizenship to justify the withholding of ownership rights; it also links that justification to the idea that noncitizens without land cannot be loyal to the state, thereby buttressing earlier laws forbidding access to citizenship. This circular logic maintains the elite power structure that keeps Japanese immigrants in a precarious position in relationship to the state.

---

3. Azuma, *Between Two Empires,* 92.
4. Ibid., 93–94.
5. Ngai, *Impossible Subjects,* 39.
6. *Terrace v. Thompson.*

Several of these same concepts are evident in the governmental, public justifications for the later incarceration during World War II. For example, the U.S. Army's propaganda film *Japanese Relocation* (1943) attempts to explain the act of incarcerating people of Japanese descent—two-thirds of them U.S. citizens—as though it were a thoughtful, orderly maneuver that was undesirable but necessary. The narrative logic positions the government with an unspecified "we" making these choices: "We are protecting ourselves without violating the principles of Christian decency," the narrator states, calling into question for whom the United States is a place of refuge and indirectly emphasizing that American exceptionality is tied to an exclusionary Christian ethos. Significantly, the propaganda utilizes frontier ideals as well, and yet there is no discussion of landownership as the "evacuees"—as they paternalistically labeled the incarcerees whom, via this term, they claimed to be protecting—irrigated, tilled, and harvested the U.S. interior until "the raw lands of the desert turn green." This statement supposedly points to a hopeful future, similar to the promises to homestead farmers in the interior that "rain follows the power," but instead seems to be a reminder of the interminable length of this incarceration, since turning a desert into this supposedly green paradise is akin to saying that their stay in the camps will last "until hell freezes over."[7]

By looking at this history and its literary representation in Julie Otsuka's *When the Emperor Was Divine* (2002), I argue that this wartime displacement reveals how a preexisting governmentality equating citizenship and landownership that disenfranchised people of Japanese descent was transformed into a claim to authority during a wartime state of exception and emergency. With this claim, the government disempowered and moved people based on ethnicity directly without regard for their rights, turning residents and citizens into stateless bodies without any obligation to protect them. The violence of this imposed movement and of the hyper-controlling rules then extended beyond the space and time of the camp to become an internalized biopolitics among the incarcerees and their descendants. Giorgio Agamben's explanation of the state of exception via the space of the concentration camp helps to elucidate this issue; while the camp seems to represent a space where the law is suspended outside of normal jurisdiction, this violent application of power actually undergirds modern notions of sovereignty and law in their regular functioning, so that the camp's "spatiotemporal" nature escapes its boundaries, "overflowing outside them" and "coincid[ing] with the normal order."[8] Alexander Weheliye's recent discussion of Agamben adds that these seemingly

---

7. Wilber, *The Great Valleys and Prairies,* 69.
8. Agamben, *Homo Sacer,* 19–20, 36–37.

exceptional moments themselves are always already part of the quotidian existence of people of color, revealing that the camp does not reduce individuals of Japanese descent to an undifferentiated bare life but to a racialized bare life through the perception of foreignness. By extending Agamben's and Weheliye's notions of the way that biopolitical power shapes everyday life, I argue that the imposed displacement during World War II became a self-imposed governmentality after the war when the people of Japanese descent left the concentration camps and attempted to return to normal rules. In other words, the imposed physical limitations of the camp became their own internalized restrictions on themselves no matter where they were placed.

It is important to note that these imposed governmental limitations were implemented in part along gender lines. That is, when the government assumed patriarchal power, it caused the breakdown of male-centered families, diminishing the men and granting women only illusory power. Eventually this patriarchal imposition caused people of Japanese descent of both genders to lose their sense of place and self in a process I call "disorientation." The historical and fictional incarcerees attempted to resist in a variety of ways. I employ Edward Soja's concept of Thirdspace (i.e., the combination of real and imagined spaces to create new possibilities) and Homi Bhabha's concept of third space (i.e., a place of positive hybridity) to show how Otsuka's novel presents a "Thirdspace" that does not lead to social justice for the characters but that challenges the racializing discourse that the government imposes on the displaced.[9]

When the Emperor Was Divine tells the story of a family of Japanese descent that endures a forced migration from their home in Berkeley, California, in a convoluted path both to and from U.S. concentration camps during World War II.[10] Readers follow the unnamed mother, sister, and brother to

---

9. See Soja, *Thirdspace* and Bhabha, "Third Space."

10. The nomenclature for the camps has been discussed at length, and I recognize that there is no unproblematic name for these places. Roger Daniels explains this issue in *Prisoners without Trial*, 46. He states that the government most commonly called the camps relocation centers as a palliative, but it has been stated that even Roosevelt himself called the camps "concentration camps" (46). Additionally, he comments that although camps did not become death camps like the German concentration camps, their goal was to concentrate particular people in these locations, so I will often use this label as well as "incarceration" over the term "internment," which has been demonstrated to be an anachronistic term as well as inaccurate, since Daniels has stated that it was not used during World War II as a totalizing label, since it refers only to "a legal process [. . .] to be applied to nationals of a country with which the United States was at war," (Daniels, "Words Do Matter," 183). For further discussion about the use of these terms, see Hirabayashi, "Incarceration." Additionally see National JACL Power of Words II Committee's *Power of Words Handbook*, which lists the group's views on terminology and some implications related to terminology.

the so-called Topaz Relocation Center in Utah and hear indirectly about the father's imprisonment as an enemy alien. Told from the shifting perspectives of different family members, this minimalist novel subtly revisits the psychological and cultural effects of a racist government policy on a group of people.

The government emptied people of Japanese ancestry from the West Coast, with many losing their land and possessions, as it tried to deplete the people themselves so that they would have no effect on the Anglo-American United States. The removal was an attempt to change the people themselves. As Michel Foucault has noted, "penal imprisonment, from the beginning of the nineteenth century, covered both the deprivation of liberty and the technical transformation of individuals."[11] Mae Ngai adds to this concept of transformation through imprisonment by describing additional stages to this process for people of Japanese descent during World War II: "Internment was a crisis of citizenship, in which citizenship was first nullified on grounds of race and then reconstructed by means of internment, forced cultural assimilation, and ethnic dispersal."[12] Otsuka's novel is significant, as I show, because it indicates how this transformation occurs through the space of the camp itself, as well as through the movement and government policies that literally and figuratively "evacuate" people, emptying them of their self-worth, individuality, and any connection not only to Japanese culture but to the United States as well. The very namelessness of the characters, in contrast to the individualized, concretized narratives of Hurston and Babb, points to the underlying challenge to identity and citizenship faced by people of Japanese descent. This targeted "emptying" of Japanese immigrants and citizens has continued consequences for Japanese Americans negotiating the legal and political aspects of their heritage.

A LEGAL HISTORY OF IMMIGRATION AND INCARCERATION

The idea that Japanese immigrants were not assimilable motivated much immigration law; the racist policies behind these laws became more visible during the war. Although seemingly justified by a state of emergency, the unconstitutional actions of federal government and the public support of the West Coast farmers showed a continuity with previous policies that were motivated by racism and greed. Critical race theory shows that U.S. laws regulated the immigration and rights of this group long before World War II. The Naturalization Act of 1870 opened up the possibility of naturalization

---

11. Foucault, *Discipline and Punishment*, 233.
12. Ngai, *Impossible Subjects*, 201.

to "those of African descent" in addition to "free white persons," but, by not addressing Asian immigrants, the act led to Supreme Court cases that judged the categorization of Asian immigrants through the black/white binary. For instance, the Supreme Court ruling on *Ozawa v. United States* confirmed that Japanese immigrants could never gain U.S. citizenship because they were neither white nor of African descent, creating a negative legal space from which their statelessness could be constructed. Other laws also supported this prohibition against Japanese immigrants' access to full rights. In 1913, with the passage of the Alien Land Law in California, Japanese immigrants, in addition to being prohibited from owning land, were labeled "aliens ineligible to citizenship," with only their children, the Nisei, able to gain the rights of citizenship through their birth in the United States; the first-generation Issei were marked as alien.[13] Additionally, the Johnson-Reed Immigration Act of 1924 halted immigration for Asians by prohibiting U.S. entry to those who were "ineligible to citizenship."[14] As critical race theorist Angelo Ancheta affirms,

> rather than being centered on color, which divides racially between the superior and the inferior, anti-Asian subordination is centered on citizenship, which divides racially between American and foreigner. Asian Americans are thus perceived racially as foreign outsiders who lack the rights of true "Americans."[15]

This perception of Asian immigrants and their descendants as perpetual foreigners presents a legalized nativism—"intense opposition to an internal minority on the ground of its foreign (i.e., 'un-American') connections"— whether or not there are any grounds for that perception.[16] Additionally, this freezing of Asian immigration, as David Palumbo-Liu has convincingly argued, refocused U.S. policies from regulating the Japanese immigrants attempting to come into the country to regulating those who were already in the country.[17]

---

13. Because the Issei were not allowed citizenship, I use phrases like "people of Japanese descent" or "people of Japanese ancestry" to attempt to include both the second generation and beyond who were able to gain citizenship (Japanese Americans) and those who were not. It was not until the Immigration and Nationality Act of 1952 (the McCarran-Walter Act) that first-generation Japanese immigrants were able to become naturalized citizens.

14. For more on the Johnson-Reed Immigration Act of 1924, see Ngai, *Impossible Subjects*, 21–55.

15. Ancheta, *Race, Rights, and the Asian American Experience*, 15.

16. Higham, *Strangers in the Land*, 4.

17. Palumbo-Liu, *Asian/American*, 18.

After the Japanese attack on Pearl Harbor on December 7, 1941, this "patriotic racism" became a "formal governmental policy," marking a distinction between Japanese immigrants and other Asian immigrant groups.[18] The new specificity denotes a change in the racial formation process, what sociologist Howard Winant calls the "socially constructed status of the concept of race" based on a historical context.[19] New restrictions were soon posted stating where and when people of Japanese descent could go (making no distinction between citizens and noncitizens). At the start of these regulations, immigrants of Japanese descent were grouped together with Italian and German immigrants under the rubric of "alien enemies," but the enforcement of regulations against these other "enemy" groups was more limited; after all, the argument went, did we want to stop Joe DiMaggio's father from being able to go about his life as usual? The political power of the East Coast Italians and Germans, the celebrity of DiMaggio, and racial views determined who was a threat.[20] Eventually, President Roosevelt signed Executive Order 9066 on February 19, 1942, imposing wartime demarcations on civilian spaces, with his secretary of war able to mark the West Coast as entirely made up of military areas "from which any or all persons may be excluded." This change meant that who the "enemy" was became even more specific and spatialized.

The position of people of Japanese descent as enemy, however, was not so much a military concern, but one determined by economic and racist motivations, as shown by the inconsistent application of the executive order and by the rhetoric of some of the proponents of the removal. On the one hand, although the largest population of people of Japanese ancestry (150,000) was located in the territory of Hawaii, the site of the Pearl Harbor attack, this area was not depopulated because the loss of the workforce would have devastated the local economy. (Importantly, though, more than 1,000 were still imprisoned.)[21] On the other hand, on the West Coast, with some Japanese Americans running farms and local businesses, their economic power was a threat to whites. In particular, the U.S. Department of Agriculture crop-report statistics detail that Japanese farmers during 1941 grew one quarter of

18. Ancheta, *Race, Rights, and the Asian American Experience*, 11–12.

19. Winant, "The Theoretical Status of the Concept of Race," 181.

20. Daniels, *Prisoners without Trial*, 51. This "more limited" removal of civil rights is no less worthy of study because of its smaller scale. For further information on this topic, see texts such as DiStasi, *Una Storia Segreta* and Krammer, *Undue Process*. A related incarceration worthy of study was that of the Aleut after the Japanese attacked Dutch Harbor, a U.S. military outpost on the Aleutian chain in the Alaskan territory, on June 3, 1942. See White, "The Lost Internment."

21. Ogawa and Fox, "Japanese Internment and Relocation," 132. For a particular experience in Hawaii, see George and Tamae Hoshida, *Taken from the Paradise Isle*.

the fresh berries and vegetables from California, including 90 percent of the strawberry crop and 75 percent of the onions, spinach, and cucumbers.[22] The Grower-Shipper Vegetable Association even admitted the desire to profit by throwing their competitors off their land when they sent their managing secretary to Washington to petition Congress to remove all people of Japanese descent from the West Coast:

> We're charged with wanting to get rid of the Japs for selfish reasons. [. . .] We do. It's a question of whether the white man lives on the Pacific Coast or the brown men. [. . .] If all the Japs were removed tomorrow, we'd never miss them in two weeks, because the white farmers can take over and produce everything the Jap grows. And we do not want them back when the war ends, either.[23]

Greed and racism came together in a way that allowed a resurgence of the idea that individuals seen as un-American did not have a right to landownership, and while the law had already withheld that right from Japanese immigrants, incarceration would take that right away from even Japanese American citizens who had to sell quickly or not gain any money at all for their land and their labor. As even the U.S. Army's propaganda film admitted, "quick disposal of property often involved financial sacrifice for the evacuees."

The government, too, had its own economic desires tied to the ongoing development of farmable land, planning that the interior land near the concentration camps would "become, through the efforts of the internees, economically self-sustaining" even though it was nonarable.[24] This liberal capitalistic vision, recalling the ideology of farming and the yeoman myth that led to the Dust Bowl, was rendered all the more disjunctive to reality since, "in many cases, such as at Topaz, where the majority of the internees were urbanites, the internees were found to have 'no previous experience in agriculture' at all."[25] The people of Japanese descent in the camps were on nonproductive land, often did not have the necessary farming skills, and were not able to own

---

22. Frank J. Taylor, "The People Nobody Wants," 64.

23. Ibid., 66.

24. Lye, *America's Asia*, 161.

25. Ibid., 171 quoting Ernest Reed, "Termination Report," 22. Otsuka's own grandparents fit this categorization. As she explained to me, "They did not do agricultural work. My grandfather was a businessman so he was the general manager of a Japanese export/import company in San Francisco. Life was fairly comfortable for them before the war but not afterward" (in an interview with the author, August 14, 2016).

the land or the true value of their labor in any case, as they were transformed into prison workers able to be hired at greatly diminished pay.[26]

Although the government may have been in denial about the possibilities for this interior land, government officials did acknowledge the hardship of financial loss for people of Japanese descent and their own discomfort over "evacuating" American citizens; they also revealed their knowledge of the unconstitutionality of their actions at the time. A diary entry by Secretary of War Henry L. Stimson about the incarceration order indicates his awareness of its implications for the American system of government:

> The second generation Japanese can only be evacuated either as part of a total evacuation, giving access to the areas only by permits, or by frankly trying to put them out on the ground that their racial characteristics are such that we cannot understand or trust even the citizen Japanese. This latter is the fact but I am afraid it will make a tremendous hole in our constitutional system to apply it.[27]

Stimson's worries from the perspective of the executive branch about creating a hole or exception in the "constitutional system" were echoed by some in the judiciary. In *Hirabayashi v. United States* (1943), for instance, which challenged the curfew component of Executive Order 9066, Justice Frank Murphy, who initially dissented, wrote in his finalized concurring opinion, with the unanimous court, something that continued to read like dissent. He stated that the curfew creates "two classes of citizens for the purposes of a critical and perilous hour—to sanction discrimination between groups of United States citizens on the basis of ancestry."[28] These grudging acceptances of "military necessity" relied on an assumption either that in a time of war the government must combat its enemies through solidarity or that people of Japanese descent were disloyal to the United States.

This second point, however, was strongly undermined by the Munson Report, which, utilizing evidence from the Office of Naval Intelligence and the FBI, concluded in 1941 that "we do not believe that they would be at least any more disloyal than any other racial group in the United States with whom we went to war" and "the Japanese are loyal on the whole."[29] Thus, while multiple government officials questioned their own actions, they comforted themselves

---

26. As Sandra Taylor in *Jewel of the Desert* states, "Most earned $16 a month for a forty-four-hour week, at a time when other Americans made $150–$200 a month" (157).

27. Hodgson, *The Colonel*, 259.

28. Irons, *Justice at War*, 244. In note 68 he cites Murphy, draft dissent, box 132, Murphy Papers, UML and *Hirabayashi v. United States*.

29. Munson, *Report on Japanese*, 15–16.

through using the language of the state of emergency to justify their breaking of the rule of law. As Caroline Chung Simpson explains, though, these
actions were a part of a longer history of controlling the power and rights of
its populace:

> Critics have depicted the Japanese American internment as part of an
> ongoing early twentieth-century policy of labor management through land
> reform and the dispossession of racialized populations. [. . .] This emerging
> critique has established internment less as an isolated historical event or
> ideological crisis than as part of the very logic of U.S. democratic capitalism,
> which reproduces its inevitability in the regulation of categories of citizen-
> ship and alienage.[30]

That is, not only was the government aware of its racist policies, but also
this displacement strongly demonstrated the ongoing trend of such actions
to maintain the empowerment of the few that is often hidden under
"exceptionality."

In the months after the presidential order, civilian exclusion orders followed that were addressed "to all persons of Japanese ancestry" with accompanying maps, illustrating both visually and linguistically the systematic erasure
that encircled the "offending" persons and excluded them from that space.[31]
These orders led to the mandatory mass removal of the entire Japanese and
Japanese American population from the West Coast. These people, labeled as
a threat, were tagged and shipped en masse to various concentration camps in
desolate spots, from the deserts of Utah to the swamps of Arkansas, to separate them from the rest of the population. The sites of the camps were know-
ingly located on "desolate, nonproductive" land, mostly already owned by the
federal government in locations such as portions of Native American reservations and forfeited property.[32] In other words, the government attempted to

---

30. Simpson, "Internment." See Lye, *America's Asia*.

31. One such example of the space-related specificity is from Civilian Exclusion Order No.
27, dated April 30, 1942:

> All of that portion of the County of Alameda, State of California, within that
> boundary beginning at the point at which the southerly limits of the City of Berke-
> ley meet San Francisco Bay; thence easterly and following the southerly limits
> of said city to College Avenue; thence southerly on College Avenue to Broad-
> way; thence southerly on Broadway to the southerly limits of the City of Oakland;
> thence following the limits of said city westerly and northerly, and following the
> shoreline of San Francisco Bay to the point of beginning. (United States Commis-
> sion, *Personal Justice Denied*, figure A)

32. Wallinger, "Dispersal of the Japanese Americans," 78 quoted in Lye, *America's Asia*, 161.
War Relocation Authority, *A Story of Human Conservation*, 20, 22. I owe the combination of

quantify, categorize, and contain the people of Japanese descent on the West Coast by geographically delimiting, tagging, and then moving them to the wastelands of the interior. These spatializations tried to perform a metonymic substitution—exchanging, as it were, the Japanese American citizens' valuable property and land on the West Coast for desert land and the regimented space of the concentration camp. While the journeys taken by individuals differed vastly, many remained in some type of camp until 1945, with the last relocation center, Tule Lake, not closing until March 20, 1946.[33] This spatial control had long-term effects on how individuals regulated their own bodies and identities, since the government did not acknowledge the demoralizing and illegal construction of this substitution for decades. Those who were incarcerated were never tried for their alleged crimes—most were not even told what their crime was—even though the entitlement to a trial is a constitutional right; redress was not made for these actions until 1988. By being treated as stateless displaced persons, the people of Japanese descent highlight one of the central concerns of this book, namely how to theorize rights with movement in a manner beyond white capitalist logic.

INCARCERATION NARRATIVES

This governmental approach has a literary parallel. While the initial impetus of complete "evacuation" of Asian American literature by the Anglo-American mainstream has been replaced by a "multicultural" acceptance, some Asian American literature is still sold through its focus on the individual's need to change before being accepted and feeling acceptable.[34] Palumbo-Liu has noted this trend of marketing Asian American literature as "the literature of an assimilated group now at peace after a 'phase' of adjustment."[35] The adjustment is an inward assimilation that "is necessary for the suture of the ethnic subject into an optimal position within the dominant culture," or what he labels a "model minority discourse."[36] By embracing this discourse, the reader

---

these two examples to Lye, *America's Asia*, 160–61.

33. Daniels, Kitano, and Miller, *Japanese Americans*, xxi.

34. This denial of Asian American literature was fought against most famously by the editors of *Aiiieeeee!* (Chin et al.). For more on the gendered and racial implications of this complex fight for recognition, see Ling, *Narrating Nationalisms*, 3–30.

35. Palumbo-Liu, *Asian/American*, 410.

36. Ibid., 397. Chris Vials has noted how Palumbo-Liu's account accords with other work by recent scholars: "In their own respective ways, David Palumbo-Liu, Robert G. Lee, Christina Klein, Elaine Kim, and more recently Colleen Lye have seen these decades as a bridge between the prevailing pre–World War II view of Asians/Asian Americans as the Yellow Peril

experiences a sense of resolution that neatly wraps up the problem and blends Japanese American characters into whitewashed "Americans."[37]

Incarceration narratives in particular attempt to escape this model minority discourse because their subject matter addresses such imposed alterations of self. As Lisa Lowe has pointed out when looking at some incarceration narratives, they "refuse, in different manners, to develop, reconcile, and resolve."[38] In contrast, scholars Fu-Jen Chen and Su-Lin Yu argue that many of these narratives are written with a linear structure, enabling readers to conclude that there were few long-term repercussions to those who were incarcerated merely because the narrative is linear with a sense of "finality about 'returning' and 'being free.'"[39] Admittedly, the first memoir about the camps, Miné Okubo's *Citizen 13660* (1946), possesses a strict linearity and quick resolution: it ends with Okubo's release and her statement, "I was now *free*. [. . .] My thoughts shifted from the past to the future," as though separating those times were that simple.[40] It is reasonable, however, that a narrative published immediately after the experience could not give a long view on the subject, and even the narrative's existence belies that she could so easily turn her thoughts from the past.[41] Narratives written with any distance from World War II reveal even more fully that the incarceration experience continues to haunt the story and its subjects. For instance, Yoshiko Uchida's chronicle *Desert Exile: The Uprooting of a Japanese-American Family* (1982), while following a narrative structure similar to Okubo's account that ends with the narrator's departure from the concentration camp, adds an epilogue that discusses the history beyond the camps for readers of the next generation, giving the *longue-durée* view. Also, in Jeanne Wakasaki Houston's memoir about her experiences at one of the concentration camps, *Farewell to Manzanar* (1973), the story extends beyond the time at Manzanar and even includes nonlinear segments, such as a proleptic chapter, delaying the expected release from the camp and again showing how its effects continue after their expected end date. Therefore, while a basic linear structure may allow for a simpler reading, how these texts break up those narrative expectations shows in varying ways that the story cannot be neatly contained.

---

and the reigning postwar discourse of Asian Americans as 'model minorities'" (*Realism for the Masses*, 114).

37. Palumbo-Liu, *Asian/American*, 410.

38. Lowe, *Immigrant Acts*, 48. Lowe analyzes Monica Sone's *Nisei Daughter* (1953), John Okada's *No-No Boy* (1957), and Joy Kogawa's *Obasan* (1981).

39. Fu-Jen Chen and Yu, "Reclaiming the Southwest," 552.

40. Okubo, *Citizen 13660*, 208–9.

41. Additionally, Okubo's piece, through its use of medium, resists resolution through narrative dissonance. Okubo tells the facts plainly, accompanied by illustrations like a children's book, yet the content remains very adult.

The inability to resolve the texts is structurally demonstrated in fictional work about the concentration camps as well. Early writers such as Hisaye Yamamoto in her short story "The Legend of Miss Sasagawara" (1950) and John Okada in his novel *No-No Boy* (1957) frame their narratives with an observer who remembers the characters, thus breaking up a straightforward presentation. In "The Legend," the narrator is an incarceree who relates Mari Sasagawara's story, but she reflects on the story many years afterward as a graduate student who survived the camp but has not erased the experience from her mind, revealing that, as the author herself states, "It is an episode in our collective life which wounded us more painfully than we realize," staying with them all their lives.[42] Similarly, in *No-No Boy* the story is framed by a Japanese American soldier who is thinking about the novel's protagonist, "his friend who didn't volunteer for the army because his father had been picked up in the second screening and was in a different camp from the one he and his mother and two sisters were in."[43] The reflections of the unnamed soldier show that his spatial distance from the concentration camps is not an erasure of what happened there. Both stories align with the nonfiction retellings and show that narratives about the incarceration disrupt the simple progression of these stories through time and space, leaving characters of Japanese descent, whether incarcerated or not, dwelling on these events long after their conclusion.

The works discussed thus far were composed by those who lived through the experience of the concentration camps, but now the narratives of the next generation (most often the Sansei—the third generation) are appearing, such as Otsuka's novel.[44] With these additions to the canon, we should consider how the new authors draw upon or depart from earlier texts. Otsuka is certainly indebted to those who came before her in content and approach (and she credits many of these sources at the end of her novel, including some of those listed above), but with crucial distinctions.[45] Structurally, Otsuka follows Houston's lead by including what happens to the characters after their return

---

42. Yamamoto, *Seventeen Syllables*, 69.

43. Okada, *No-No Boy*, xi.

44. This focus does not intend to occlude, of course, that others outside of this heritage are also writing novels about the Japanese American concentration camps. Recent popular novels such as Jamie Ford's *Hotel on the Corner of Bitter and Sweet* (2009), Susan Choi's *American Woman* (2003), and David Guterson's *Snow Falling on Cedars* (1994) show interest in this history and narrative from multiple perspectives.

45. In addition to "A Note on Sources" at the end of her novel, she also mentions in interviews the large amount of research that she did:

> I spent months and months reading oral history collections, secondary source books about the internment, and old newspapers from the 1940s. I had to know how things happened, and when, and how things looked, and what kind of plants grew where, and what the dimensions of the barracks were, and what a dust storm felt like—all these things I had to know more for myself really, than for the book,

FIGURE 1. Dorothea Lange, "Family of Japanese ancestry arrives at assembly center at Tanforan Race Track," San Bruno, California. National Archives, April 29, 1942.

from the camps, and many of the details that she relates are based on her close reading of earlier works. However, what separates her work is that each chapter is narrated by a different character so that time and space are experienced distinctly depending on the perspective.[46] Her motivations for writing also differ from those who came before her. Otsuka's purpose is not to relate her own per-

so that I felt I could tell the story confidently. (Kawano, "A Conversation with Julie Otsuka," n.p.)

46. Like Min Hyoung Song states in *The Children of 1965*, who is also interested in this generation of writers, I agree that Otsuka "clears space for occupying a present that cannot simply look to the past as a possible source of healing or as something long past, unrelated to current struggles or aspirations for the future" (219), but I will also show the specific ways that Otsuka uses time and space to reflect the psychological impact of the camps.

sonal experience, nor is she writing to advance the political goal of reparations for those who had been in the camps, since that goal had already come to pass.[47] Instead, Otsuka's novel raises generational questions about the ramifications of incarceration and the continued threat of state-sponsored racism.

Although Otsuka's mother, uncle, and grandmother had been incarcerated, she was born years after their release, but she has more than once circumspectly addressed the implicit reasoning behind her writing *When the Emperor Was Divine*.[48] As she describes it, she began her research around the same time that her mother began to experience dementia and seemed to be using her work to try to connect to her mother and her past when she saw her mother slipping away. The separation Otsuka felt from her mother's experiences during her incarceration was enhanced because of the irrevocable nature of the illness, but it was a disjunction she had borne throughout her life. During her childhood she had heard stories about "camp" but did not fully comprehend their meaning, and even upon her discovery of a Dorothea Lange photograph of her mother, uncle, and grandmother on the day they had arrived at the Tanforan Racetrack, the obscuring angle of her mother stands for her own uncertain position in relationship to this historical yet intimate moment (see figure 1).[49] In the photo her grandmother is the central figure and her uncle is the eight-year-old boy in the foreground who is standing in front of a ten-year-old girl who is barely visible—Otsuka's mother. The man pictured is not a relative since her grandfather, like the father in the novel, had been arrested four months earlier, but his presence and the photo's awkward framing show the confusion of displacement. The novel's existence thus underscores the fact that the next generation continues to be affected by the

---

47. *When the Emperor Was Divine* was published after the U.S. commission report that conceded the government's wrongdoing and after the Civil Liberties Act of 1988 was signed by Ronald Reagan, giving $20,000 to each living camp survivor. The reason for the monetary redress, a symbolic token, was unequivocally stated in the final findings of the United States Commission on Wartime Relocation and Internment of Civilians report, *Personal Justice Denied*, made public on February 24, 1983:

> In sum, Executive Order 9066 was not justified by military necessity, and the decisions that followed from it—exclusion, detention, the ending of detention, and the ending of exclusion—were not founded upon military considerations. The broad historical causes that shaped these decisions were race prejudice, war hysteria, and a failure of political leadership. (459)

Both the words and the reparations by the U.S. government acknowledge that the concentration camps were wrong.

48. The details from Otsuka, "Julie Otsuka on Her Family's Wartime Internment In Topaz, Utah" were also part of the Gluckauf-Haahr Annual Lecture in Literature I heard her give at Yeshiva University on April 17, 2013.

49. Otsuka, "Julie Otsuka on Her Family's Wartime Internment In Topaz, Utah."

trauma their parents and grandparents experienced; they experience "post-memory," Marianne Hirsch's term for an "experience of those who grow up dominated by narratives that preceded their birth, whose own belated stories are evacuated by the stories of the previous generation shaped by traumatic events that can be neither understood nor recreated."[50] Therefore, this generation may feel themselves in a "spatial and temporal exile," not the exile of their parents in the U.S. concentration camps, but the exile *from* the camps, the site of the trauma.

Even now Otsuka is uncertain if she is done with this material, stating in an interview with me how elements from *When the Emperor Was Divine* returned in her next novel, *Buddha in the Attic*:

> I thought when I finished *Emperor*, "Well, I'm done with World War II and the camps." I never thought I'd go back to it, but the little piece of unfinished business for me [. . . came back in *Buddha's*] last chapter. That was what I was wondering about when I finished *Emperor*: "What about their neighbors? What did they feel?"[51]

Additionally, Otsuka has written the short story "Diem Perdidi," which is connected to the concentration camps through a character similar to her own mother, who is dealing with dementia as well as strong memories of her past. In our interview, Otsuka viewed this story as her most "personal" "merger" of the camps with her own family's history, indicating that the material is not growing more distant for her over time, but rather is an ongoing working through of this history and its relationship to her family.[52]

Part of the next generation's writing then becomes an attempt to understand what they can never fully grasp and yet still feel, showing that there

---

50. Hirsch, *Family Frames*, 22. Rea Tajiri, the Sansei director and narrator of *History and Memory: For Akiko and Takashige* (1991), states her own sense of generational displacement in a voiceover:

> I had known all along that the stories I had heard were not true, and parts had been left out. I remember having this feeling growing up that I was haunted by something, that I was living within a family full of ghosts. There was this place that they knew about. I had never been there, yet I had a memory for it. I could remember a time of great sadness before I was born. We had been moved, uprooted. We had lived with a lot of pain. I had no idea where these memories came from, yet I knew the place.

51. Julie Otsuka in an interview with the author, August 14, 2016.
52. Ibid.

has not been an easy resolution to the story and the history.[53] While the Nisei have not been completely silent on the subject since a substantial earlier canon exists, the next generation continues to write about the concentration camps, showing that people of Japanese descent are still sorting through the forced movements that affected their community and themselves.[54]

Significant identity issues resulted from the forced displacement of Japanese people in the United States, because, as I show, the cultural identities of people are inextricably tied to migration and space. Discussing other Japanese American incarceration texts, Lowe has noted that "Japanese Americans were forced to internalize the negation of Japanese culture and to assimilate to Anglo-American majority culture."[55] While she does not speak as much about the geographic elements of this cultural shift, she does point to the self-negation involved in this process. By adding the spatial element, I examine this shifting of place and self in relationship to movement. In the specific instance of the 1940s U.S. concentration camps, the governmentality is what I term "disorientation" because it resulted in the migrants' loss of a sense of place and self through a complex pattern of movement and alienation from space.[56] The government's policy attempts to "dis-orient" by compelling the incarcerees to turn away from the East—here, it is not the compass direction but any Japanese cultural connections—and to instead adopt an imagined communal binary view of "us vs. them," American versus Japanese.[57] *When the Emperor Was Divine* shows how this practice of disorientation disassociated physiognomy, cultural practices and objects, and cultural/national identities from one another at a particular point in U.S. racial history, resulting in an alteration of

---

53. Chu, "Science Fiction and Postmemory Han," 97. Otsuka, for instance, was partly trying to expand the one-sided story she discovered in a box of letters her grandfather had written to her grandmother while he was incarcerated (Kawano, "A Conversation with Julie Otsuka," n.p.).

54. Some Nisei have actually returned to the topic now that the next generation is writing. For instance, Jeanne Wakatsuki Houston's 2003 fictional epic about three generations of women and the camps is an example of such a revitalization. Houston had coauthored the renowned *Farewell to Manzanar* in 1973 and *The Legend of Fire Horse Woman* is her first novel. At the same time, Sansei author Perry Miyake's *21st Century Manzanar* (2002) tells the story of a dystopian near future where Japanese Americans are again incarcerated (ReVac) when the United States engages in an "economic war" with Japan. For this next generation, both the past and the future remain haunted by the camps.

55. Lowe, *Immigrant Acts,* 49.

56. Using the base of "oriental" is of course loaded since this term has a history of racist usage as a means to dehumanize people from Asia. For a discussion of this topic, see Edward Said's classic, *Orientalism.* I call upon this term precisely to point to the racist implications of the actions toward Japanese immigrants and Japanese Americans during incarceration.

57. This idea of disorientation can be tied to Palumbo-Liu's literary perception about the model minority discourse, but here the government and not the literary agent or audience is the one forcing the discourse.

identity with effects into the present day for those who were incarcerated and their descendants. As this chapter illustrates, the alteration of self based on movement, community, and government shows that external oppression and the imposition of statelessness can easily slip into internal oppression when the environment is so unforgiving that the individual cannot maintain a separation between the oppressors' tactics and his or her own internal thoughts. When characters lose their sense of place, they also lose their sense of self, resulting in self-hatred or disappearance, which weaken both the individual and the community in which he or she resides.

In order to explain the disorienting effects on Otsuka's characters, I first discuss how the novel introduces the orientation of these characters before their movement. Then I demonstrate how the separate movements of the father to various prison camps and those of the mother and children to a concentration camp confuse these characters because of their oppressive surroundings. The characters attempt to resist through imagination, using dreams and magical thinking, but the Thirdspace that the novel creates only fully exists outside of the text on the level of reception, with the family remaining oppressed. The novel's Thirdspace challenges the distinction between foreign immigrant and internal citizen via the bare, racialized life of the camp. That is, the mapping of physiognomy onto the citizen/foreign binary exposes the racist and inequitable policies at the heart of the government itself. Even when the family returns home, internalized disorientation continues to affect how they view themselves and their community, thus indicating that the migration narrative remains unresolved for Japanese Americans.

ORIENTATION AND PLURALISM BEFORE DISPLACEMENT

Before incarceration, *When the Emperor Was Divine* presents an example of a Japanese American family successfully functioning in U.S. society. Even with the racism that predates World War II, the novel's family has learned to navigate these issues, whether literally going to different places or interacting outside of the Japanese American community. At this point, they are able to feel comfortably situated in a pluralistic society, but this feeling will change as state-sponsored racism undermines their relationship to their spatialized world and their sense of self.

In the beginning of the novel, the mother is clearly oriented in her world and assumes without discussion her new role as head of the household. Although Pearl Harbor and her husband's removal from their home had occurred months before the novel starts, she and her children still live in their home, enabling them to maintain a sense of stability. She is grounded in space and time and has positive interactions with her neighbors while being able to incorporate Western and Eastern ideologies into her everyday life. Historically, some of this stability might have also come from the larger sense of a Japanese community, since the vast majority of U.S. residents with Japanese ancestry lived in the state, enabling a cultural support system.[58] Within the novel, many of her movements take her through Japanese Town, as it was then called, so that a connection to an ethnic community was possible. Specifically, the book starts with the mother running errands, and she has no trouble traversing and understanding the space around her: "At the corner of Shattuck she took the streetcar downtown. She got off at Kittredge and went into J. F. Hink's department store" (6).[59] She easily moves between modes of transportation, sometimes walking, sometimes riding the streetcar. She systematically understands how her current location connects to her desired destination. Additionally, she has an understanding of her place in time, based on her quick movement to start packing as soon as the evacuation notice appears and on her reading the news stories of the day: "The Burma Road had been severed and one of the Dionne quintuplets—Yvonne—was still recovering from an ear operation. Sugar rationing would begin on Tuesday" (4). These stories tell of the ramifications of World War II at home (food rationing) and abroad (Japan's success on the Burma Road), but they also juxtapose trivial details by bringing to the forefront the mention of Yvonne Dionne, one of the first-known surviving quintuplets.[60] The mother is able to handle the military, economic, and social aspects of her time and place. She has the time and the ability to comprehend both political and popular culture.

Moreover, the mother's interactions with whites remain convivial.[61] When she is at the hardware store, the owner Joe Lundy chats with her amiably, tries

---

58. Daniels, *Politics of Prejudice*, 1. Of course, this population in Hawaii was even larger, but it was still a territory.

59. Julie Otsuka, *When the Emperor Was Divine*. (New York: Anchor, 2002). All citations are from this edition.

60. This reference is also symbolically important since the Canadian government seized these children from their parents because they feared that their impoverished parents would exploit them. The government then kept them under surveillance until 1943, when they were nine years old; the government had quickly become the exploiters. Tourists could come to visit them while they played outside within a wire-fenced confine. These children, although celebrities, were themselves imprisoned like the mother in the text would soon find herself and her family.

61. Later in the text, the reader learns that neighbors did not say goodbye when the mother and her children were finally required to leave. Even so, the mother, because she still has a grounded sense of self, is able to explain away their lack of support by saying, "They're afraid" (115).

to stop her from paying, gives her a treat "for the children" (6), and compliments her attire. At the same time, this scene reflects the changing atmosphere, since Joe's actions further reveal his sense of collective guilt, as he tries to wipe away an invisible stain on his cash register in order to avoid discussing her family's impending incarceration. In spite of this underlying tension, she maintains a solid, healthy sense of space, time, and self and relates to others with ease, even as those interactions become racially tinged.

Eastern and Western cultures intermingle in the mother's daily routine. As she stands in her kitchen, she listens to the radio:

> Enrico Caruso was singing "*La donna é mobile*" again. His voice was full and sweet. She opened the icebox and took out a plate of rice balls stuffed with pickled plums. She ate them slowly as she listened to the tenor sing. The plums were dark and sour. They were just the way she liked them. (9)

She happily eats a Japanese snack while listening to Italian opera and enjoys them both with no sense of inner conflict. Of course, in this case not only is she enjoying transnational cultures, but she is also enjoying two items from perceived U.S. enemies. Additionally, we see that her home contains material objects that come from both cultures, from a bonzai tree (7) and ivory chopsticks from her mother in Kagoshima (8) to a wind-up Victrola and Westminster chime clock (7). The mother has embraced a pluralistic existence where various cultural elements sit side by side. She is comfortable in her own skin and in the world that surrounds her.

Although the mother's actions are told as they happen, accounts of the father focus on memories of him from before the war, since he is already imprisoned when the novel begins. In them, he too seems happily connected to his community and his children, singing songs and making time for his family. Like his wife, he combines Western and Eastern cultures. On the one hand, his food of choice is American: "The thing that he loved most about America, he once confided to the boy, was the glazed jelly donut" (63). On the other hand, the boy also remembers his using a distinctly Asian implement to do some yard work: he watched his father "plucking the caterpillars one by one off the snow pea plants with his long wooden chopsticks" (68). Without internal conflict, both parents have comfortable relationships with their environments and themselves.

The children similarly start off in a much more grounded place than where they end up. Before the camps, they are able to maintain close interracial relationships on the school grounds and at other children's homes. "*Your house or mine?*" (120), the children remember their classmates calling out to them.

Although they were born and raised in the United States, they too combine Eastern and Western ideas in their lives. As Sandra Taylor notes about the historical children of Japanese immigrants, "the Nisei were truly Japanese Americans, growing up with one foot in each culture," but she also mentions children who were not invited to Caucasian children's houses after school; this prewar acceptance was not universal.[62] The children, both in the book and historically, were integrated at school, but the record shows that for some segregation took over after school hours while for others integration continued after school but with elements of racism still experienced.[63] In the novel, the children do have a foot in each culture, since after school, the pop culture references that fill the characters' world are all Western, from the boy's desire to hear *Speaking of Sports* on the radio (14) to his sister's fondness for Dorothy Lamour and "Don't Fence Me In" (13), but when they are at home they both drink "barley water" (14, 16). The children's blending of cultures works more on the public versus private level of generational assimilation, but the entire family fits into their community while not being afraid to enjoy personal likes and dislikes that may fall outside of U.S. cultural norms. The family has a "stone lantern covered with moss in the garden, and the statue of the fat round Buddha with its head thrust back" resting in the yard alongside a "red Schwinn" and the ubiquitous "white picket fence" of the American Dream (68). Further, they maintain positive relationships with people outside of their own race, such as the boy's friendship with a girl with "long yellow hair" named Elizabeth Morgan Roosevelt (68). Even so, the book shows that these easy relationships should be questioned. After all, President Roosevelt betrays them when he signs Executive Order 9066, and later fences stand as obstacles to their dreams.

When the Emperor Was Divine does not romanticize the time period by saying that there was no racism toward Japanese Americans before World War II. The boy remembers that his father always "knew which restaurants would serve them lunch and which would not. He knew which barbers would cut their kind of hair" (62–63), pointing to the very real limits on spatial and social interactions. The boy also recalls his sister coming home from school with her new jump rope to report: "'They let me turn the handle,' she said, 'but they wouldn't let me jump'" (70), a historical detail that Otsuka probably gathered from her reading of *Jewel of the Desert*, a scholarly work on Japanese Americans in the World War II era, showing how her assiduously researched book presents factual particulars that connect the reader closely to the events

---

62. Sandra C. Taylor, *Jewel of the Desert*, 13.
63. Ibid., 12, 43.

of the time.[64] Racism is passed through the generations so that children speak it. These painful moments remind the reader that Pearl Harbor did not create anti-Asian racism in the United States, but with a firm sense of place and time, Otsuka's characters before World War II were still able to be integrated into their community and to have a strong sense of self despite the racism they did experience. As the war progresses, however, that racism, accompanied by widespread state sponsorship that uproots these characters, alters the characters' view of themselves.

The first chapter of the book ends with the characters' current clarity of time and place shifting toward the uncertainty of the future. The night before the family leaves, the mother tells herself, and her daughter's pet macaw, "I am right here, right now" (19), as if she is trying to remember this moment for the future, when the here and now might not be as grounded. The chapter's final sentences speak to the changing perception of time and space as the forced removal begins:

> In a few hours [the boy] and the girl and their mother would wake up and go to the Civil Control State at the First Congregational Church on Channing Way. Then they would pin their identification numbers to their collars and grab their suitcases and climb up onto the bus and go to wherever it was they had to go. (21–22)

Concrete directional and time markers at the start of this quotation give way to things that are new and strange: being identified by numbers attached to their clothes like luggage tags and going "wherever it was they *had* to go." Beyond the necessity of the movement, they do not know their destination, and the circularity of the phrase that starts and ends on "go" further accentuates a sense of constant movement without an end or arrival.[65] Historically, they are about to become part of a mass forced migration that extended along the West Coast as just one of hundreds of families in their specific "evacuation

---

64. Ibid., 12.

65. This repetition of the word "go" is a leitmotif that guides *When the Emperor Was Divine.* The mother uses this word to refer to the family's forced migration (9) and tells their pet macaw to "go" several times as she pushes him out into the night on his own forced migration; since pets are not allowed to be "relocated" (20), he becomes a domesticated pet without a home just like the family is separated from their home. At the camp, the men play the ancient Asian board game Go, which is about the conquest of territory. Then, once the family returns to the West Coast, the children comment, "We were free now, free to go wherever we wanted to go" (113), a slight alteration to show how *want* has replaced *need* based on their freedom. Finally, "go" is the last word of the book (144), turning any sense of an ending into an incomplete arrival. The characters remain in a constant state of movement that cyclically disorients them. They are kept on the go throughout the novel.

region" to be moved that day. This experience was repeated at the same scale in 108 separate areas, each moving an average of 1,000 individuals.[66] The end to the chapter marks a shift that parallels the historical details. The characters are about to begin their physical dislocation, and this journey will be characterized by force and vagueness. From now on, the government tells them that their identity is only to be externally perceived; they will have little say about who they are.

DISLOCATION AND PATRIARCHY

This governmentally forced movement demonstrates the power of the United States over the places people occupy, a fact that bears out Foucault's statement that "space is fundamental in any form of communal life, space is fundamental in any exercise of power."[67] In this case, for people of Japanese descent, the government "shattered their sense of community and replaced it with another one, a somewhat prisonlike [sic] existence where they lived under Caucasian domination."[68] In this new space, the military ruled and the inhabitants needed to submit to the sovereign authority of the government; the path of the journey itself further accentuates their disempowered position.

After the mother and children begin their physical journey, the details of the father's journey already underway are more fully articulated. Unlike the rest of his family, the father is arrested and tried, although the details of his treatment remain vague. What is explained is that the father has already made several moves, including four states, since his arrest on December 7, 1941, even though for the first four days, the family had no idea where he was.

The father's zigzagging forced migration functions to keep him unsettled and his family uncertain of and disoriented concerning his whereabouts. Taken in the middle of the night, still in his pajamas and slippers, he is not given the time to put on his shoes or his hat before they push him into the back of a police car (83). (Seven hundred Japanese resident aliens were arrested the day Pearl Harbor was attacked.)[69] The government was rounding up the perceived heads of the Japanese American community. The publically stated reason was that these individuals would lead acts of sabotage and espionage (even though the Munson Report, written just prior to Pearl Harbor, showed "there is no Japanese 'problem' on the Coast"), but they were

---

66. Daniels, *Concentration Camps, North America*, 87.

67. Rabinow, "Space, Knowledge, and Power," 252.

68. Sandra C. Taylor, *Jewel of the Desert*, xviii.

69. Levine, *A Fence away from Freedom*, 231.

also rounding up the heads of Japanese American families.[70] As the daughter notes, her father was in a camp where "only fathers lived" (61). Conflating fathers with men, and their perceived threat, underlined many actions by the United States. By removing these patriarchs, the government quickly forced their own governmental patriarchy onto fatherless and husbandless families.[71] As Chuh explains, incarceration in general aimed at redirecting loyalty to the United States: "Internment speaks of knowledge produced by racism and patriotism, the promulgation of devotion to the father(land) that demands different demonstrations of loyalty from the nation's would-be sons and daughters."[72] In history and in Otsuka's novel, we can see how the father of the family is replaced with the fatherland. That is, the government appeared to believe that without the fathers, these families would be more easily maneuvered—a reversal of earlier immigration policies that kept wives from their husbands as a means to bring in workers from abroad while controlling the population of immigrants. Supposedly, without the "Japanese" fathers, these families would renounce what the United States viewed as the truly threatening father figure—the emperor. The United States wanted people to turn away from Hirohito and metonymically from Japan.[73] As the novel's title suggests,

----

70. For further analysis of the Munson Report, see Weglyn's *Years of Infamy*.

71. Removing the men also furthers stereotypical gendered perceptions of Asians as feminine and submissive since the camps included mostly women, children, and the elderly. Men in the camps were already disempowered because the males who were seen as "powerful" had been arrested and imprisoned separately. David Eng might even add that this feminization leads to sexualization that marks these men as homosexual. See Eng, *Racial Castration*. Lisa Lowe ties this gendered perception to the foundational laws of the United States that first only granted citizenship to males and to whites, inextricably connecting gender and race, but "as the state extended citizenship to nonwhite male persons, it formally designated these subjects as 'male,' as well" (*Immigrant Acts*, 11), leaving Asian immigrants in an alien and feminine position until after World War II. Susan Koshy also points out that at the start of the twentieth century, gendering Japan had separated male and female into two pieces with "'the color and poetry that is Japan' [. . .] associated with the feminine subject and the political and economic power of Japan [. . .] associated with the masculine subject," the "object of desire and object of threat" (*Sexual Naturalization*, 43).

72. Chuh, *Imagine Otherwise*, 61.

73. The characters' dreams reflect the government's own occupation with the father figure; they are filled with references to their absent father. The boy dreams that his father will return to sit next to him on his cot and put on a pair of regular shoes—therefore regaining his dignity, including his masculinity. The daughter dreams that her father will come and sweep them away on a boat in an amalgamated European space, and the mother dreams of her own father in Japan. Literally they hope for the return of the father, but from the U.S. governmental perspective this desire also contains a threat. That connection among father, country, and power actually plays out in one of the boy's dreams. He dreams he is trying to see a picture of the emperor, whom he labels as a god, but something always goes wrong. These repeated failures blend in his dream with the idea that "he was miles from home, and his father was not there" (73). His father and his emperor are unreachable while he is far from his home—in his disempowered

the government wants the emperor to no longer be seen as divine and thus lose the power of a patriarch and, by extension, god.

Once in the camps, the family is further undermined. Because meals are not served family style but in group mess halls, many of the children eat together and quickly disassociate themselves from what was once the primary bond of family, a connection that is stressed in Japanese communities as the way that society coheres.[74] The camp instead becomes the-father-that-sees-all from the watchtowers, Foucault's panopticon and the replacement "god," with the family almost fully replaced by the military culture where people sleep in "barracks" and go to the bathroom in the "latrines." Otsuka's characters live in a military space as the enemy within. The armed guards on the towers stare at them with binoculars and searchlights just as they surveilled the enemy during their recent "tour of the Pacific" (52). The U.S. patriarchy can attack those who are living under its gaze, but for the incarcerated it stands as the only acceptable father figure.

Since the family's actual father is mostly absent in the story except through flashback, his postcards, and his final return at the end of the novel, we do not hear directly about the effects of each movement on him. What we do see are the effects on his family. While they track his progress from afar, even with specific postcards marking his location by state, his family feels disconnected from where he is. The vacation tone of postcards clashes discordantly with the father's prison experience. He is not visiting the pueblos, the riverbanks, or even "the world's largest stack" shown on the postcards. He does not "wish you were here," as many travelers write on such cards, as even his daughter cannot help but write on her postcards to friends on the outside (54). The language he uses is vague (where he is, the weather is "fine" [10]) and the landscape alien (in New Mexico he reports that there are no trees [34]). Partly, of course, this shorthand form of information is caused by the genre of postcard writing and by the father's desire not to send his family any of his troubles, but his narrative is also limited by the censors that obliterate lines of his writing—many of his short notes include full lines of blacked-out language. At other points his lines have actually "been cut out with a razor blade" (59), marking the violence of such silencing of voice. Both the movement of the father from place to place and the limiting of his communication remove the family's ability to clearly "place" him anymore.

The one time the mother is allowed to see him, she tells the children that he looks like a "hobo" (91) because he had not been allowed to change clothes

---

position, he cannot hold onto these standard patriarchal figures for himself. It is not just the government that recognizes an established connection between power and patriarchy.

74. Sandra C. Taylor, *Jewel of the Desert*, 9.

or shower, still in the pajamas and slippers he was wearing when he was taken away. The government forces this altered view of the father by not allowing him to take care of his body nor allowing him to remain in one place, turning the father into what Sherene Razack, referencing Samira Kawash, calls the "homeless body": "Through its presence as a material body that occupies space, but as one that is consistently denied space through a series of violent evictions, the homeless body confirms what and who must be contained in order to secure society."[75] The government now controls the father's body, and their rendering of that body creates a new view of him in the family's eyes: a nomadic statelessness that is also tied to a lack of hygiene.

Later, the daughter reinforces this ambiguous placement of the father. Although she knows the names of all the places he has been, she still ends the list of named locations with "wherever it was he happened to be" (30), echoing the language at the end of novel's first chapter that says that they will go "wherever it was they had to go" (22). As in that original statement, here her specifics begin to yield to vague generalities of the unknown. The separation of the father from his family and his constant movement isolate him and make it more difficult for his family to clearly identify him. By making the physical body impossible to locate in a specific place, the cultural body is undermined. Under the policies of the government, space and movement become weapons of disempowerment against identity and the family by displacing the father and positioning itself in his stead.

DISLOCATION AND DISORIENTATION FOR THE REST OF THE FAMILY

The space of the concentration camp, in history as well as in the novel, is the destination of a displacement that is designed to dehumanize and confuse. By treating residents and citizens as bare life, as animals that can be disposed of, the government imposes upon the incarcerated a warped sense of time, while the barbed-wire space of the camp in the desert reinforces the starkness of their constitutionally displaced existence.

In the novel, the mother and the two children, like the father, feel fully displaced because they are moved more than once. We learn, through information given out of linear order and adding to the disorientation, that they are first taken by bus to a temporary detention facility at the Tanforan Racetrack near San Francisco. From there they are moved by train to Utah, with the final leg of the journey by bus to the Topaz Relocation Center. None of these char-

---

75. Razack, *Race, Space, and the Law,* 10.

acters is merely relocated. Each is taken on a convoluted ride that promotes confusion through indirect paths and different means of transportation. This constant movement is part of the disorientation process. They can never be completely certain where they are going or when they will be moved next.

At the Tanforan Racetrack, their first stop, the mother and the children are housed in horse stalls. They have lost their home and are being treated in the same manner as an animal. The space itself is still marked for the purpose of holding horses instead of housing humans: the boy pulls some horse hair from the walls and looks to where the wooden door had been chewed by the former inhabitants. They sleep on mattresses stuffed with straw and even wash their faces in "long tin troughs" (30), so that not only does the space look like a horse stall, but they are also supposed to act like horses, a process of dehumanization. As David Sibley points out, "to animalize or de-humanize a minority group [. . .] legitimates persecution."[76] If people are not people but horses, they "logically" lose the rights and protections of humans under the law.

Next, the mother and children are moved to Utah. While the train to Utah has windows that allow the family to see the country they are traversing, each time they pass a town the soldiers who "guard" them tell them to pull down their shades. This separation between the external and internal space is supposed to protect them because so many people see them as enemies. On two separate occasions, however, a stone and then a brick are thrown through the window regardless of whether the shades are up or down (29, 43). These physical attacks highlight that the threat comes not just from the government—here represented by the soldiers who appear to be kind while carrying weapons —but also from the country at large that allows the government to take such actions against an entire group of people in the first place. The danger is from both inside and outside the train.

Looking at one attack, this moment is the first time in the text when a character is fully disoriented. The girl wakes up to the crashing glass:

> She was sweating and her throat was dry and sore and she wanted a glass of cold milk but *she could not remember where she was.* At first she thought she was in her yellow bedroom in the white stucco house in Berkeley but she could not see the shadow of the elm tree on the yellow wall or even the yellow wall itself so she knew she was not there, she was back in the stalls at Tanforan. But at Tanforan there were gnats and fleas and the awful smell of the horses and the sound of the neighbors on either side fighting until late in the night. At Tanforan the partitions between the stalls did not reach all the way up to the ceiling and it was impossible to sleep. The girl had slept. Just

---

76. Sibley, *Geographies of Exclusion*, 10.

now she had slept. She had slept and dreamed about her father again so she knew she was not at Tanforan, either. (43–44; italics added)

An attack causes her not to know where she is, a type of confusion that has been historically noted at the camps: "Whenever the community was racked by a disturbing event the younger children became disoriented."[77] In the girl's case, she wakes to being threatened, which makes no sense to her; therefore, her surroundings make no sense either. She works logically through her environment to try to ascertain her location using sight, sound, and smell. Her continued inability to uncover her current location turns her to the past and a positive memory of her father. She recedes from the current place and time because of its hostility and instead returns to a better place and time—one where her father was more dominant than the attacking community. Her disorientation on the way to the camp is only an early signal that these characters are being individually altered by their physical movement.

Once at Topaz, all of the major characters experience disorientation. This confusion is brought on by the destabilizing movement that makes them unable to resituate themselves, by their imprisonment, and by the hostility of the environment. As though their first stop at the racetrack was not bad enough, the concentration camp where these characters have been brought differs vastly from their West Coast home, which had moderate temperatures, easy access to the ocean, and an urban community. Space in this novel is not romanticized, as Chen and Yu state often occurs when literature discusses the Southwest as "something sublime, spiritual, or therapeutic, all founded on images of sun, desert, blue skies, dramatic canyon lands and mesas, [. . .] and other symbols of a different ethnicity."[78] Underlining this removal of the romantic, the boy comments on how his previous knowledge of the desert does not match the reality he experiences: "It was not like any desert he had read about in books. There were no palm trees here, no oases, no caravans of camels slowly winding across the dunes. There was only the wind and the dust and the hot burning sand" (53). The family members find themselves in a barren desert that not only lacks the basic elements of their former lives, but physically affects them as well. The glare off the sand is so bright that it blinds them temporarily (48), and the dust storms take their breath away, leaving them no means of avoiding the environment (64). Like the dust storms that I discussed in the previous chapter, these storms are of great importance, but because the circumstances are different, so too is the symbolism. The way that

---

77. Sandra C. Taylor, *Jewel of the Desert*, 126.
78. Fu-Jen Chen and Yu, "Reclaiming the Southwest," 553.

the dust permeates their space shows that while they are being contained, their space is still being invaded, leaving them no sense of privacy:

> The dust got into your shoes. Your hair. Your pants. Your mouth. Your bed. Your dreams.
>
> It seeped under doors and around the edges of windows and through the cracks in the walls. (64)

The dust is invasive, but also violent. It "made your skin burn. It made your nose bleed. It made your eyes sting. It took your voice away" (64). The harsh environment parallels the harsh treatment of the incarcerated. Historically, people recalled: "The dust storms were the worst. Everyone would become white."[79] This dust is not made from topsoil, so that the alkaline ground of the desert ironically speaks to the underlying desires of those who put them in the camp. Either they would be attacked and destroyed or they would become "white" through assimilation.

The bleak desert climate surrounds them, yet the space accessible to them is even more strictly confined, from the small size of their rooms to the borders of the camp—the barbed-wire fences: "The rules about the fence were simple: You could not go over it, you could not go under it, you could not go around it, you could not go through it" (61). These rules show how clearly imprisoned the characters are by the boundaries of their physical world and the rules imposed on them. Otsuka herself spoke of the contradictions of the camp, "It's a confined space, but it's also, in a way, an enormous space because when you actually see it, it's just endless. [. . .] If you were to try to escape there was no place you could go to."[80] Therefore, incarcerees could see the wide world beyond the camp but knew that they were required to stay within the contained spaces of their tiny barracks and the barbed-wire fences. Even the few times that they are allowed outside the camp they are reminded again of their place: "They said they'd been shot at. Spat on. Refused entrance to the local diner. The movie theater. The dry goods store. They said the signs in the windows were the same wherever they went: NO JAPS ALLOWED. Life was easier, they said, on this side of the fence" (66–67). They are being trained to stay within their confines both through physical and psychological means; they are being taught to know their place.

In keeping with the spatiotemporal nature of the camp, the constraints of the environment are also temporal. Min Hyoung Song notes that time in the

---

79. Levine, *A Fence away from Freedom*, 50.
80. Julie Otsuka in an interview with the author, August 14, 2016.

camps functioned in "estranging, non-Euclidean ways," which he calls "desert time," but the use of time does more than create an ambiance of boredom and emptiness; instead, it speaks to the process of emptying of self for the characters.[81] The characters still remember "the bright green grass, the roses, the house on the wide street not far from the sea," but now home is so distant that it seems "like a dream" and "another time" (93). Their view contrasts with the established sequencing at the camps. The government sets up a regimented, linear time while the characters gradually experience time as repetitive, stalled, and eventually dreamlike. At first, the characters hope that their incarceration, when it is over, will be just an "interruption" (114) in their lives, a limbo that they desire to escape. This hope and its subsequent defeat are tellingly represented in the novel by the symbol of a watch. For instance, time already begins to stall on the train to the camps, where a formerly wealthy man carries "a handsome gold watch that no longer told the correct time" (32). The hands on his watch might be still moving, like they are on the train, but that movement fails to correlate with actual experiences. Their lives are regulated by someone else even to the point of controlling when to raise and lower the shades on the train. They feel trapped in a repetition that they do not dictate and that does not move forward. The girl's watch further illustrates the characters' sense of time. This watch is not functioning, just like the other watch on the train, but in this instance time is consciously stopped, like the clocks in a house after a death. She "stopped winding it the day they stepped off the train" (65).[82] Once she arrives in the camp time, she lives in a space of mourning.

Even though the girl stops her watch, she repeatedly looks at it, as though she gains new information from her analysis. While the characters, like the watch, are technically stuck, they attempt to recapture a productive sense of time by thinking about the past as something they can return to in the future. In this way, the watch, which belonged to the girl's father and thus represents the family unit now lost, becomes a device of recollection and hope. When asked by her brother for the time, she carefully reads her unmoving watch and announces that it is six o'clock. To them, that time was another empty marker in days filled with regimented waiting: "For the mail. For the news. For the bells. For breakfast and lunch and dinner. For one day to be over and the next day to begin" (54). Even so, the brother wants to know what that hour means "at home," and the sister replies, "I bet they're having a good time" (66). There

---

81. Song, *The Children of 1965*, 217, 219.

82. Other instances of stalled time include the calendar that has fallen from the wall and the tin clock that was stopped literally by the environment, "its gears [. . .] clotted with dust" (103).

is hope in this response that they, too, can return home to a "good time." The brother seizes this hope, and from then on, "when he thought of the world outside it was always six o'clock. A Wednesday or a Thursday. Dinnertime across America" (66). He visualizes the time his sister briefly describes, and it includes the entire family.

The other characters also embrace dinnertime as a time that recreates a complete sense of their family, but later in the story the characters start to confuse past, present, and future. The sister in a delirium states that the father is coming to rescue them, but then, looking at her stopped watch, says, "It's six o'clock. [. . .] He should have been here by now" (98). She seems to be expecting her father, and because he has not arrived, we see her hope running out. The mother similarly confuses her memories and hopes with her present state:

> "Sometimes," said [the boy's] mother, "I'll look up at the clock and it's half past five and I'm sure that [the father is] on his way home from the office. And then I'll start to panic. 'It's *late*,' I'll think to myself. 'I should have started the rice by now.'" (85)

Although the wish for a reunited family helps these characters to live for the future, as their anxiety rises at the camp, their sense of time is confused. They recede from the spatiotemporal reality, partly as a survival mechanism to avoid the horrors of their contemporary space and time, but this retreat into spaces of delirium and dream becomes a threat because they may not return from them. Their disorientation may become permanent, and we see signs in both of the parents that this may be the case. The mother states at the camp, "Sometimes I don't know if I'm awake or asleep" (94), and even after the camp the father calls out to see the children because "otherwise he wouldn't know if he was really awake" (133). Their dreams about different times and places give them a refuge from reality, but as this location between a dream world and their lived world becomes blurred, it is also a sign that they have lost their sense of reality and orientation.

The novel aligns the characters' confusion about time with their confusion about their physical space and selves. Iris Young states that during Western exploration, "the 'edge' of civilization was marked by the presence of grotesque peoples" in stories and images; in *When the Emperor Was Divine*, the characters have been moved to the "edge" of civilization, to a desert wasteland, and start to see themselves as grotesque and culpable for their confinement.[83] The characters are most susceptible to this disorientation, which leads to self-

---

83. Young, *Justice and the Politics of Difference*, 126.

negation in the hazy location at the edge of sleep, delirium, and daydreams. In this borderline space of the psyche, the characters state that they do not know when, where, and eventually, who they are. Specifically, the boy often wakes in the night, "crying out, 'Where am I?'" (57); he fears that he has deserved this banishment to an unwelcoming and unfamiliar desert where "the wind blow[s] through the sagebrush" (57). The mother also misses her environmentally based ties to home and daydreams that one day she could "look out the window and see the sea" (94). Without that connection, she feels ill at ease, constantly jolted back to the moment of crisis when her husband was taken. She confuses the bell that announces mealtimes with the doorbell that brought the strangers to arrest her husband. She asks, "What is it?" and "Who's there?" (93) each time she hears the bell. This military procedure for meals, resembling Pavlovian conditioning, repeatedly draws a reaction from the mother, but she hungers for her husband, not the food that is available to her.[84] The mother and her children have been psychically uprooted at the same time that they have been physically uprooted; time and space are out of joint. Although they use their imagination, they are not in control of synthesizing the real and imagined elements of their spatialized world.

TURNING AWAY FROM THE EAST

The family is not just disoriented in their sense of their specific location and time, but they are also disoriented in the sense of being turned from the East. A U.S. ideology demonizing the East is progressively forced upon the characters in the novel and real people in the camps. This hatred, which does not distinguish between the Japanese enemy and the internal inhabitants, is turned inward by the fictional incarcerees and eventually results in loathing not only where they come from but who they are. Despite their acts of resistance, Otsuka's characters come to "mirror" the racist thinking that the government employed in order to justify their incarceration and denial of citizenship rights in the first place. By showing the damaging potential to the characters, the novel's presentation of this warped mirror reveals to the reader the failed logic of the governmental policies that alienate the country's own subjects.

---

84. The mother becomes disoriented in other ways as well, such as through a sense of malaise when she loses interest in current events: "She had stopped keeping track of the days. She no longer read the paper or listened to the bulletins on the radio" (93). In contrast to her newspaper reading in the beginning of the novel, her current inability to try to stay acclimatized shows how broken she has become.

The family quickly learns that they are threatened because of their physiognomy and their cultural connections to Asia. The day after the father is taken, the mother

> lit a bonfire in the yard and burned all of the letters from Kagoshima. She burned the family photographs and the three silk kimonos she had brought over with her nineteen years ago from Japan. She burned the records of Japanese opera. She ripped up the flag of the red rising sun. She smashed the tea set and the Imari dishes and the framed portrait of the boy's uncle, who had once been a general in the Emperor's army. She smashed the abacus and tossed it into the flames. "From now on," she said, "we're counting on our fingers." (75)

The mother's immediate response to the attack on her family is to destroy the material objects that connect them to Japan. This destruction of Eastern material objects was a response that was noted several times in the historical record.[85] In some cases, such destruction may have been intended to show patriarchal loyalty to the United States, but in many instances it was because of the fear that "the FBI may come" and Japanese objects might "incriminate."[86] In a conversation I had with the author, she spoke of this moment as "an act of rage" and "self-harm" where "she's destroying a part of herself at the same time that she is expressing rage towards the government." But she importantly also noted, "It's the safe thing to do. You know that too. You have to do that. There's really no question about whether or not you should get rid of those objects. You just should because you don't want to be found with anything on you."[87] Disavowal of self becomes a strangely distorted protection of self.

In the novel, the mother then goes on to alter the food she makes for the children, giving them peanut butter and jelly sandwiches instead of rice balls in order to show that the children are "American," which is ironic since of course they are U.S. citizens. Finally, she tells the children to disavow their ethnicity. She says, "If anyone asks, you're Chinese" (75). Even though it is not a full geographic dis-orientation, this alteration of identity is significant because China and Japan were political enemies (they had been at war since 1931) and were and are culturally distinct.[88] This last disavowal has the mother

---

85. For examples, see Sone, *Nisei Daughter*, 155; Levine, *A Fence away from Freedom*, 24; and Cheung, "Interview with Hisaye Yamamoto," 80.

86. Levine, *A Fence away from Freedom*, 24; Sone, *Nisei Daughter*, 154.

87. Julie Otsuka in an interview with the author, August 14, 2016.

88. Although the United States had a long history of disenfranchising Chinese immigrants as well as Japanese, during World War II the United States helped the Chinese to battle against the Japanese, viewing the region as a "second theatre" of attack on the Japanese enemy. There-

telling her children to claim the identity of her home country's adversary because it is a feasible direction their physiognomy and U.S. culture will allow them to turn, even though, of course, antagonism toward Chinese Americans also existed. The mother asks her children to pretend to be Japan's enemy as a means to avoid being seen as an enemy in the United States.

This attempt at passing as Chinese as a way to escape attack was counterbalanced by white America's desire to demarcate the races. Historically, *LIFE* magazine reported that Asians in America were being beaten, and, therefore, the magazine's December 22, 1941, issue published pictorial representations of a Chinese and a Japanese face that were itemized for comparison. The following is the stated reason for this decision: "To dispel some of this confusion *LIFE* here adduces a rule-of-thumb from the anthropometric conformations that distinguish friendly Chinese from enemy alien Japs."[89] The article does not oppose violence against citizens. Instead, *LIFE* wants to make sure that readers are attacking people of Japanese descent, who are categorically marked as "enemy aliens," based on supposedly scientific phenotypical markers. Although the article does not acknowledge anti-Chinese sentiment, which certainly did exist in the United States at the time, it does stress the particular, popular focus on anti-Japanese sentiment. In the novel, the mother's advice that the children disavow their Japanese identity constitutes an attempt at self-preservation in a country where even the major magazines are advocating violence against Japanese Americans. Destroying possessions, changing habits, and disavowing identity may be invoked as elements of self-preservation, but they are disorienting elements as well that force assimilation and cause internalized oppression.

Even though the mother burns the family's belongings to attempt to keep them safe, she holds back some items. Later, as she packs up the house before the move, we see that she still has the wedding chopsticks that her mother sent her from Japan (8). While this is a small token, she has not completely obliterated her ties to Japan. Similar historical examples exist, such as Monica Sone's statement that she saved a doll from her grandmother as a sign that she had "rebelled."[90] Defying the government's orders, both women, historical and fictional, erase just enough of their cultural connections, they think, to keep themselves out of trouble.

While at the U.S. concentration camp, the boy takes on the new rules while also resisting them. When the boy's mother tells him, "Never say the

fore, China was now considered to be an ally in opposition to Japan as the enemy, making Chinese heritage a less threatened position.

89. "How to Tell Japs from the Chinese," 81.

90. Sone, *Nisei Daughter*, 155.

Emperor's name out loud" (52), sometimes as he passed the guard tower he would whisper "Hirohito" over and over again. These moments of resistance are small acts of defiance by the mother and her son that show a shift in self-worth but not a total erasure of it, and they support Foucault's claim that "there always remain the possibilities of resistance, disobedience, and oppositional groupings."[91] While these small feats demonstrate the attempts of the characters to remain intact, they are also tied to magical thinking, which, like dreams, is the withdrawal from logical causation to the symbolic when faced with an uncontrollable time and place. Therefore, the boy's belief in the power of repeated phrases illustrates both his attempts to control his environment and his inability to do so.[92] Although the boy resists more often than the girl, much of his resistance is tied to irrational thinking.

Even when thinking positively about these acts, they are more than balanced by acts of acquiescence. For instance, the girl finds herself also repeating language, but the language she speaks is that of the oppressor. After the brick is thrown through the train window, she repeats to herself the words she had just heard from a soldier, "Shades down" (46). In this moment we see the act of internalization. She sees that there is a threat outside, and that a potential solution to that threat is merely to pull down the shades as the soldiers recommend. While this symbolic separation between the outside world and the internal one has larger and more dangerous ramifications, the girl only sees the immediate relief caused by compliance, and, more importantly, she has repeated a lesson previously demonstrated so that it has become ingrained. She has begun to believe the oppressor's viewpoint, which contains hatred and fear of herself. She continues to accept the government's view of space and cannot imagine her own Thirdspace as a resistive practice to their biopolitics.

We see this internalized oppression not just in the acceptance and repetition of the rules that the characters face but directly in their acceptance of others' hatred. Early in the book, the girl's racist exclusion from playing jump rope angers her (she even cuts up her rope), but in the camp, she takes out that anger on herself instead of on a rope. She states about her jump roping abilities and most likely herself, "I'm terrible. I don't even deserve to hold the rope" (97). In her exile, the girl has lost her ability to resist racism. In this conversation she also says, "I'm not here" (98). That same night she falls into a delirium and asks questions such as "Where are we?" and "What country is

---

91. Rabinow, "Space, Knowledge, and Power," 245.

92. Other instances when the boy uses magical thinking include when he thinks that if he does not look at a lock of his father's hair, "his father will be all right" (79) or that if his mother takes the key off her neck, their house "would fall down, or go up in flames, or simply disappear. The war would last forever. Our mother would cease to be" (108).

this anyway?" (98). She is spatially disoriented in such a way that emphasizes their manufactured statelessness. After losing her sense of place, she is unable to hang on to a positive sense of self. Although the specific catalyst for this event is not named, the girl struggles from the beginning of their incarceration as she internalizes, and then expresses such ideas as "Nobody will look at you [. . .] if your face is too dark" (58). Dislocation and racism combine to defeat her resistance to racist ideology.

The boy also has to deal with the confusion that surrounds him. At the camp, he learns to play war, where he shouts "*Kill the Japs!*" (54), showing his internalization of the Japanese as the enemy that he needs to destroy. Additionally, the clothes given to the incarcerees are U.S. Army surplus from World War I, and when the boy puts on the uniform and looks in the mirror, he "narrow[s] his eyes and [sticks] out his two front teeth" (87), speaking in imitation of a stereotypical Japanese voice where l's and r's are swapped: "*I predge arregiance to the frag* [. . . .] *Solly. So so solly*" (87). This painful reversal of identification shows the complexity of vilifying the enemy and then seeing the enemy as yourself. He both wants to kill the enemy and sees himself as that enemy wearing a bullet-ridden, military peacoat.

The mirror then acts as the place where his internal self and external perceptions collide, spatializing the collapse of the boy's interiority. He looks into the glass and sees an image that resembles that of the enemy Japanese: the dark hair, the brown skin. Once he sees that image, he wants to heighten it into a stereotype by altering the shape of its eyes, teeth, and voice. The problem, of course, is that the image he mocks is his own. He is no longer shouting to kill the Japanese who are over there somewhere, because, in the case of the mirror, the over there is Foucault's classic example of a utopia, a no-where, that merely reflects the physical self here.[93] Therefore, his external perception of the enemy in the mirror collapses into his perception of himself. The spatial distance deceives him into an altered perception of himself in a "broken mirror" that is rooted in external racist perceptions he has heard. Whereas the boy remains trapped within this internalized racism, his position as an American citizen in the U.S. concentration camp being reflected to the reader opens the possibility of a Thirdspace in the narrative. The Thirdspace of the mirror reveals the racist stereotype and constitutional displacement imposed by the U.S. government by reflecting the distorted image of this monstrous creation. The performance of the pledge of allegiance points to a deserved citizenship right that is wrongly being withheld.

---

93. Foucault, "Of Other Spaces," 24.

The use of the mirror reveals how the boy sees himself and his body through the eyes of the oppressors who stereotype his body. As Young states, "When the dominant culture defines some groups as different, as the Other, the members of these groups are imprisoned in their bodies. Dominant discourse defines them in terms of bodily characteristics and constructs those bodies as ugly, dirty, defiled, impure, contaminated or sick."[94] The boy and the girl, who is sometimes the source of information for the boy, recognize certain speech patterns, skin color, narrow eyes, bulging teeth, and dark, straight hair as markers of the enemy, and they are trained to see the ugliness in those stereotypical phenotypes and then in themselves. It begins with the repetition of racist statements like "For it was true, they all look alike" (49) when the boy sees the men in the camp. Although he sees his father in their bodies, he still separates himself from them. Eventually, though, the children become so repulsed by themselves that they pronounce, "We looked at ourselves in the mirror and did not like what we saw: black hair, yellow skin, slanted eyes. The cruel face of the enemy. [. . .] We tried to avoid our own reflections whenever we could" (119–20). Through the characters' experience leading up to and in the concentration camp, we see how they have fully incorporated the racism aimed at them in such a way as to disorient their identities. The hyper-controlling rules and exceptional space of the camp, where sovereign authority enacts its power on subjected bodies, become a mirror of larger U.S. cultural racism so that the characters are overwhelmed and cannot imagine themselves in an alternative fashion. On the level of the narrative, however, the Thirdspace of the novel is a place where such hybrid cultural identities are acknowledged and accepted as part of the United States and its principles. The mirror Thirdspace reflects the government's fragmenting policies back on us and demands ethical action.

THE RETURN HOME

When the family finally returns home to Berkeley, they return with a changed sense of self because the space of the camp has overflowed its boundaries; no longer contained by a state of exception, it is now a self-imposed governmentality that exists everywhere, especially in their home. In the traditional narrative form of incarceration stories that Chen and Yu analyze, the return home resolves the tale, but, for this family, that return does not create a positive sense of closure. Instead, the characters realize that their dream that "the world would be ours again" (126) cannot exist as they imagined it. Their

---

94. Young, *Justice and the Politics of Difference*, 126.

dreams were delusions. Because of the disorientation that they have endured, their sense of place, self, and community has been altered, even though the place and the people outwardly appear very much the same as they did before the family's incarceration. The return home fails to bring resolution; this homecoming shows only more clearly the racism that this family has endured because now they are outside the prison walls but the prison persists.

Historically, the War Relocation Authority did attempt to relocate everyone in a dispersed fashion in order to break up Japanese communities and prevent the reformation of farming communities that originally had led to Japanese prosperity and Caucasian anger. Still, many returned to their previous communities, just like the family in the novel, but that did not mean a return to the same experience of that environment and relationships.[95] Even though "the town seemed much the same as before [and] Grove Street was still Grove, and Tyler Street still Tyler" (114), their home retains only its former shell. Many people had lived in their house while they were gone, and they had stolen most of the belongings and destroyed everything else. Even the yard had been ransacked, with the stone Buddha knocked over and the mother's rosebush purloined. While they had dreamt that on their return their "phone would ring off the hook" (126), instead, silence greets them, and they observe that the community is no longer to be trusted. The children themselves eventually start to question their neighbors as they think they see their belongings elsewhere: "Wasn't that our mother's Electrolux Mrs. Leahy was pushing back and forth across her living room floor? Didn't the Gilroys' mohair sofa look awfully familiar?" (123). Their suspicions are neither confirmed nor denied, bringing the reader into this ongoing process of questioning the honesty and connection between neighbors. Distrust leads to a disconnection where even a neighbor who nods to the mother is ignored because who knows the possible intention of a nod? The family feels isolated from their neighbors because of the physical change to their home, their space.

They have also learned direct lessons from the government prior to their reentry—telling them how they are supposed to relate among themselves, their neighborhood, and their neighbors:

> Keep your head down and don't cause any trouble, we'd been told, weeks before, in a mess hall lecture on "How to Behave in the Outside World." Speak only English. Do not walk down the street in groups of more than three, or gather in restaurants in groups of more than five. Do not draw attention to yourselves in any way. (122)

---

95. Sandra C. Taylor, *Jewel of the Desert*, xix.

"We followed the rules" (122) is the children's tactic, which they are taught by the government and their parents. They are told not to be individual and to turn away from being Japanese, through their language and associations. With these rules, the children beg for acceptance:

> We would join their clubs, after school, if they let us. We would listen to their music. We would dress just like they did. We would change our names to sound more like theirs. And if our mother called out to us on the street by our real names we would turn away and pretend not to know her. (114)

Here, acceptance becomes directly tied to disavowal. They use the language from the mess hall lessons to negate themselves. Assimilation becomes a direct disorientation.

The mother advises her children that this type of assimilation is to their advantage, while she, too, disappears into her new role as a servant. When she first returns home, she attempts to reacclimate herself by reading the newspaper again, but the articles that seem to attract her attention are the popular culture news such as a celebrity's marriage and the lack of stockings; that trivia is not paired with an investment in any larger issues. The mother also turns to it because it is "safe" knowledge, unlike possible fear-inducing headlines, which would take her back to the trauma and blind fear thrust upon her by the government. So she reads about the symbol of mindless amusement and white acculturation, Shirley Temple.[96]

Even with this small attempt to reconnect herself to the outside world, once she discovers that she cannot find employment at the places where she had formerly been a customer, she begins to recede into herself, eventually taking a job as a housecleaner. "*You just smile and say yes ma'am and no ma'am and do as you're told*" (129). She takes on a role that is clearly marked as inferior and non-threatening. Historically, the job of the domestic would have allowed women returning from the camps to be both seen and not seen by their employer. As Ruth Frankenberg discusses, racialized domestics are often forgotten and remembered at will because, although they work within the home, they are not considered part of the domestic experience of the homeowner.[97] This job was still available to those who had been incarcerated because of its demoralizing position of constant subservience and occasional erasure.[98]

---

96. Using Shirley Temple as a symbol of a desire to attain whiteness is an often used allusion from Toni Morrison's *The Bluest Eye* to Mitsuke Yamada's poem "American Son" in *Desert Run*.

97. Frankenberg, *White Women, Race Matters*, 49–50.

98. The mother is now in the same position as Mrs. Ueno, her former housekeeper, who carries the mother's water at the camp (56).

While the children try to hide themselves behind the rules they had been given, the mother tries to hide in her job. Still, they all continue to hope that things will return to normal, but interconnected changes in place, self, and community will not allow that type of homecoming. Two climactic scenes play out this disjunction. The first is the return home of the mother, girl, and boy. They tell the reader, "We were free now, free to go wherever we wanted to go, whenever we pleased. There were no more armed guards, no more search-lights, no more barbed-wire fences" (113).[99] Yet, although the symbols and realities of imprisonment have been removed, they continue to act as though they are imprisoned. Specifically, they reconfigure the home space into the barracks space because they have become so acclimatized to their prison. The home has become their prison: "Without thinking, we had sought out the room whose dimensions—long and narrow, with two windows on one end and a door at the other—most closely resembled those of the room in the barracks in the desert where we had lived during the war" (111–12). At this point, to borrow Henri Lefebvre's spatial terms, they "perceive" the space of their home as the "conceived space" of the camp. In other words, the abstract purpose of the concentration camp, to confine and sequester, has filtered into the way they experience the space around them.[100] They have incorporated these elements of imprisonment in the spatial practices of their home. No longer are guards and barbed wire necessary because they have so internalized others' fears that they constrain themselves. The characters have adopted the government's view on their incarceration, so much so that they have recon-figured their real house into an imagined Thirdspace of imprisonment, whose implications remain a challenge to American policy and audiences rather than a site for social justice.[101]

This self-vigilance, however, does not imply that outside threats have van-ished for this family. Even though they reconfigured the home into a bar-racks, the community continues to harass them with late-night phone calls and by throwing a whiskey bottle through the window. This physical break-ing of the barrier between private and public space forces the family to even further sequester themselves. Talking about the role of the home, Samira Kawash states:

> Traditionally, the house has been taken to name the putative interiority of
> the domestic, the private, the feminine, and separates those forms of interi-

---

99. Note another reprisal of to "go to wherever it was they had to go" (22). Here the focus is on choice and pleasure.

100. See Lefebvre, *The Production of Space*.

101. Soja, *Thirdspace*.

ority from their exterior counterparts. The house is itself the boundary figure, the containing wall that by its physical presence materializes and secures the separation between interior and exterior, private and public.[102]

Now, however, the separation has been broken down, with the dangerous "outside world" able to intrude on their private space. The symbolic boundary of their house has been broken just like the barrier to their own internal and external perceptions has been besieged.

The house has lost its connection to the symbolic American Dream even though the white picket fence still stands. As Amy Iwasaki Mass states, from her position as someone who had lived through the camps, "Our ideals about America were [. . .] shattered. We had believed the American dream of freedom in a democratic nation. We had been socialized to believe that by working hard and being good citizens we, too, could realize the American dream."[103] With this lost respect for this aspiration, the characters experience how the house loses its positive symbolism and the fence of dreams begins to take on the containing elements of prison walls.

The walls and fences keep them in and yet are penetrable to attack. With this knowledge, after the whiskey-bottle attack, the family moves upstairs to a room that does not have windows that face the street. Then the mother puts rice sacks on the windows "so no one could see in," and at night she turns out all the inside lights "so no one would know we were home" (118). The mother reacts by enacting the advice of the soldiers on the train—"Shades down." The division between the outside world and this family continues even though they have supposedly returned to the "outside world." In addition to this repetition of the oppressor's spatial solution to a racist "problem" invented by the U.S. government, the room to which they retreat had been vandalized before their return home. While we are not told the words that are scrawled on the walls, the text implies that these words are racial slurs because of their impact on the family: "For years we could not get those words out of our heads" (111). The family is trapped inside a space filled with racism. The house literalizes the racism that has now been internalized. The self-negating lesson of the train has been fully learned—they need to hide themselves and expect anti-Asian attacks.

These lessons are also learned by the father, who had been separated from his family throughout the novel, thereby building in the historically appropriate gendered separation that occurred for many adults, with the mother being sent off with the children to a camp while the father was imprisoned

---

102. Kawash, "Safe House?," 188.
103. Mass, "Psychological Effects of the Camps on the Japanese Americans," 160.

elsewhere. This separation created additional distinctions between how men and women responded to the end of their incarceration. While the mother attempts to reclaim her family and her home by assuming the position of a servant, the father must deal with his return in a different manner because he cannot get a job anywhere. Additionally, he clearly has been physically harmed at the government camp (now walking with a cane and missing all his teeth). His response, then, is not even the temporary reacclimation that the mother makes; instead, his identity continues to disintegrate after his return. He, like the mother when she was in the camp, will not read the newspaper or listen to the radio, no longer plays with the children the way he had in the past, and keeps to himself. Although internally he rages, externally he has been silenced—"the handwriting in his notebook grew smaller and fainter and then disappeared from the page altogether" (137). Since the children had known him so long only through postcards, this disappearance of the written stands in for the disappearance of his identity in general. His sense of place and self has been dissolved.

As stated earlier, the gap between dream and reality has become confused for the father; he has become disoriented even in his dreams so that the internal and external spaces of perception cannot even be separated while he is asleep. In his recurring dream,

> it was five minutes past curfew and he was trapped outside, in the world, on the wrong side of the fence. "I've got to get back," he'd wake up shouting.
>
> "You're home now," our mother would remind him. "It's all right. You can stay." (137)

His wife, misunderstanding his dream, tries to comfort him with the knowledge that he has returned home, but his incarceration has upended his personality: he is so fearful of punishment that he wants to return to his imprisonment. For the father, there is no return home; he remains in prison. Even in his thoughts at the end of the novel, we see that he remains trapped, asking his captors, "Now can I go?" (144). He wants to leave the confinement the government created for him, but that prison has long extended beyond the camp's fences into the community's space and into the characters' own minds.

Nonetheless, the anger he demonstrates in his final soliloquy, "Who am I? You know who I am. Or you think you do" (142), shows that his submission is not total. He asks the same kinds of questions we've seen other characters ask when they are disoriented, but he also provides his own extensive answer. This final chapter, told from the first-person point of view of the father, has received wide-ranging responses because it is tonally distinct from the more observational third-person perspectives of the rest of the novel. Here the father is talking without interruption, and as he speaks he refers to his captors as "you," implicating the reader as one of those who think poorly of him. While critics such as Michiko Kakutani viewed this ending as "a shrill diatribe," scholars Tina Chen and Rajini Srikanth have noted the potential of this accusation of the reader.[104] Srikanth says that the last chapter "restores to the father the dignity of his personhood."[105] Chen states that this section sets up a place where "readerly empathy as unexamined site of feeling and response can be transmuted into an engaged, accountable critical sympathy that acknowledges alterity not through an impulse towards mastery but through an ethical component to reorienting the self in relation to Otherness."[106] In addition to this final chapter offering more of the father's humanity and emotion resulting from his being granted a voice, this section also shows how he has and is resisting his disorientation.

I suggest that this final chapter, titled "Confession," provides the novel's most direct attempt at finding a Thirdspace through which incarcerated people of Japanese descent can confront U.S. racist policies and, by implication, the populace who tacitly supported them. It does so by locating the father's final speech in the exceptional space of the interrogation room—a room that "was small and bare" and "had no windows" (140)—though this room has become unmoored from the bounds of space and time to become an indistinct address to all. That is, the fact that we are unable to locate the father's litany of accusations as well as impossible confessions and threats in any real time within the story highlights the interminable nature of his interrogation and response to the questions of loyalty demanded by the U.S. government that continue to be posed internally long after his official release. As Otsuka herself told me, "I have no visual for where that scene would be set—to me that's all aural, it's all about the voice. It's almost existing in the middle of nowhere."[107] Even for Otsuka, this space becomes a potential utopia—a "nowhere" of a potential Thirdspace beyond the current possibilities. In one respect, the father's response, as with that of the rest of his family, shows the same disorienting confusion evident earlier in the novel. In another way, however, the father uses the bare space of the interrogation room to repeat the racist fears of his interrogators back to them, saying, "You were right. You were always right. It was me. I did it" (140), reflecting their absurdity and hollowness. The father's mirroring of governmental policies recalls and extends his son's performance

104. Kakutani, "War's Outcasts Dream of Small Pleasures."
105. Srikanth, *Constructing the Enemy*, 124.
106. Tina Chen, "Towards an Ethics of Knowledge," 169.
107. Julie Otsuka in an interview with the author, August 14, 2016.

of Japanese stereotypes in front of the broken mirror, exposing the evacuative logic and the ideological contradictions of U.S. constructions of citizenship and loyalty. So when he says, "I'm the traitor in your own backyard" and "Assign me a number" (143), he shows how people of Japanese descent have been emptied of their identity through a forced "evacuation" movement and how this violation of constitutional rights undermines the citizenship protections of all Americans. This challenge does not lead to direct action in the world of the novel because the father has been broken by his incarceration and because there is no escape through confession; in the end he asks for forgiveness for his imaginary crimes and betrayals, seeking only to be released. The novel's ending on his question "Now can I go?" thus demonstrates a yearning for his release as well as a lack of complete escape from these suspicions and internalized surveillance for his family and for future generations, who are still asking the same thing.

The family returns to a home that remains the same structure it was four years earlier, but because of their journey, their feeling about that space and therefore how they feel about their community and themselves is fundamentally changed. The country's government has questioned their loyalty and, hence, they now question the society's loyalty to them. Although the family does eventually move back into separate sleeping quarters, the damage is done, and although the children might be able to partially recover from their incarceration because of their young age while at the camp, the parents have slipped into their new invisibility and now self-inflicted imprisonment.[108]

This chapter has demonstrated that the four-year journey that finally returns the characters to their initial physical starting point is not a simple circle, and it most certainly does not end with a "final synthesis which denies the damage of the internment or which reconciles the Japanese American subject divided by the 'enemy/not enemy' logic of the state."[109] Agreeing with Lowe's idea of this disjunction for the characters, I have added to it the idea of disorientation and its effects on how they see the space around them, in their community, and within themselves. With this knowledge, we can better understand the continued ramifications of this displacement. As Mass details, "the psychological impact of the forced evacuation and detention was deep and devastating" because people felt betrayed by their country to the point

---

108. As Jeanne Wakatsuki Houston states about her own experience, "That hollow ache I carried during the early months of internment had shrunk, over the years, to a tiny sliver of suspicion about the very person I was. It had grown so small sometimes I'd forget it was there. Months might pass before something would remind me" (Houston and Houston, *Farewell to Manzanar*, 195–96).

109. Lowe, *Immigrant Acts*, 50.

where it affected not only their trust of their environment but also their own self-worth.[110] This wartime displacement has not ended on the last page of this book written by the child of an incarceree. Instead, it is "a continuing project of suspicion and survival" that lasts to this day for many Japanese Americans who underwent this trauma, and, as *When the Emperor Was Divine* shows, for their children as well.[111]

Governmentalities directly affect people and their relationship to the spaces around them even across generations. Otsuka's characters, like their historical counterparts in the U.S. concentration camps, experience disorientation from the racist policies forced upon them as wartime necessities, and although in the novel they fight back with dreams and magical thinking, ultimately this disorientation points to limits of the logic of citizenship and naturalization that can lead to precarious peoples being rendered stateless foreigners. The family has been reunified, but who is in charge is left uncertain, because the specter of the government looms as the ongoing surveillant and dominant force. On the narrative level, though, through the use of the Thirdspace of the mirror and the interrogation room, a space has been constructed to reveal the flaws of the government. For the younger generations that did not live through the camps and are now writing these narratives, this novel shows how such an imaginative project engaged with narratives of past migrations provides potential for change in the present.

---

110. Mass, "Psychological Effects of the Camps on the Japanese Americans," 160.
111. Lowe, *Immigrant Acts*, 49.

CHAPTER 4

The Economic Displacement of Mexican American Migrant Labor

Disembodied Criminality to Embodied Spirituality
and Viramontes's *Under the Feet of Jesus*

PRECEDING CHAPTERS have surveyed several types of internal displacements: environmental, economic, and wartime. In some cases, these types
have overlapped. What has become evident from this examination is how
they share large structural similarities despite the notable differences in race,
region, and circumstance. Citizenship and landownership were tied to views
of American-ness, a concept utilized by those in power to exclude different
groups over time through various forms of governmentality. For example, the
displacement of people of Japanese descent during World War II discussed
in the previous chapter was a wartime event invoking a state of emergency
to remove citizenship rights. Their incarceration in the heart of the country
ironically was an attempt to render them foreign and external—a constitutional displacement.

Other displacements built upon and extended this same logic of foreignness and exclusion in order to continue to disenfranchise. During World War
II, because of the 15 million enlisted, there was a fear of a farm labor short-
age, though in reality, as Mae Ngai argues, this fear masked a desire to keep
wages low by creating a surplus of laborers.[1] While many people of Mexican
descent had long been working in farming, as discussed in chapter 2's analysis of the effects of the Dust Bowl migration in California, a new program

---

1. Ngai, *Impossible Subjects,* 137.

began in 1942 between the United States and Mexico that utilized many of the H-2 visa protocols for obtaining transnational farmworkers that were mentioned in chapter 1's examination of African American and Caribbean labor in Florida. This new "'emergency' migration policy lasted twenty-two years," until 1964, showing again how the concept of emergency is employed by the government to create an unquestionable normalcy.[2] The Bracero Program, as it was labeled, was the largest guest worker program in the United States, involving 4.6 million laborers over the course of its history.[3] Alongside those workers were undocumented immigrants as well as United States citizens of multiple ethnicities, including many Mexican Americans. Those immigrant workers were welcomed for their work, whether through open governmental policy or silent acceptance of the even cheaper undocumented labor, but they were required to return to Mexico when their work was complete. This transnational workforce had none of the protections of citizenship, and the citizens working next to them were often treated as though they too had no rights. The Bracero Program thus facilitated and expanded an already ongoing economic displacement by regularizing the idea that people of Mexican descent were temporary aliens who could never become citizens, and this stereotype continues to the present day.

In 1962, César Chávez, a prominent Mexican American labor activist from Arizona, founded the National Farmworkers Association labor union in response to the Bracero Program after his own experience working in the fields. Chávez wanted to bring together farmworkers so that they might more effectively bargain as a collective for their rights as workers and citizens. Most memorably, he led the Delano Grape Strike and Boycott from 1965 to 1970, where he and his union joined forces with Filipino American workers. Since it was already the end of the harvest, a field strike could not be successful. Instead, the workers asked consumers to boycott purchasing grapes until they were allowed to unionize and their demands were met. While this boycott was effective against one corporation almost immediately, some corporations held out because grapes were only one of their products or they sold their grapes through other company names, making them harder to track; Chávez's union, which merged to become the United Farm Workers (UFW) union, thus expanded their boycott to all grapes as the years passed. Part of their strategy was to have local churches and national church organizations sign on to support the boycott to show that they were "a mainstream, nonradical

---

2. Snodgrass, "The Bracero Program, 1942–1964," 79.

3. Ngai, *Impossible Subjects*, 138. The label "guest worker," as Ngai explains, is "today's euphemism for the federally sponsored importation of contract labor" (129).

cause."[4] This spiritual support for workers showed that they were moral people and therefore deserved economic support as well. Chávez himself performed a kind of Catholic penitential pilgrimage, what he called a *perigrinación*, when he walked barefoot from Delano to Sacramento (approximately 300 miles).[5] As he described it, the journey was both spiritual and political, a "religious pilgrimage and a plea for social change for the farm worker" to benefit both "body and soul," where the participants were calling on divine support and solidarity just as with "our Negro brothers in Selma."[6] By 1969, "retail grape sales were estimated to be down 12 percent nationally and down more than 50 percent in major cities," but the government undermined this progress through President Nixon's public support of growers and his public eating of grapes.[7] Additionally, the Defense Department quadrupled their purchasing of grapes for soldiers in Vietnam. Even so, the UFW eventually triumphed because they expanded their boycotts, explaining that harmful pesticides were being used on the grapes; these effects were felt by growers, and in 1970 they finally signed a contract with the union.[8] Overall, the UFW as it was run by Chávez operated as a "struggle in spiritual rather than simply economic terms, as a new national civil rights movement."[9] That is, the UFW's combination of church support and spiritual beliefs with economic activism effectively combated capitalist and racist views that served to restrict citizenship rights.

Even after the formal conclusion of the Bracero Program, however, many of the same policies and attitudes underpinning it continued. Cultural views on Mexican immigration remained much the same around the time of the 1994 passage of the North American Free Trade Agreement (NAFTA) and the bills leading to it, such as the Immigration Reform and Control Act of 1986. NAFTA in particular promoted trade between countries without the human bodies that are likely to come with that trade. Douglas Massey calls the U.S. policy with Mexico "schizophrenic" because "borders are rendered permeable with respect to movements of goods [. . .] but impermeable with respect to the movement of workers."[10] This approach divorces the economic prosperity linked to an opening of borders from the workers who are part of the expanded market.

---

4. Shaw, *Beyond the Fields*, 36–37.
5. Ibid., 80.
6. Sullivan, *Blue Collar—Roman Collar—White Collar*, 66.
7. Shaw, *Beyond the Fields*, 43.
8. Ibid., 43–46.
9. Ibid., 2–3; additional background on the Delano Grape Boycott is found in Shaw, *Beyond the Fields*, 13–50.
10. Douglas S. Massey, "Understanding America's Immigration 'Crisis,'" 310.

This chapter addresses how historical Chicana/o migrants are forced into cycles of movement based on their economic need that place them into a bare life that renders them invisible with respect to rights and marks them as criminals whose bodies need to be eradicated from the land while they are also being sought for their labor. The migrant laborer, as seen throughout this book with African Americans in Florida and Anglo-Americans on the West Coast, points to a particular configuration of the displaced person. Recognized neither as an international refugee nor as an internally displaced person moved by a single event, the repeated movement of the migrant laborer through its very regularity serves to reinforce a precarious status without citizenship rights or protection. These ongoing nonproductive movements of Chicana/o workers are part of a history of mass movements of people that are affected by governmental choices that alter self, space, and community. Because this status, however, falls outside the UN's eventually codified legal protections and internal state aid, this particular arrangement of the workers' lives and movement ignores the full embodiment of these individuals and creates a disenfranchised community without positive visibility.

This history shows the ongoing struggle for economic and civil liberties between workers and migrants of Mexican descent, on the one hand, and corporations and the U.S. government on the other. Literary texts, by contrast, show not only the effects of that history but also the possibility for an alternative future. Chicana author Helena María Viramontes, born in East Los Angeles in 1954, accompanied her parents to the fields of Easton, California, during her childhood summers to pick grapes with those immigrant workers. Viramontes has said that those experiences and her involvement with the United Farm Workers Support Coalition while she was in college during the early 1970s formed the basis of her 1995 novel *Under the Feet of Jesus* and its fictional representation of migrant workers. She even dedicates the book to her parents, "who met in Buttonwillow picking cotton," as well as to the memory of César Chávez. Elsewhere Viramontes reflected on this early political involvement, stating that she learned about fighting for the collective good while participating in the grape boycott.[11] In this chapter, I examine Viramontes's portrayal of the plight of some of these workers, which, although grounded in her experience in the 1970s, nonetheless occupies an indefinite present, since her book is located in an unspecified moment in the latter half of the twentieth century. In general, Viramontes's novel shows that although the government policies change, the result is often the same for the workers,

---

11. Viramontes, "Scripted Language."

who are treated almost exclusively as criminals who need to be eradicated from the land even as their bodies are sought for labor.

Under the Feet, which concentrates on a Chicana/o family who is part of this continual economic displacement through their migrant labor in the fields of California, addresses citizenship's tie to racial identity, which was prominent in the national discourse nearly twenty years ago when the novel was first published, but which remains recognizable even today. Over the course of the book, individual characters feel harassed by the Border Patrol, are poisoned by pesticide sprayings ordered by those who disregard the effects on workers' bodies and their water supply, and are labeled thieves if they eat the fruit they pick. These actions remind them of their bare life in the eyes of the state and that their ownership of even the fruit of the land, not to mention the land itself, is impossible, as well as reminding them that their labor is desired but not their bodies. Hence, Viramontes's text portrays the ramifications of such biopolitical policies that restrict workers' movement and deny their existence.

Under the Feet also shows not just how outside forces are imposed on the characters but also how they respond. My analysis of this response begins with political geographer Edward Soja's general concept of "Thirdspace," which views the combination of real and imagined space as creating new livable possibilities.[12] In this chapter, I rely on one of the theorists that Soja used to build his larger argument, critical scholar Homi Bhabha, whose related term "third space" emphasizes postcolonial and historical elements, showing that the intermingling of various cultures can create a positive hybridity.[13] Finally, I draw heavily on *mestiza* writer Gloria Anzaldúa's argument about the conflicts of space for people of Mexican heritage who live along the U.S.–Mexican border.[14] My thinking is informed by her concept of the borderlands, the space "where the Third World grates against the first and bleeds," and even more specifically her idea of *Nepantla,* the in-between space.[15] *Nepantla* clarifies that her borderlands theory about the ambiguities of physical space can also be understood on a more mental and spiritual level, a topic scholars often avoid. Viramontes herself has discussed this kind of overlap in her own thinking. She has said that as a child, she would learn by overhearing adults talking in her house as well as by reading the few books available to her—the encyclopedia and the Bible—leading her to develop a thought process that required

---

12. Soja, *Thirdspace.*

13. Bhabha, "The Third Space."

14. Soja's spelling of the term "Thirdspace" differs from Bhabha, who spells it "third space." In quotations I will spell it as each scholar does, but when I am employing the term, I will use "Thirdspace."

15. Anzaldúa, *Borderland/La Frontera,* 25.

intellect, spirituality, and a connection to people.[16] *Under the Feet* embraces such theoretical positions that move beyond binaries by having its characters, particularly the female heroine Estrella, find ways to respond to the governmental forces imposed on them by integrating and reforming cultural and religious connections in order to develop their own symbolic response that reimagines the spaces that erase and harm them into safe havens that embrace and protect them. This reimagining is accomplished by searching for a new place that blurs physical and spiritual boundaries as well as the boundaries of linear time—inverting what I am calling their "disembodied criminality" into an "embodied spirituality" that acknowledges their complex cultural heritage. Whereas my chapter on the Dust Bowl migrants demonstrated how their utopian solution based on class and shared ownership left behind many people of color, and while my chapter on the incarceration of people of Japanese descent showed how the racial discourse of the government was challenged via the exceptional space of the camp and interrogation room, in contrast, in Viramontes's book we see a fuller potential of Thirdspace as a site for social justice that combines the political with the spiritual.

I first briefly discuss the history of the U.S.–Mexican border and then how it underlies the disembodied criminality imposed on real migrant workers and on Viramontes's characters. Next I examine the complex role of spirituality in the novel before turning to Estrella's symbolic response of embodied spirituality, which creates a Thirdspace via *Nepantla* that utilizes layered histories, spaces, and spiritualities—reflecting Viramontes's own development of the kind of spiritual and spatial reimaginings utilized by Chávez and the UFW. By demonstrating the disruptive possibilities of the overlaps and synchronicities of time and space, *Under the Feet* reveals the resistive power available to those perceived as living in the margins both in an ethnic and a gendered context. While the doctrines and practices of Christianity work in some ways to create a distinct view of community for the largely Catholic migrant workers that is not strictly limited by national boundaries in the novel or in reality, organized religion is not presented as the text's solution to the problem of national borders because the coercive power of the church continues to colonize as well as oppress some of its followers. Instead, Estrella demonstrates how the characters must draw on their own complex spirituality that includes and then transforms their ties to Christianity, Aztec religion, and local customs into a space for social justice. In the end, through the representation of an adolescent girl, the novel continues to hope for a new community and a feeling of home that emphasizes each person's own internal strength. Though this resolution does

---

16. Viramontes, "Scripted Language."

not emphasize a sense of New Tribalism that expands to other ethnic groups, it is one that includes the present and the past, the imagined and the real.[17]

A HISTORY OF THE BORDER:
COLONIZATION AND MIGRATION

The physical border between the United States and Mexico has long been contested and shifting, and with that movement has gone the dominion of hundreds of thousands of miles of land and the people residing on it. In 1521, the Spanish conquered Mexico-Tenochtitlán and the Aztec people; this defeat of the native population, accomplished by allying with local enemies and then later turning on them, became a model for the assault on dozens of other Native American tribes over the years. Throughout these assaults, religion was linked with conquest. The Spanish brought Christianity, specifically Catholicism, and as the land was dominated, so too was the religion of the original inhabitants. At the same time, the rituals of the local people informed and altered the Catholic tradition. The Virgin Mary became the Virgin of Guadalupe, who was herself inflected with the lineage of Indigenous religious and mythical women: la Llorona, "The Weeping Woman"; Coatlicue, "Serpent Skirt"; and Tonantzin, "Our Lady Mother," establishing early on the cross-cultural connections that point to the possibilities of hybridity and Thirdspace.[18]

Eventually the Mexican people were able to win their independence from the Spanish Empire in an eleven-year war that ended in 1821. Their control of much of this land, however, only lasted a few decades because the United States was pushing west under the ideology of Manifest Destiny.[19] Texas's revolt against Mexico in 1836 and its subsequent annexation by the United States in 1845 helped to instigate the U.S. war with Mexico from 1846 to 1848, when Mexico lost even more of its land. The boundary between the two countries officially moved south 150 miles from the Nueces River to the Rio Grande,

---

17. See Anzaldúa on New Tribalism: "It's a kind of mestizaje that allows for connecting with other ethnic groups and interacting with other cultures and ideas" (Hernández-Ávila, "Quincentennial," 185).

18. Anzaldúa, *Borderland/La Frontera*, 50–52.

19. del Castillo and De León, *North to Aztlán*, 15. The idea of Manifest Destiny had been circulating since the beginning of the Republic but was coined in 1845 by newspaper editor John O'Sullivan: "Americans had believed they had the *right* to spread over the entire continent and display their republican system for the world to admire" (Wheelan, *Invading Mexico*, 30). This "expansion of freedom," of course, hides the fact that there were people already living on the land who thus had to be viewed as inferior. The expansion of land also allowed for the expansion of slave territory (Wheelan, *Invading Mexico*, 97). See also my discussion of Manifest Destiny in the introduction and chapter 2.

with the United States claiming modern-day Texas, California, Utah, and parts of Colorado, Arizona, New Mexico, and Wyoming. The document that followed the war, the Treaty of Guadalupe Hidalgo, incorporated the Mexicans living there into the United States, promising them citizenship and the protection of their property.[20] This treaty resulted in Mexico losing over half of its territory and was followed a few years later by the Gadsden Purchase of what is now southern Arizona and New Mexico.

The people who resided on this ground that changed hands continued to feel the conflict over their space, with those of Mexican ethnicity often being viewed by other U.S. inhabitants as foreign. As immigration became more systematized at the turn into the twentieth century, people of Mexican heritage were labeled as "alien" and sometimes "criminal" based solely on their heritage. Immigration studies scholar Juan Perea explains:

> The public identification of "illegal aliens" with a person of Mexican ancestry is so strong that many Mexican Americans and other Latino citizens are presumed foreign and illegal. When citizens and aliens look alike, then all are presumed to be alien and foreign and undermining of the national character. This is an old theme in American politics.[21]

Although criminal alien-ness was the general perception, Mexican immigrants were granted access to citizenship because of the previous Treaty of Guadalupe Hidalgo. Therefore, Mexicans were considered "white by treaty," producing a conflicted notion of belonging at the U.S.–Mexican border as the dominant culture codified this racialized notion of white citizenship into law and argued that the nation's borders needed to be watched.[22] The Border Patrol was established in 1924, "inspired by the notorious Texas Rangers which had a long, violent history with ethnic Mexicans living in Texas."[23] The same year, the Johnson-Reed Immigration Act of 1924 excluded many other immigrant groups but created exceptions for Mexican immigrants to fill work positions. This conflict between the United States' desire for workers and the violence against these workers told Mexicans that their labor was desired but not their presence—an impossible request.

In the early part of the twentieth century, the United States formalized its migration laws, making entry into the country without a visa illegal. Mexican immigrants, however, were able to enter both permanently and as seasonal

---

20. Acuña, *Occupied America,* 19–20.
21. Perea, *Immigrants Out!,* 2.
22. Gross, *What Blood Won't Tell,* 253–54.
23. Jurado, "Alienated Citizens," 53.

workers. Because of their comparably unclear status, Mexican immigrants could be even more easily viewed by the Border Patrol as problematic. Thus, "the Border Patrol stood at the forefront of the reconceptualization of Mexicans into foreigners, aliens, and presumed criminals," legally demonstrating the United States' "fear of the foreigner within."[24] In addition to patrolling the borders, so-called repatriation programs were common throughout the century, with many Mexican Americans being deported along with undocumented immigrants; the fervor of such programs can be seen under the derogatorily named Operation Wetback, which, at its start in the 1954, was "apprehending 3000 undocumented workers a day."[25] As Robert Chang and Keith Aoki explain, "For the United States, which is not at much risk of literal invasion by another nation-state, its cultural identity and national sovereignty may be at great risk of 'invasion' by immigrants and would-be immigrants."[26] Although these authors are discussing a point later in U.S. history, this fear has long resided in the dominant culture. Instead of looking outward for a threat, the nation frequently looks internally for enemies and racializes the announced fear. Thus, the United States replicates in its "discourse of citizenship" the postcolonial conversation that Bhabha analyzes:

> The language of rights and obligations, so central to the modern discourse of citizenship, must be questioned on the basis of the anomalous and discriminatory legal and cultural status assigned to migrant and refugee populations who find themselves, inevitably, on the other side of the law. [. . .] Cultural and political identity is constructed through a process of othering.[27]

By marking citizenship as an either/or binary, many are left on the "wrong" side even though they are within the boundaries of the country.

These ethnically and racially based governmental policies affected not only new immigrants, but also those already living and working within the country. They, however, resisted this imposed, restricted identity through a variety of means. People of Mexican descent working as migrant laborers on the West Coast participated in a series of protests against the injustices produced by this construction of movement and self that were ultimately undermined by the increasingly corporatized farm owners and the government. Even before the predominantly white Dust Bowl migrants arrived in California, migrant laborers had performed many strikes. In total, there were more than 140

---

24. Stern, "Nationalism on the Line," 305; Chuh, *Imagine Otherwise*, 83.
25. See Balderrama and Rodríguez, *Decade of Betrayal* and Ngai, *Impossible Subjects*, 157.
26. Chang and Aoki, "Centering the Immigrant in the Inter/National Imagination," 1407.
27. Bhabha, "The Third Space," 218–19.

strikes in the 1930s.[28] Furthermore, people of Mexican descent "participated in twenty-three strikes in California in 1933 and 1934, many of which were successful in raising wages."[29] The owners responded through acts that show the workers in the position of bare life, with violent incidents such as the shooting of strikers and the formation of an industry coalition that lobbied the government and pressured workers. These pressures included paying poverty-level wages, ignoring or removing workers' civil rights, and physical assaults, to which the government responded with only a bureaucratic report.[30] In this way, a general governmentality linking citizenship and ownership thus acted to disempower workers in the time leading up to the Bracero Program, which would formalize these conditions.

These issues derived from the immigration of those near readily crossable borders and from the larger history of U.S. farming that has been discussed throughout this book. For instance, during the New Deal, as Mae Ngai explains, the Agricultural Adjustment Act (AAA) "assisted the largest farmers and encouraged the further consolidation of landholdings through programs that accelerated mechanization and paid benefits to farmers to restrict production" while at the same time excluding the workers themselves from "social and labor legislation" so that they were not seen as workers.[31] This erasure of farmworkers' rights eventually led to the reinstitution of foreign contract labor, which had been outlawed for decades because it was seen as comparable to slavery; the workers were turned into the precariat as they could not "bargain over wages or working conditions, either individually or collectively" and "did not have the right to choose [their] employer or to quit."[32] Thus, the United States reinstituted a system that denied labor protections as well as any potential for citizenship, harkening back to a system of slavery and colonialism that denied rights based on perceived ethnicity no matter the person's actual status.

Because of these long-term conflicts, people with Mexican heritage who live in the United States, whether U.S. citizens or not, often feel liminal both spatially and culturally. They are on the U.S. side of the border, but they continue to reside in a borderland, as Anzaldúa describes it. Whereas "a border is a dividing line, a narrow strip along a steep edge. A borderland is a vague and undetermined place created by the emotional residue of an unnatural bound-

---

28. Shaw, *Beyond the Fields*, 15.
29. Battat, *Ain't Got No Home*, 42.
30. Shaw, *Beyond the Fields*, 15.
31. Ngai, *Impossible Subjects*, 136.
32. Ibid., 137–38.

ary. It is in a constant state of transition."[33] Oppressed by the governmental notion of disembodied criminality, which imagines economic and national space through techniques of abstract mapping that occlude Chicana/o bodies and their lived experience of travel, people with Mexican ancestry are viewed as alien no matter what their citizenship. Because of their placement in a borderland, their relationship to space and identity is not as simple as standing on one side or the other of a firm line. As the characters in *Under the Feet* will demonstrate, a Thirdspace must be sought by interjecting alternative possibilities and continuing the struggle for social justice.[34]

THE DIFFICULTY OF MOVEMENT AND DISEMBODIED CRIMINALITY

Helena María Viramontes's *Under the Feet of Jesus* follows the predicament of Chicana/o migrant workers through a family unit made up of the mother Petra, the daughter Estrella, two sons Ricky and Arnulfo, twin toddler girls, and Petra's companion Perfecto Flores that must move with the harvest. The novel is less interested in a specific historical moment than in how time in many ways stands still for these migrants. This story could take place during any moment in the second half of the twentieth century.[35] This indistinctness illustrates that the characters' situation is a perpetual one that continues in much the same fashion as it has for decades, with specific governmentalities that shift but create the same results. As Kathy Jurado states, "One cannot help but interpret the ambiguity of the time frame in Viramontes's novel as an intentional effort to make a point about the static, abject working conditions of migrant workers in the U.S."[36] The characters' difficulty traveling epitomizes this stagnancy. When they do move, the path is mostly circular—back and forth to the fields and through the seasonal pattern of crop picking. This nonproductive movement of itinerant laborers marks them as invading criminals without permanent homes, a view reinforced by U.S. policies throughout the twentieth century to the present.

---

33. Anzaldúa, *Borderland/La Frontera*, 25.

34. Soja, *Thirdspace*, 5.

35. The text's present moment could be 1990, extrapolated from the year the father-figure Perfecto dreamed that he was born, 1917 (25), and his stated age of seventy-three (79). Other descriptors, however, create a more indefinite twentieth-century picture. For instance, posters of Marilyn Monroe and Elvis Presley (110) could indicate any time from the 1950s onward, given the ongoing celebrity of these icons. Other cultural markers also connote the iconic rather than the historically specific, including automatic sliding doors (156), invented in 1954; crop dusters (42), used for the aerial application of pesticides since the 1920s; and Quaker Oats oatmeal (18), first marketed in 1901.

36. Jurado, "Alienated Citizens," 113.

Viramontes's characters are trapped in the cyclical pattern of incessant movement, are tied to the polluted land that is killing them, and are denied a sense of belonging in public and private spaces. This enforced disembodied criminality aligns with the historical fear that many Anglo-Americans had and continue to have of the "foreigner within." Within the novel, for example, Estrella directly confronts her own insecurities about how she is or is not perceived when she witnesses a baseball game near the U.S.–Mexican border. While the novel consistently demonstrates how the Chicana/o characters acknowledge each others' physical presence, at the baseball game, Estrella feels distanced from it since she is alone, unobserved by players and spectators alike, in her position on the railroad tracks instead of in the bleachers or on the field. As she starts to leave, however, she believes the Border Patrol has arrived and flees, fearing being seen as a criminal merely because of her ancestry.

In this spatialized scene, the field represents America's pastime while also showing Estrella's ongoing symbolic search for a "home base." The sporting event illustrates the difficulty of getting into this American "game," with the team members all "behind the tall wire mesh fence," but the field's "chalked boundaries" also reveal the arbitrary nature of such demarcations (58).[37] The location of Estrella, the unseen spectator on the train tracks, compounds the symbolism of this spot. She sits on a means of motion that is getting her nowhere. The tracks extend further north into the United States as well as south into Mexico, but though she is connected to both locations, she is grounded in neither:

> Estrella turned to the long stretch of railroad ties. They looked like the stitches of the mother's caesarean scar as far as her eyes could see. To the north lay the ties and to the south of her, the same, and in between she stood, not knowing where they ended or began. (59)

Just as she was born from her mother's abdomen, she was born from this land, but she stands "in between" because she is not "bleached white" like the baseball uniforms on the field (58). She is made to feel like an intruder on the land. Her outsider position instills a fear in Estrella so that the presence of floodlights is directly tied in her mind with the Border Patrol: "She tried to remember which side she was on and which side of the wire mesh she was safe in" (59–60). Unable to determine if she is "safe," she runs away even though she is a U.S. citizen; she knows her raced body is seen as criminal and therefore must be kept moving. The interstitial location of Estrella and her family at the edge of the United States and Mexico reveals how motion and

---

37. Helena María Viramontes, *Under the Feet of Jesus* (New York: Plume, 1996). All citations are from this edition.

stasis lead to the same uncertain space of the borderland for all of Viramontes's Chicana/o characters. They feel the ongoing pressure to repeatedly prove their legal identity.

Citizenship implies that you have a home base, but for Viramontes's characters movement is necessary to get to each migrant camp. That movement is almost always circular or failed. We see workers in trucks driving to and from the fields, but mostly we see how these families are both literally and figuratively stuck with "the tire sp[inning] and sp[inning] without moving an inch" (130). *Under the Feet*'s characters lack the money and power to change their situation, so they struggle to move from job to job even as their strained movement divulges their instability. Although they are migrant workers, there is little productive movement in this novel. The novel displays that smooth traveling is less about destination and more about a sense of belonging, legality, and identity, qualities that are suppressed by the governmentality of disembodied criminality.

Put another way, characters who can move easily are those who do not need to do so. Their ease of mobility shows their stability. The lime green Bermuda convertible that Estrella observes at the gas station is a case in point:

> The white plush carpeting was so white, it was obvious no one ate in the car. She envied the car, then envied the landlord of the car who could travel from one splat dot to another. She thought him a man who knew his neighbors well, who returned to the same bed, who could tell where the schools and where the stores were, and where the Nescafé coffee jars in the stores were located, and payday always came at the end of the week. (105)

This description, interspersed with the family's own visit to the gas station store, flaunts the opportunities of movement that they do not possess for a vehicle whose "whiteness" resonates with racial privilege. The image of the car contrasts with the earlier description of the inside of Petra's family's car:

> Perfecto steered away from the potholes but still the car dipped and bumped and the empty water bottle on the dash and coffee cups and sun visors flapped down and the maps spilled onto the mother's lap. Be careful, she scolded, bracing her arm against the sun-cracked dashboard. (6)

The clutter of the car and the precarity of their passage differentiate their two travel experiences. The convertible is not a home—Estrella imagines the driver has a permanent bed, neighbors he knows, and a table at which to eat. Even so, she still refers to the car's owner as a "landlord." A car is the only piece of "land" that her family owns. He can also place the gas nozzle into the tank and wait for it to "trigger [. . .] off," instead of watching for it to hit a limited dollar amount like her family does in hope of getting Alejo to the hospital on their minimal funds (105, 148–50). Although this car owner may presumably live somewhere nearby, close to the border of the United States, he is not living in the "borderlands" like Estrella's family.

Nor does the car owner have to worry about the hills, valleys, and traffic patterns missing from the symbolic realm of maps but felt when traveling with more limited means. As we learn,

> Petra knew the capricious black lines on a map did little to reveal the hump and tear of the stitched pavement which ascended to the morning sun and through the trees and no trees, and became a swollen main street and then a loose road once again outside the hamlets that appeared as splat dots on paper. (103)

Travel is difficult in the material world, and the family's movements reveal the limits of the symbolic spaces that describe the "facts" of travel as well as mark the boundaries that limit their lives. Maps lie. They suppress certain details, such as the very existence of the borderlands, yet they claim to represent an objective and totalizing view. Representational maps reflect the imagined lines that designate national identity and colonial power, but these imposed demarcations hide the complexities of the borderlands and fail to reflect the lived experiences for Viramontes's characters.

STRUCTURING THE BORDERLAND: NONLINEAR INTERSECTIONS

The borderland, the novel demonstrates, may be seen by many as the edge of society, but the space can also be seen as the "spinal cord of this continent."[38] As Guillermo Gómez-Peña explains, "The border is the juncture, not the edge, and monoculturalism has been expelled to the margins."[39] Like Anzaldúa, he sees the borderland as a place where various cultures come together, and because of that it should not be viewed as liminal but as the location that structures the society. He continues his argument by saying that to analyze border culture, one must "look at the past and the future at the

---

38. Gómez-Peña, *Warrior for Gringostroika*, 44.
39. Ibid.

same time."[40] Bhabha combines these ideas about place and time in his own view of third space:

> The importance of hybridity is not to be able to trace two original moments from which the third emerges, rather hybridity to me is the 'third space' which enables other positions to emerge. This third space displaces the histories that constitute it, and sets up new structures of authority, new political initiatives, which are inadequately understood through received wisdom.[41]

Bhabha emphasizes the combination of various ideas across time and the generative capabilities of hybrid space, ideas that Viramontes dramatizes. The novel employs religious elements from different traditions and periods that are grounded in both historical and mythological locations, also employing a version of Soja's real and imagined spaces. Time no longer exists only in its linear form; instead, the past, present, and future need to be spatialized themselves, placing each moment side by side and then surpassing each. This connection of the complexity of the borderland with the blending of time periods appears in the structure of the novel.

Under the Feet demonstrates this Thirdspace of overlapping times through its replication of the cyclical movements of the characters, creating a circularity by starting and ending with the image of the barn. The first line of the novel asks, "Had they been heading for the barn all along?" (3), and it turns out that the rickety façade was the destination, since the last scene displays Estrella standing on its roof. Beyond that largest of frames, however, are the scenes that cinematically jump readers from place to place with a quick line break, jarring us for a moment until we recognize the new site. In addition to the change of location, there are changes from linear time. In some cases, a simple image provides the catalyst for a leap to a memory in another time and place. For instance, in one scene in the present, Alejo makes shadow animals for the deformed boy he finds in the barn. The boy, however, hurts himself when he chases after the shadow of an eagle "sprinkling droplets of blood [. . .] until it zigzagged across the dented trough and finally returned to the tower from where it first appeared, and vanished" (23). After a line break, the story continues several years earlier, when Estrella's father was leaving the family: "Not even a few drops of menstrual blood in his coffee would keep him from leaving" (23). Blood ties these two scenes across not only time but also space:

---

40. Ibid.
41. Bhabha, "Third Space," 211.

one in a barn and the other in the family's home.[42] Also connecting them is a disappearance; the bird transfixes the boy until it disappears, just as the father's disappearance confuses and saddens Estrella and Petra.

The escape of the father figure in the past and the eagle in the present symbolizes the lack of accessibility to a reliable patriarch both on the familial and the national level, since the eagle represents the United States and the mythical Aztlán. Viramontes's characters cannot find security, and in the temporal hybridity created by these overlapping experiences, we feel this loss in a new way that links the deformed boy's experiences with Petra's and Estrella's. This is a displaced community. Like Marcel Proust's episode of the madeleine, objects can create involuntary memories, altering time and place. But in this book, that memory is not stirred solely by individual recollection. It is also stirred by the unseen narrator's knowledge of all these characters, creating for them a type of collective consciousness. After all, the example just mentioned rapidly takes the reader from a scene written from the limited omniscient point of view of Alejo to the limited omniscience of Petra, yet they connect through their borderland location.

Linear time is also affected in the novel through the repetition of the same moment from different perspectives. Sometimes this shift is marked by a line break, but at other times the shift happens in the unmarked space between paragraphs. For example, in the first sequence of scenes, the reader observes the arrival of the family to their new home at the same time that Alejo and his cousin Gumecindo pick peaches in a field. Estrella and her twin sisters investigate the barn and scare out some birds that "shriek" along with the girls' surprised "screams" (10). Back in the field, Alejo comments that the sound must be "cats fighting," although he later admits he was also thinking about the animals trapped in the tar pits (10, 88). Meanwhile, his cousin fears that the noise is la Llorona, a mythic woman who drowns her children in retaliation for a man leaving her. In this moment, we get three different interpretations of the same sound. Interestingly, two of those views contain references to history or long-believed cultural myth, so that even these multiple perspectives on the same instant reveal how the present and the past overlap.

The other key scene that plays out from two perspectives occurs near the end of the book when Petra accidentally breaks her Jesus statue and Estrella overhears her mother. This important symbolic loss is timed with both Petra's loss of religious faith and Estrella's sudden realization that Alejo may not be all right: "It only now occurred to her that perhaps she would never see him alive again, that perhaps he would die" (170). Intersecting time and place here

---

42. The common link of the blood also shows that these families, although not literally related, have cultural bloodlines uniting them.

connect to religious beliefs with a long history. Petra's response is to turn to Perfecto for an answer—a traditional one of a woman turning to a man. Estrella's response, however, moves the reader to a new location and possibility, as I will explain shortly.

Although reviewer Valerie Miner makes note of the novel's style as a "poetic, fragmented narrative [that] mirrors her characters' dislocations," I extend this idea because the novel does more than dislocate its characters; it relocates them through a new sense of space and time.[43] The postmodern introduction of various perspectives and the unexplored ties of a historic-spatial narrative allow the characters to reclaim the past moments that have led up to the current one. By setting those time periods side by side, Viramontes allows for the possibility of moving beyond those moments to a beneficial Thirdspace.

THE POTENTIAL AND LIMITATIONS OF ORGANIZED RELIGION AND RITUAL

While the Border Patrol and the corporations biopolitically affect these workers to make them homeless, criminalized, alien bodies that are only useful for labor, spirituality is incorporated into characters' lives as a potential, even political, solution, echoing Viramontes's own experiences with the UFW. Organized religion and ritual offer the building blocks for a Thirdspace because of the solace they provide and the ways that they can be used to bring together not just different spaces but also different times. The use of organized religion and ritual in *Under the Feet* presents the possibility for this type of symbolic conception, but such practices ultimately fail to create a hybrid space that reconfigures authority when uncritically accepted.

Religious figures play a prominent role in this novel, starting from the title itself, but the title's conflicting meanings, which range from the literal to biblical interpretations, also reveal the ambiguous nature of religion in this text. The literal meaning of the title is twofold: the family's legal documents lie under Petra's Jesus statue and the earth naturally lies under Jesus' human feet. The former point highlights concerns about questioned citizenship and national landownership rights, as Petra directly states: "If they stop you, if they try to pull you into the green vans, you tell them the birth certificates are under the feet of Jesus, just tell them" (63). The latter point about the earth indicates ecological concerns that scholars such as Mitchum Huehls have

---

43. Miner, "Review: Hopes, Fears and Secrets," 19.

noted in relationship to the pesticide use in this text—a concern that again echoes the boycott led by Chávez and the UFW.[44]

In addition to these literal meanings that point to the plight of the workers, there are also religious interpretations of this title that provide the characters with hope through Catholicism. The title invokes a set of biblical passages that portray a conflict between humans and serpents, where the serpent is crushed underfoot. In Genesis 3:15, for instance, God himself establishes that there will be eternal conflict between Eve, the mother of humanity, and the earthy, devilish serpent: "I shall put enmity between you and the woman, / between your brood and hers. / They will strike at your head, / and you will strike at their heel."[45] The "brood" that will be born to crush the serpent has been interpreted by Christians as Jesus, but other quotations from the Old and New Testaments often leave open the identity of the treader. Psalm 91:13 states, "You will tread on asp and cobra, / you will trample on snake and serpent," and Luke 10:19 declares, "And I have given you the power to tread underfoot snakes and scorpions and all the forces of the enemy. Nothing will ever harm you." In all these examples, God gives his followers the permission and the power to destroy their opponents as a way to remain safe. The novel's title thus appears to present organized religion as promising the migrant laborers an eventual triumph over their oppressors.

The characters in Viramontes's novel, however, discover they are interchangeably both the treader and the trod upon. They may walk with Jesus in their belief, allowing them to symbolically destroy those who attack them, just like "Perfecto's boot pop[s] the scorpion" under his shoe (8). At the same time, the manual labor that exhausts them every day and leaves them without even basic acceptance by their country shows how cruelly they are stepped on. Being on the road makes them feel like the "perfectly crushed" snake, run over by a truck, that they "couldn't even scrape [. . .] off the pavement with a butterknife" (106). After all, behind this entire religion are the Spanish conquerors who once trampled their ancestors. The characters can be identified as the snakes and scorpions—the *niños de tierra*, the children of the earth—who were sacrificed in the past for land and wealth and continue to be sacrificed in the present for the same reasons. Although religion is sometimes tied to nationality, the land upon which Jesus walks theoretically should not be limited by country or by citizenship. Therefore, violence to the characters and the land upon which they walk replaces the inclusive, accepting space that should

---

44. Huehls, "Ostension, Simile, Catachresis," 352.

45. All citations from *The Oxford Study Bible*, eds. M. Jack Suggs, Katharine Doob Sakenfeld, and James R. Mueller (New York: Oxford University Press, 1992).

be beneath Jesus' feet. In the ambiguity created just by analyzing the title, the text already highlights its multifarious relationship with Christianity.

Under the Feet specifically questions too much dependence on Christianity to "solve" the plight of the Mexican American migrant, thereby attempting to incorporate and then even go beyond Chávez's pilgrimage. When the statue of Jesus falls and his head breaks off, "[Petra] was surprised by the lightness of the head," and shortly thereafter she comments on her "broken faith" (167–68). Perhaps, the novel says, this ideology does not hold as much weight as it should. Yet, while the text questions relying too much on organized religion, Petra's devotion is sincere, and it does create positive results such as her caring for Alejo because "she did it for the love of God" (124). For Petra, Christianity acts as an anchor that helps her to make positive moral decisions for her family and to broaden that definition of family to include others who need the support of the community. In the book, Christianity has its benefits and limits.

There are, however, representations of the kind of hybridity that Bhabha and Soja desire across time and space, but they fail to lead to a productive Thirdspace because they have become popularized and uncritically accepted. Christianity and its blending with Mexican tradition appears even at the grocery store in a poster of the Virgin of Guadalupe:

> A lopsided poster of the holy Virgen, Our Lady of Guadalupe was tacked between the posters of Elvis Presley and Marilyn Monroe holding her white billowing dress down. La Virgen was adorned by red and green and white twinkling Christmas lights which surrounded the poster like a sequin necklace. Each time the lights blinked, Petra saw herself reflected in La Virgen's glossy downcast eyes. Unlike Marilyn's white pumps which were buried under the shriveled pods of Chile Negro, La Virgen was raised, it seemed to Petra, above a heavenly mound of bulbous garlic. (110)

This image, like the book's title, is fraught with complexity. Its "lopsided" angle shows that religion has been skewed. The gaudy Christmas lights, out of season in the midst of summer, illustrate how Christianity has been commodified and refocused on decorations and material goods rather than on the birth of Jesus. The other posters also highlight the commercialization of religion, since the Virgin is hung as a celebrity of popular culture just like the Hollywood and music stars beside her.

Even so, the Virgin most reflects how Catholicism had to adjust in Mexico. As Anzaldúa explains, the Virgin of Guadalupe, while seemingly a Catholic representation of Spanish culture in Mexico, also brings Mexican culture to Spanish symbols. She is "a synthesis of the old world and the new, of religion and culture of the two races in our psyche, the conquerors and the conquered" because she is a blending of the Virgin Mary with the Aztec religious figure of "Our Lady Mother" Tonantzin.[46] Worshipping the Virgin of Guadalupe disguised a continued worshipping of Tonantzin.[47] Because of this combination, the Virgin of Guadalupe is sometimes called the First *Mestiza*. She symbolizes the Chicano/*mexicano* "rebellion against the rich, upper and middleclass; against their subjugation of the poor and the *indio*."[48] Therefore, the poster in the novel suggests a positive combination of cultural elements in the Virgin of Guadalupe. Nevertheless, here in the gas station where the children are forced to stay outside and the fruits are the "relics" of what they had been in the fields, a positive Thirdspace cannot be found (110). Although cultural hybridity and spiritual possibility are presented, they are the commodified shell of a Thirdspace. The Virgin may hide Tonantzin within her, but this poster ultimately points out the restrictions of organized religion. The church, Anzaldúa states, like any institution, "come[s] with agendas and trappings which lull you into not challenging things"; through dogma it "eliminates all kinds of growth, development, and change."[49] When this idea is applied to the scene, one recognizes that the static images of Marilyn Monroe and Elvis from their youth reveal that the Virgin, too, is unchanging. She may give Petra comfort, but she does not provide any major transformation, revealing the necessity to constantly reimagine ways of making the past relevant to the present.

Petra also reveals this type of stagnancy through her non-Christian rituals, which she uses to protect their home and bodies. She believes in drawing a line in the sand to keep the scorpions away from the house, and she believes in home remedies for Alejo when he becomes ill. Though Petra feels secure in her practices through most of the book, warding off "white rationality," one wonders if she performs these acts to keep the scorpions away or if she does so, like her Christian prayers, as a ritual that, through its mere repetition, gives her a sense of ease.[50] Again, like organized religion, rituals can be productive. They can create a sense of calm where there is only anxiety, but they can also cause harm when they are the only long-term solution. After all, when Alejo is poisoned by the pesticides, he needs medical attention, not

---

46. Anzaldúa, *Borderland/La Frontera*, 52, 50.

47. On December 9, 1531, the Virgin of Guadalupe is said to have appeared in the same place where Tonantzin had previously been worshipped. See Lafaye for more on the ties between these two figures, including the linguistic and symbolic overlaps (*Quetzalcóatl and Guadalupe*, 211–17).

48. Anzaldúa, *Borderland/La Frontera*, 52.

49. Weiland, "Within the Crossroads," 73, 98.

50. Anzaldúa, *Borderland/La Frontera*, 58.

folklore remedies. By getting "stuck" in religion and ritual, Petra reflects the larger stagnancy in their lives.

The characters' cultural grounding in Aztec beliefs extends beyond the worship of Tonantzin to Aztec beliefs about the space they inhabit. Though the characters themselves may not directly mention this historical tie, their location in the Southwestern United States invokes this past. The Aztecs viewed this region as Aztlán: "According to myth, Aztlán is the ancestral homeland in the north that the Aztecs left in 1168 when they journeyed southward to found the promised land, Tenochtitlán (Mexico City), in 1325."[51] This "mytho-historical" tie, as Lee Bebout labels this important narrative that counters the U.S. ideology of Manifest Destiny, was also connected to politics when in 1969 at the Denver Youth Liberation Conference this idea of the Southwest as the mythic Aztlán was reenvoked under the preamble of "El Plan Espiritual de Aztlán," a foundational document for the Chicano Movement that fought for Chicano civil rights.[52] Additionally, this same concept was used by Chávez and the UFW in their pilgrimage, since they marched with banners of the Virgin of Guadalupe as well as of the ever-present symbol of the cause, the Aztec eagle flag representing the mythic Aztlán.[53] By connecting themselves to a cultural history as well as a claim to the land, "this narrative [of Aztlán] positioned Chicanos and their struggle both geographically and historically."[54] It disrupted colonization, built a tie and respect for Indigenous cultures, and fought colonial mapping while "imagining community and mediating the heterogeneity of the movement," and, according to Rudolfo Anaya, brought together "spiritual and political aspirations."[55] People of Mexican descent thus are linked to this culture through their native bloodlines and through the land itself. Of course, even this tie to a pre-Conquest culture has its own problems, since it "romanticizes an era marked by war and conquest and a rigorous class hierarchy, an Aztec culture that had eradicated a matriarchal Mayan culture."[56] In other words, all of these cultural belief systems provide Viramontes's characters with the material to construct hybridity. Viramontes's awareness of this connection is evident when Estrella is handed "white leaflets with black eagles on them" (84), but active engagement on the part of her characters continues to be needed to produce a Thirdspace that moves beyond the stagnancy of the present along the contested space of the U.S.–Mexican border.

---

51. Arrizón, "Mythical Performativity," 23.
52. Bebout, *Mythohistorical Interventions*, 1–5.
53. Shaw, *Beyond the Fields*, 80–81.
54. Bebout, *Mythohistorical Interventions*, 2.
55. Ibid., 3–4.
56. Grewe-Volpp, "'The oil was made from their bones,'" 73.

ESTRELLA'S EMBODIMENT OF SPIRITUALITY IN MEXICAN AMERICAN TRADITION

In *Under the Feet*, Estrella synthesizes and adapts spiritual elements from Catholic and Aztec beliefs to create a symbolic response that addresses the problems of disembodied criminality. This embodied spirituality acknowledges the need to change preexisting stories so that individuals have a way to understand their bodies and move beyond the criminalization imposed on them by the United States. Petra's daughter personifies the complications beyond the binary, starting with what Anzaldúa labels "folk Catholicism," which blends Catholic and Indigenous elements. Reclaiming female strength from various sources, Estrella is, at various times in the novel, the Virgin of Guadalupe and la Llorona, Eve and Coatlicue.[57] Since many of the Christian and Indigenous female figures are already "telescoped onto the other," as Sandra Cisneros phrases it, Estrella needs to find a way to alter these stories to rewrite the past and reimagine the future, or, as Norma Alarcón states, "It is through a revision of tradition that self and culture can be radically reenvisioned and reinvented."[58] Estrella's work aligns with that of Chicana feminists; by containing the supposed binaries, she creates a new Thirdspace for understanding that surpasses each individual religious tradition and demonstrates her willingness to assume the multiple roles of being in-between.[59] She knows that finding a new resolution is a matter of survival, and although only a teenager, she tries to save Alejo and then her larger community, developing over the course of this *bildungsroman* from innocent girl to potential savior through her transformation at mythically resonant locations such as the canal, the tar pits, and the barn.

This integration begins in Estrella's connection to the story of la Llorona. While scholars such as Ana María Carbonell and Wendy Swyt have pointed to the use of la Llorona mythology in short stories by Viramontes, this theme has not been fully explicated in *Under the Feet*, despite its importance.[60] Some early versions of the myth of la Llorona focus on a goddess named Chihuacoatl, "serpent woman"—itself a telling name in connection to the other reli-

---

57. Anzaldúa, *Borderland/La Frontera*, 58.

58. Cisneros, "Guadalupe the Sex Goddess," 50 and Alarcón, "Traddutora, Traditora," 71. Alarcón investigates the changing role of Malintzin, but Viramontes finds Guadalupe more "tractable" than might be first imagined.

59. Other Chicana authors have also sought ties to Aztec goddesses. For instance, Sandra Cisneros's poem "It Occurs to Me I Am the Creative/Destructive Goddess Coatlicue" states her desire to claim the breadth of Coatlicue's powers.

60. Carbonell, "From Llorona to Gritona" and Swyt, "Hungry Women."

gious elements of the story—and reveal that this story has its foundation in the reign of the Aztecs:

> According to [an] Aztec codex, just a few years before Spanish ships first landed on the Mexican coast of Vera Cruz in the sixteenth century, a woman circled the walls of the great Aztec city of Tenochtitlán. Late at night she was heard weeping in mourning for the impending destruction of the great Mexican civilization, and especially for her children: "My children, we must flee far from this city!" The Aztecs took this as the sixth of eight omens warning of their imminent ruin. Because of her signaling doom, the Weeping Woman, or La Llorona [sic], became a perennial avatar of Snake Woman.[61]

This story of an Indigenous woman who warns about the impending arrival of the *conquistadores* was altered after the actual arrival of the Spanish to a distraught woman killing her children after her husband leaves. That change disempowers the woman and demonizes her as a child killer, something Viramontes revisits.[62]

La Llorona first appears only a few pages into the novel, when Alejo and his cousin hear the screech of birds and Estrella's sisters scream in response to those birds. Spooked, the cousin says, "I always thought la Llorona was just a story" (11). Later the narrator notes, "[Alejo's] cousin had not stopped talking of la Llorona and the ghosts of her drowned children" (39). After these two mentions of la Llorona, the novel focuses on Estrella. In the first instance, the scene changes to a previous time when she is with her father, stealing an orange, just as the boys in the previous scene stole peaches. This memory leads to the statement, "It was her father who'd ran [sic] away," and the male betrayal that Estrella experiences parallels la Llorona's betrayal by her husband (13). After the second mention, Alejo watches Estrella swim naked in the canal after a watermelon. Associated with water, Estrella again replicates a feature of la Llorona's story, but whereas la Llorona is said to haunt the waterways where she drowned her children, Estrella's aquatic link is one of both seduction and innocence. She attracts Alejo with her body, even though she is innocent of doing so.

Both connections of la Llorona and Estrella indicate the disparity between the myth and its current reimagining. Not an evil temptress, Estrella is a young girl for whom a watermelon may easily become a child. As Petra observes, "Estrella cradled a watermelon like a baby and this vision saddened her" (40).

---

61. León, *La Llorona's Children*, 7.

62. For more details about the various versions of the story of la Llorona and her connection to other female goddesses, see Luis D. León's *La Llorona's Children*.

This formulation of Estrella as pregnant without sexual contact recalls the pregnancies of two other religious figures, the Virgin Mary and Coatlicue.[63] Through her embodiment of such cultural stories, the child alters them and rewrites history, eventually realizing this symbolic mother role in her relationship with Alejo. He becomes the child she must sacrifice when she hands him over to the hospital, and she becomes the mother figure who loses her child because of the power of those above her.[64] She is a renewed la Llorona, one with whom the reader can empathize instead of fear.

Connecting Estrella to well-known figures but adapting familiar images, the novel stresses her transformative role in relation to both native ritual and Christianity. On the basic level of listening to various spiritual narratives, Estrella supports her mother's Catholicism by reading her catechism chapbook and her non-Christian rituals by drawing the line in the ground: "Her mother believed scorpions instinctively scurried away from lines which had no opening or closing. Estrella never questioned whether this was true or not" (42). She even tells her mother when the line has become faded, showing that she willingly participates in these rituals.

Estrella, however, moves beyond these rituals that draw lines in the sand, invoking the flawed logic of national borders. She also looks beyond the act of merely praying for a solution, breaking with convention in relationship to organized religion and ritual. Early in the novel, she reads with a friend when she "was supposed to be in church," and later she watches a lunar eclipse with the men even though she "should have been safely tucked away like the other women of the camp because the moon and earth and sun's alignment was a powerful thing" (38, 69). She begins to break cultural traditions when she sees how they limit her as a woman. It is during this same scene, though, when she recalls her chapbook reading. Seeing a bonfire set by the men "like a beacon for them to find their way back to their beds [. . . with] the sizzling red sparks spear[ing] up into the night," Estrella recites, "*The Holy Spirit came in the form of tongues of fire to show His love*" (68).[65] She sees this moment with

---

63. Arrizón, "Mythical Performativity," 37.

64. In this moment, she is also rewriting the historical figure of Malinali Tenepat (*Malintzín*), who was a Mayan woman sold as a slave to Cortez. She functioned as his translator and has been presented as a betrayer of her people. Anzaldúa, along with many other feminists, marks her as a mother figure instead of a whore, "la Chingada." She says that this version of history has made women "believe that the Indian woman in us is the betrayer" (*Borderland/ La Frontera*, 44). With this figure in mind, Estrella's actions rewrite this narrative. Though we see her functioning as a translator for Alejo and her family at the clinic, this time she is giving voice to her Indigenous family, and this time her giving up Alejo is in the hopes of saving him.

65. Although Estrella does not state it, the second part of her remembered chapbook reading also has relevance in this scene. When Estrella feels afraid after Alejo leaves her, she hears "*wind groaning over the mouth of the bottle, notes far and wayward in the night*" (71; italics

people together beneath the stars, the barn as the only structure in sight, as a holy moment with the potential to bring together all of those around her. Unfortunately, this tradition is one not intended for women. Estrella begins searching for a new remedy that would include women, but one that continues to draw upon her spiritual heritage, including Catholicism, folk rituals, and Aztec religion, to create a new space and spiritual identity for herself and her community.[66] In this way, Estrella echoes Viramontes's sense of the spiritual achieved through reading and community in her own personal growth.

Her actions have ramifications on the individual and communal levels. As Bhabha explains, these "in-between" spaces where cultural differences are distinguished "provide the terrain for elaborating strategies of selfhood—singular or communal—that initiate new signs of identity, and innovative sites of collaboration, and contestation, in the act of defining the idea of society itself."[67] Estrella's combination of spiritual elements, far from being a garbled conflation of religious practices and symbols, actually produces her identity in a way that exposes rather than conceals the space's history and tensions for her community.

While Bhabha stresses the political and social aspects of these spaces, Anzaldúa's spatial view of a culturally specific "in-between" space, a translation of "Nepantla" from the Aztec language of Nahuatl, adds a spiritual dimension:

> Nepantla [sic] is kind of an elaboration of Borderlands. I use nepantla to talk about the creative act, I use it to talk about the construction of identity, I use it to describe a function of the mind. [. . .] I find people using metaphors such as "Borderlands" in a more limited sense than I had meant it, so to expand on the psychic and emotional borderlands I'm now using "nepantla." With nepantla the connection to the spirit world is more pronounced as is the connection to the world after death, to psychic spaces. It has a more spiritual, psychic, supernatural, and indigenous resonance.[68]

---

added). As Alejo walks into the distance, he continues to practice the method of blowing in the cola bottle that she had just taught him. His "wind" becomes the *great wind* [of the Holy Spirit] *to show the power of His grace*" (31).

66. After all, Estrella herself has been associated with fire even at the start of novel, when "her chest breathed and crackled like kindling" and "her cheeks [were] as red as hot embers" (15). Estrella is that spirit come to earth.

67. Bhabha, *The Location of Culture*, 1–2.

68. Keating, "Making Choices," 176. I italicize and capitalize *Nepantla* as Anzaldúa does in *Borderlands/La Frontera*. In other interviews, the word is often not marked in this way, but since the discussions were presumably spoken, I defer to Anzaldúa's written text.

The spiritual space of *Nepantla* exists beyond the confines of established religion in the body, beginning in the gendered space of birth. *Nepantla* is "this birthing stage when you feel like you are reconfiguring your identity and do not know where you are."[69] This renewal is difficult, but it resolves the body/spirit dichotomy and uses it as a place for metamorphosis.[70]

Estrella continues her own journey toward rebirth when Alejo tells her about the La Brea tar pits, which formed millions of years ago, turning the bones in them into consumable oil. The novel creates corresponding images of women screaming in order to show the importance of saving women from being silenced by unearthing their stories. The text first associates Estrella with mythic characters like la Llorona through Alejo's cousin's fears and then later aligns Estrella with the buried girl in the tar pits after she considers the larger human ramifications stemming from Alejo's concerns about animals being enveloped by the earth. Alejo's comment, "Once, when I picked peaches, I heard screams. It reminded me of the animals stuck in the tar pits," leads Estrella to ask, "Did people ever get stuck?" (88). The voices of la Llorona and the girl in the tar pit have been reduced to inarticulate screams, burying the former's warnings about the coming conquest and the latter's lessons about how bodies and their work are consumed. Their anger against oppression goes unheeded as they and their stories are figuratively and literally buried. Estrella, struck by the image of the fragmented remains of the young girl, later repeats her story when she, too, is buried in mud: "They found her in a few bones. No details of her life were left behind, no piece of cloth, no ring, no doll. A few bits of bone displayed somewhere under a glass case and nothing else" (129). By making a connection between their situations, Estrella demonstrates that she wants to save herself and this girl so that they both are not merely used up as expendable bare life. To achieve this goal, she seeks to return voice and body to these lost and disempowered women.[71]

Although Estrella feels a specific tie to the women who are repeatedly silenced, such as the girl in the tar pits, she wants to find a home and a recon-

---

69. Blake and Abrego, "Doing Gigs," 225.

70. For an extended analysis of the spiritual elements of Anzaldúa's theories, see Delgadillo, *The Spiritual Mestizaje.* In this text, the focus is on the term "spiritual mestizaje" and only briefly touches upon the idea of *Nepantla,* which she states is the "active engagement in a stage of spiritual mestizaje," or, as she quotes Anzaldúa, it is the "site of transformation" (Delgadillo, *The Spiritual Mestizaje,* 8).

71. Estrella plays out what Viramontes says is her own goal through her writing, to first "conjur[e] up the voices and spirits of women living under brutal repressive regimes" and then "do justice to their voices. To tell these women in my own gentle way that I will fight for them, that they provide me with my own source of humanity. That I love them, their children" ("Nopalitos," 34–35).

nection to the earth for all her people. The land should not poison; if you pick the fruit, you should be able to eat it; if you walk the land, you should be able to live on it freely. As Estrella continues on this path, she draws on the story of Coatlicue, the Aztec Earth Mother who "represents duality in life, a synthesis of duality, and a third perspective—something more than mere duality or a synthesis of duality."[72] As Coatlicue, whose name means "serpent skirt," she is the goddess who creates and destroys, the guardian of the womb and grave.

At the clinic, Estrella puts her destructive side into action when the nurse takes all of the family's money. At this moment, Estrella thinks, "If only God could help," and while at first it may seem that God does not answer, her spiritual connection to the women before her does help her to make a decision (147). First, she draws on the history she has learned:

> She remembered the tar pits. Energy money, the fossilized bones of energy matter. How bones made oil and oil made gasoline. The oil was made from their bones and it was their bones that kept the nurse's car from not halting on some highway [. . . .] It was their bones that kept them moving on the long dotted line on the map. Their bones. Why couldn't the nurse see that? Estrella had figured it out: the nurse owed *them* as much as they owed her. (148)

She invokes the past to talk about the pain of the present, showing her political awareness that the current governmental practices and their abstract mapping of space without bodies give benefits only to the dominant group. Her internal theorizing then leads her to the duality of Coatlicue. She grabs a crowbar and demands their money back: "She felt like two Estrellas. One was a silent phantom who obediently marked a circle with a stick around the bungalow as the mother had requested, while the other held the crowbar and the money" (150). Here, the destructive side emerges. She finds that she has to choose just the aggressive side of herself to take action. As Anzaldúa explains,

> The male-dominated Azteca-Mexica culture drove the powerful female deities underground by giving them monstrous attributes and by substituting male deities in their place, thus splitting the female Self and the female deities. They divided her who had been complete, who possessed both upper (light) and underworld (dark) aspects.[73]

---

72. Anzaldúa, *Borderland/La Frontera*, 68.
73. Ibid., 49.

Estrella is still trying to find an integrated self that allows for a balance between the opposing forces inside her. Even so, this is a major scene of change because she begins to recognize the power she has within.

Estrella again sees this doubling of herself when she enters the barn a few scenes later: "She spoke to her shadow as if she were not alone" (172). Here her shadow stands in as the "dark" side of her new strength, but she embraces that darkness with an "Okay" said "to her other self" (172). Then the two sides of Estrella work together to climb the chain in the barn. By entering the space she has vowed to destroy in order to birth herself, she presents the full complexity of the Coatlicue figure, where the both/and of destruction and creation are joined.

In this way, Estrella reforms the female goddess who, along with other female deities, has been demonized under patriarchal power. Alicia Arrizón articulates the specificity of this historical transformation:

> After the conquest, Tonantzin/Guadalupe was established as the "good" mother, while Coatlicue and her female deities Cihuacoatl and Tlazolteotl were rendered into defiant beasts. They are the transgressors of *marianismo* (the cult of the Virgin Mary and her subject position as the mother of God), imposed by an entrenched Christianity. Thus, as an opposing force, Cihuacoatl's legacy helps to explain the whore-virgin dichotomy that has shaped gender relations and sexuality in post-Spanish colonial sites.[74]

By reincorporating the elements of all of these women, Estrella empowers herself. Through her transmogrification of the religious and cultural stories that shape the borderland, she also hopes to strengthen and reunify her people.

RETURNING TO THE BARN: A SOCIAL JUSTICE THIRDSPACE FOR THE MIGRANT LABORER

The fullest picture of Estrella's Thirdspace of embodied spirituality emerges in the symbolic final scene of the book, where it acts to blend the ethical demand of the refugee with the citizenship protections that should be afforded to the internally displaced person for the repeatedly displaced migrant laborer. This scene incorporates previous allusions to spiritual narratives in the text and imagines how not only the women that she embodies but all of the Mexican migrants can come together. Estrella searches for a communal space, and the barn becomes her choice. She is intrigued by this rickety, old building partly because she has been forbidden to enter it by Perfecto, so claiming it

---

74. Arrizón, "Mythical Performativity," 37.

asserts her newfound female authority. At the same time, she is also tied to it because it was a focal point during her spiritual experience on the night of the eclipse.[75] The barn holds many other symbolic benefits, as well. In Christian tradition, it is important as the place of Jesus' birth. Agriculturally, barns, as the storehouses for food and animals, signify fertility. In Aztec history, the barn parallels the cave-like spaces of worship and the symbolic cave space of rebirth. In the novel, it is also an internal space for reflection and a sanctuary. As Estrella states, when things have gotten so bad for Alejo that they have finally taken him to the clinic despite the cost, "all she wanted was to find a deep, dark quiet place like the barn to cry" (139–40). It is also the place where the deformed boy is seen, the symbolic and literal child of the people who have been harmed by the poisoning of the fields. All of these representations are drawn upon in this ending scene.

Early in the text, the barn evokes organized religion when it is described as a "cathedral of a building" (9). At the end, that tie remains, but with a difference. Although the barn is still a cathedral, it is now Estrella's heart that is "like the chiming bells in the great cathedrals" (176). In an interview about the book, Viramontes herself comments that the barn is "a rejection of her mother's faith but a reemphasis as well."[76] That is, Estrella has become the heart of the "church" under a spiritually embodied viewpoint, and the barn becomes not only a place of refuge but a living entity—a Thirdspace for the migrant workers. It, in effect, represents the book's new spirituality, standing physically for all the people who seek refuge. Estrella imagines the pain the barn would feel in its humanized state if she were to tear it down like Perfecto, her stand-in father figure, has asked:

> The nails would screech and the wood would moan and she would pull the veins out and the woodsheet wall would collapse like a toothless mouth. Nothing would be left except a hole in the baked dirt so wide it would make one wonder how anything could be so empty.
>
> Is that what happens? Estrella thought, people just use you until you're all used up, then rip you into pieces when they're finished using you? (75)

Like the mythic and religious women who have been subsumed by dogma or oppressed by a masculine power, the barn would be harmed and silenced. With the reference of the barn's veins, Estrella also invokes her mother's pain-

---

75. Importantly, during the eclipse she blows on the bottle because she feels good but could not "build the house of words" (70) to express herself; she could not yet "build rooms as big as *barns*" (70; italics added). Now Estrella is trying to utilize the barn that does exist so that it can house her feelings, her spirituality, and the voice of her people.

76. Kevane and Heredia, *Latina Self-Portraits*, 150.

ful varicose veins, while the toothless mouth recalls Toothless Kawamoto, a *piscador* who stands for all migrant workers and importantly marks, through his Japanese name, a connection beyond a singular ethnic space: "She saw the bend of a back, and at first could not tell whether it was female or male, old or young" (56). The tearing down of the barn is the tearing down of all the people who are being "used up."

By embracing the barn, Estrella makes the decision to fight for the community. She chooses to avoid selfish individualism, like Perfecto's dream to return to Mexico alone or Alejo's cousin's decision to leave the sick Alejo. Instead, Estrella's connection to the barn shows that the focus should be on expanding the definition of family and a home, since, as Cecelia Lawless argues, "a home cannot be conceived as a private, protected, and individualistic place" unless through "homey nostalgia" because that definition of home has long been a place of oppression for women.[77] Estrella's expansion of the homespace imitates Petra's accepting Alejo into her family or the *piscadores'* helping her family stuck by the side of the road. They all need to work together to get unstuck and reborn.

As Michael Nieto García states, the barn in part becomes a womb for Estrella's symbolic birth.[78] Extending García's claim, I suggest that the barn becomes a womb-space tying the *Nepantla* idea of rebirth to the pre-Conquest time of Coatlicue. In myth the Mexica (part of the people later named the Aztecs) migrate, developing into the most powerful tribe in the region. On their journey, they stop at "the mount of the seven wombs":[79]

> There at Coatepec, Huitzilopochtli burst forth fully grown and armed from the womb of his mother Coatlicue, to slay his sister, Coyolxauhqui and his four hundred, or innumerable, brothers the Centronhuitznatua, the episode functioning as a metaphor for Mexican dominance over enemy peoples.[80]

Estrella, the Coatlicue figure, leaves her mother Petra, who, attempting to thwart her rebirth, "was trying to hide her back in her body" (171). She travels to the dark refuge of a cave-like space that doubles as her own womb, and in this reimagining, a son is not born from her. Instead, she gives birth to herself. She grabs onto the metal chain dangling in the middle of the barn:

> She wrapped the chain between her thighs now and jerked down to raise herself up as if she were tugging on a cord of a bell. She stopped to release

77. Lawless, "Helena María Viramontes' Homing Devices in *Under the Feet of Jesus*," 376.
78. García, "Ethnic, Feminist, Universal?," 127.
79. Austin, "Myth of the Half-Man Who Descended from the Sky," 152.
80. Boone, "Migration Histories as Ritual Performance," 134.

one hand and wipe her sweaty palm against her trousers while she hugged tight the chain against her chest with her other. (173)

As García explains, Estrella becomes the child attached to the umbilical cord of the chain, pushing through the door on the roof into life, but she is also the mother in labor, sweating and feeling the tearing between her thighs. For Viramontes, barns carry dangerous knowledge about sexuality via intercourse and birth, and for that reason are often prohibited to girls.[81] Estrella's entering the barn and reclaiming it as the site of her own birth is an entry into empowered womanhood.

Through her actions, Estrella leaves Anzaldúa's Coatlicue state: "When you're in the midst of the Coatlicue state—the cave, the dark—you're hibernating or hiding, you're in a womb state. When you come out of that womb state you pass through the birth canal, the passageway, I call nepantla [sic]."[82] Having come through *Nepantla,* she, like Huitzilopochtli who stands on the mountaintop ready for battle, stands on the roof of the barn ready for a new phase of her existence. She will not slay her sister like Huitzilopochtli did. She will look for a way to bring all of her people together, drawing on all the histories and the space out of which she has come.

In the final scene, Estrella enacts this metamorphosis of religious symbols. In her rebirth, she becomes a male figure ready to do battle to show that the Mexicans will not be conquered. She also alters the gender of the Christian story by taking on the role of the newborn Jesus figure. Assuming his characteristics from the title, she walks on the roof: "The termite-softened shakes crunched beneath her bare feet like the serpent under the feet of Jesus" (175). At the same time, she functions as Eve, who, like Coatlicue, is the mother of all. God's injunction against the serpent in the garden of Eden foretells that Jesus will eventually crush the serpent as Eve's "brood," but in the present moment Eve has that power. In this way, Estrella again complicates the timeline as she is both Eve and Jesus at once.

Estrella more fully realizes this Thirdspace when she steps out on the roof and encompasses all of time. She reflects on her surroundings:

She was stunned by the diamonds. The sparkle of stars cut the night—almost violently sharp. [. . .] Over the eucalyptus and behind the moon, the stars like silver pomegranates glimmered before an infinity of darkness. No wonder the angels had picked a place like this to exist. (175)

---

81. Kevane and Heredia, *Latina Self-Portraits,* 150.
82. Blake and Abrego, "Doing Gigs," 226.

Standing there "bathed in a flood of gray light" (175) on the roof that "reminded her of the full moon" (3), she looks like the woman of the apocalypse, "clothed with the sun, and the moon under her feet, and upon her head a crown of twelve stars" (Revelation 12:1). Estrella as Eve and as the woman of the apocalypse has encompassed the first and last books of the Bible—from creation to destruction and rebirth. Additionally, Miguel Sánchez uses the same biblical quotation to describe the Virgin of Guadalupe in his 1648 tract *Imagen de la Virgen María, Madre de Dios de Guadalupe.*[83] Estrella, like the woman of the apocalypse and the Virgin of Guadalupe, may found a new spirituality even as the apocalypse is at hand.

Estrella's multiple representations bring forth a complicated image that demonstrates the importance of a Thirdspace as a place where new ideals such as her symbolic act of embodied spirituality can develop. Through her embodiment, Estrella accomplishes Viramontes's generational goal: "As we slowly examine our own existence in and out of these cultures, we are breaking stereotypes, reinventing traditions for our own daughters and sons."[84] This final scene utilizes the traditions of Estrella's community and reconceives them to create a better future and a stronger community that asserts in the interests of social justice an unqualified belonging that is not subject to the precarity of the migrant labor movement.

To that end, Estrella "believe[s] her heart powerful enough to summon home all those who strayed" (176). Although this hope may mostly reside on the symbolic and mythical level, her desire is a real one. She sees herself as powerful as religious narratives, and she wants to use that strength. How precisely she will use that power toward social justice lies beyond the ending of the text, but as the novel closes, she stands on a roof, another boundary line between home and sky, trying to figure out how to break down barriers while building up her community.

Under the Feet, as a recent representation of the contested borderland, reveals the necessity of reimagining space by blurring the boundaries between the two sides and recognizing the complexity of interstitial locations and identities. By incorporating Gloria Anzaldúa's theory about the cultural intricacies of the borderland and about the boundary-crossing identity issues of *Nepantla, Under the Feet* demonstrates how the people who live in this space assume a borderland mentality. The novel represents the dualities of everyday life for the poor and oppressed subjected to disembodied criminality, includ-

---

83. Brading, *Mexican Phoenix,* 58. Sánchez's text has been republished in 1952 under the title *Historia de la Virgen de Guadalupe de Mexico.*

84. Viramontes, "'Nopalitos,'" 35.

ing a young girl who acts to create a third possibility that upsets binaries, expands beyond them, and shows the potential of the most disempowered.

CONCLUSION: THINKING THROUGH THE MIGRANT

The history of space and movement in the United States is not homogenous, nor are its traces visible on the map. By attending to culturally contested and semantically rich regions such as the borderland between the United States and Mexico, it is possible to imagine alternative solutions to problems caused by the binary discourses of nation, race, and gender and to avoid the pitfalls inherent in modern culture's notion of abstract, legalized, supposedly neutral space. The borderland and those who reside in it contain the potential of Thirdspace that combines the real and imagined to contemplate not just space but also how identity is affected by that space and by the economic displacements that continue to drive it. Viramontes's characters live and move within the borderland, overcoming established oppositions that mark them as bare life through the use of other women's stories and the seemingly disempowered locations of gender and race, combining what she calls "the creative process and the imagination" with their complex histories.[85] Because the governmentality imposed on them often does not allow them to feel a sense of permanency, and because Estrella still stands alone on the edge of that roof, this novel ends without having fully realized a response that touches the entire community. Estrella's embodied spirituality, however, presents the possibility of how migrant workers might start a quest for a sense of belonging and visibility in the United States through a reclaiming of their individual and collective histories, culture, and religion that will lead to a site for social justice and to an altered perspective of self, space, and community. The characters have had to embrace a "traveling identity," as James Clifford labels people for whom the question is "not so much 'where are you from?' but 'where are you between?'"[86] *Nepantla* demonstrates the creative possibilities within these uncomfortable places that can lead the migrants to embodying positive responses of their own.

This chapter, as well as the ones before it, has shown the importance of imagining beyond the spaces in which we currently reside. More broadly, this is the power of literature to help us to imagine a world outside the one as it exists, or to "imagine otherwise." Viramontes herself has invoked

---

85. Kevane and Heredia, *Latina Self-Portraits,* 150.
86. Clifford, *Routes,* 37.

Avery F. Gordon's term for the power of literature to help us to create new political and cultural possibilities:

> To imagine otherwise, [is] not to see things as they necessarily are but to imagine what can get better, giving them an awareness of the fictional dimensions of their personalities. The person before me is not simply who he or she seems to be but infinitely something more, something beyond what we could ever know. [. . .] Our lives are not set in stone, not fixed, static, dead.[87]

Viramontes's novel takes seriously this task of mindfulness that she learned by connecting her historical and cultural knowledge with her spiritual and political awareness and a compassionate and imaginative self that tries to see what has been as well as what could be. Her project, as I have shown, should be understood in the context of the history of Mexican immigration and the migrant labor of people of Mexican descent in the United States, including early visa regulations, the strikes of migrant farmworkers, the Bracero Program, the responses by the UFW, border patrols and deportation programs, and NAFTA. The paradoxical figure of the migrant laborer, who is always moving without ever arriving, most strongly emblematizes the shortcomings of the legal categories of the refugee and the internally displaced person while indicating the obligation to consider migration and movement more fully. Today the deleterious impact of migrant laborer status acutely affects those of Mexican descent regardless of their citizenship, though, as I have shown, it has undermined the rights of all the peoples discussed in this book. All of these governmental restrictions that seek to create a precarious, bare life for certain individuals and the responding oppositional fights for citizenship rights are part of a broader struggle over the meaning of landownership, American-ness, and movement. Exposing the constructedness of these terms, the connections among environmental, economic, and wartime displacements for different racial groups across the twentieth century, and the need to imagine otherwise has been the goal of this book.

---

87. From Viramontes, "Scripted Language." See also Gordon, *Ghostly Matters*, 5.

The Mobility Poor of Hurricane Katrina

Salvaging the Family and Ward's
Salvage the Bones

THROUGH THE COURSE of this book I have called attention to how internal migrations do not just happen in a flurry of confusion, naturally over time, or solely through individual choice. Instead, the governmentalities shaping mass migrations are part of a larger U.S. presentation of itself as exceptional that too often connects landownership to those empowered citizens who are seen to embody "American-ness," an abstraction that is tinged with preconceptions about race, ethnicity, religion, class, and gender, among other things. Whether it is through environmental, economic, or wartime displacements, those outside of the expected image are kept on the move as precarious, bare life to provide the labor for this nation or are imprisoned, out of sight, with their individual identities and their larger communities obscured.

Migrating Fictions addresses these disparities by reconsidering the application and scope of the terms "refugee" and "internally displaced person," with their concomitant assumptions about international and national law, space, and obligations. While applying the concept of refugee to internally displaced people can call attention to a failure in state support, it can also continue that very failure. For that reason, by comparing examples as seemingly diverse as the Mexican American migrant labor and Japanese American incarceration during World War II, this study has sought to fill in a gap in our thinking by theorizing an alternate location for the internal migrant that incorporates the ethical demand of the refugee into the disempowered status of the internally displaced person. An awareness of critical concepts such as governmentality, precarity, the state of exception, and bare life shows how inequalities in landownership and citizenship often become more prominent during internal displacements. In many respects, as I argue, forced movement, rather than being just a result of larger oppressive forces, becomes a critical factor in defining citizenship.

While internally displaced people have been constituted as an unofficial category of precarious citizens by governmental forces, migration and movement can also serve as a means to critique and reformulate such systems and policies. Thus, this book has utilized the work of historic-geographic critics as well as that of postcolonial and race scholars to develop an intersectional concept of Thirdspace that can imagine beyond past and current configurations of race, gender, and citizenship. A primary source for Thirdspace, apart from the historical migrations themselves, is in fiction, where it can function as a political site that resists dominant governmental, legal, and economic forces, that collocates the collectivity of migratory movement, and that can challenge distinctions between the refugee and the internally displaced person in the pursuit of social justice.

Even though my chosen narratives were written in distinct literary styles across the modern and postmodern literary periods, viewing these migrations and their literary inflections together enables us to see continuities often missed and corrects our association of migration with only white masculinity. From the effects on experience and narrative of African American movement from slavery to the Great Migration, as shown in Hurston's *Their Eyes Were Watching God*; to the myths of possession that created and shaped the response to Dust Bowl farmers and Babb's *Whose Names Were Unknown*; to the disorienting movement into U.S. concentration camps for people of Japanese descent and Otsuka's *When the Emperor Was Divine*; to the disembodied labor of people of Mexican descent in the borderlands and in Viramontes's *Under the Feet of Jesus*—these methods of migration constitute a broader, more inclusive history of movement in the United States. The progression of these chapters moves through the Depression, World War II, the postwar period, and beyond. Affecting all of these periods, however, is the specific moment in U.S. immigration history after the restrictions and quota system of the Johnson-Reed Act of 1924 and before immigration reform under the Hart-Celler Act of 1965. During this time, "the United States allowed in a mere 7.3 million immigrants, about the same number that had come in a single decade before World War I."[1] The governmentalities that limited immigration turned the country's focus inward

1. Gregory, *Southern Diaspora*, 22.

to watch and control the internal migrations under discussion. This history is structured by certain common elements, including the governmental and capitalist influences on landownership and movement, as well as how a perceived lack of American-ness has been linked to race and class.

These connections between the lack of landownership and disempowerment have been shown through the history as well as in each of the novels in this book through the symbols of the ground beneath the characters' feet: the mud, dirt, dust, and tar. For the black migrants in *Their Eyes Were Watching God*, the earth is perceived as valuable, but their bodies are not: "The rich black earth cling[s] to bodies and bit[es] the skin like ants."[2] The migrants are antagonized by their relationship to the land and do not gain the benefits of ownership and full citizenship. In *Whose Names Are Unknown*, the white farmers own their land at the start of the novel, so that the land's turning to dust shows how their landownership and citizenship rights are eroding, and with it their economic and overall stability. Although history reveals that the earth did turn to dust, it is through the symbolic use of the earth in California that the novel's commentary is made apparent. The earth's position as an emblem of their status in the eyes of the government is stressed when the image shifts to the representation of dirt, which indicates their "blackened" and dirty status through racialization and class-based stereotypes about cleanliness. In *When the Emperor Was Divine*, the negative presentation of the earth comes with the arrival in the U.S. concentration camp, where the dust invades the incarcerees' bodies and their rights are lost. The symbolism focuses on the real violence that the dust does to privacy and to the body, with the land as the government that is able to watch over, harm, and imprison them. Additionally, the dust is alkaline, so its whitening effects reveal the governmental desire to assimilate the incarcerees into whiteness and distance them from Japanese traditions. Finally, while *Under the Feet of Jesus* offers an idealized conception of land as a borderless, empathetic space, Estrella concretizes the current entrapping, governmental notion of how power is related to landownership through the land's representation in the tar pits. Here, the land and the fruits grown from that earth are built upon her bones, just like the oil derived from the bones of the girl trapped in the tar pit; the governmentalities that keep migrant workers in the fields use them as bare life that can be sacrificed without acknowledging their value. These various symbols of the earth and land work to expose the falsehood of societal claims that only provide full citizenship to those who own land rather than including the precariat who are working on it.

---

2. Hurston, *Their Eyes Were Watching God*, 131.

The governmental and capitalist elements that disempower citizens through notions of race, American-ness, and ownership in internal migrations have been largely overlooked, but so has resistance to them. Some of the affected individuals respond to this discrimination by contesting larger narratives with their own actions and stories, specifically by imagining how they might create new religious amalgamations, cultural and community identifications, and, in general, pathways to a sense of home through the potential of Thirdspace. The chapters of this book unfold through a historical analysis of the internal displacements that have affected the real lives of hundreds of thousands of people over the course of the twentieth century. The combination of the history with literature, however, reveals the potential for change, to "imagine otherwise."[3] The novels investigated here show different uses of Thirdspace, especially through different female attempts at empowerment. Some women craft their own sense of authority and control of movement, community, and stories, while others attempt to find inclusion in labor unions and economic communities. Some women, reduced in a prison space, escape into dreaming and magical thinking, while others imagine a potential space for community by reworking spiritual narratives into political possibilities. By showing the importance of considering women's defiance in various kinds of movement, I hope that *Migrating Fictions* has divulged not only some of those master narratives but also the narratives that challenge and reconfigure them.

I end by returning to Hurricane Katrina and the literature around it because the conversation about movement and literature is ongoing, and this story is not finished. Since I started this project, post-Katrina narratives both in fiction and nonfiction have emerged to tell us more about the experience during and after the hurricane, including columnist Chris Rose's collected stories *1 Dead in Attic: After Katrina* (2007), James Lee Burke's mystery *The Tin Roof Blowdown* (2007), Tom Piazza's novel *City of Refuge* (2008), Dave Eggers's fictional biography *Zeitoun* (2009), Josh Neufeld's graphic nonfiction *A. D.: New Orleans after the Deluge* (2009), and Sheri Fink's nonfictional *Five Days at Memorial: Life and Death in a Storm-Ravaged Hospital* (2013).[4] Jesmyn Ward's novel *Salvage the Bones* (2011), my subject of inquiry here, even won the National Book Award. In light of the other narratives and displacements discussed in this book, one might expect these post-Katrina narratives to concentrate on the movement of people from the Gulf Coast to a new space elsewhere; intriguingly, however, many of these narratives follow the stories

---

3. See Gordon, *Ghostly Matters*, 5.

4. Notable documentary films include Spike Lee's *When the Levees Broke: A Requiem in Four Acts* (2006), Tia Lessin and Carl Deal's *Trouble the Waters* (2009), and Ashley Sabin and David Redmon's *Kamp Katrina* (2009).

of those who stayed, and so I use *Salvage the Bones* as an example of this seemingly oppositional presentation of community and movement even as it continues many of the same discussions about race, gender, and class in the United States found in prior examples, revealing the ongoing nature of these problems. Particularly, the hostile perception of non-evacuators indicates racial and class dimensions surrounding the access to movement that need consideration prior to the next mass migration. A subsequent comparison of this novel and Hurricane Katrina to *Their Eyes Were Watching God* and the Okeechobee Hurricane of 1928 shows again the importance of analyzing literature and history together across the World War II divide to undermine prevailing hierarchical notions of territory that restrict ownership and safety to only certain configurations of wealth and race.

Salvage the Bones follows the Batistes, an African American family, in the fictional town of Bois Sauvage, Mississippi, during the days before and shortly after Hurricane Katrina in 2005. It illustrates the continued significance of choice in relationship to movement, reminding us that the inability to move can be just as detrimental as being forced to move. The history of slavery remains always at the periphery of this family's reaction to their environment. For instance, the book's very first mention of the storm says that "they knock against the old summer mansions with their slave galleys turned guesthouses" (4) with the knowledge that previous confinements for the enslaved now demonstrate a new generation of wealth that can afford to have guesthouses.[5] In addition, more contemporary notions of racism undermine the family's trust of the news' presentation of the impending storm because "everytime somebody in Bois Sauvage get arrested, they always get the story wrong" (6). These characters, though their family has lived for generations on this land, feel an ongoing sense of precarity and denial of their bodies and stories. They barely have enough to feed themselves, so the notion of fleeing the storm is not even considered; moreover, the "help" of the federal and local government is nothing more than a recording on the telephone that tells them that if they do not leave, the government cannot be blamed. The novel, with yet another example of a female protagonist, features fifteen-year-old Esch, who reports what she hears when she answers the automated call:

Mandatory evacuation. Hurricane making landfall tomorrow. If you choose to stay in your home and have not evacuated by this time, we are not responsible. You have been warned. And these could be the consequences of your actions.

---

5. Jesmyn Ward, *Salvage the Bones* (New York: Bloomsbury, 2011). All citations are from this edition.

There is a list. And I do not know if he says this, but this is what it feels like:
You can die. (217)

This call, which arrives on the day of the storm, does not provide the Batistes any concrete details as to how to leave; current research recommends that warning messages include specific information in order to function effectively.[6] The Batistes are not given any way to leave on public buses or trains, and yet they are told that the warning is all the help they can expect from the government. Esch feels that she is being left without consideration for her life.

Esch reacts to this warning by feeling abandoned and culpable but does not start planning for evacuation; in this sense, her experience is parallel to that of actual non-evacuators, who were labeled as "stupid and passive" and therefore at fault if harm came to them by middle-class observers, as a study specifically about Hurricane Katrina showed.[7] This attribution of blame highlights how different social and racial groups perceive "agency," which white middle-class people generally define as independent control over the environment, while black working-class people emphasize interdependence and resilience.[8] The Batiste family's seeming inaction is worthy of note on many levels, then, representing expected raced, gendered, and class patterns. They do not discuss leaving, but they are not passive, with much time dedicated to gathering water and food and preparing the house for the storm while the father, injured during preparations, gives cogent directions from his bed. The Batistes' endurance is shown through their dedication to these tasks, and they demonstrate concern for others through their sharing of resources not only with members of the family but with friends and the family dog. There are limits to this support system, however, as there is no mention of outside adult relationships to confirm the need to leave after they receive the official warning.[9] This absence makes sense, since this family has no living mother figure and the only female in the group is Esch, and women are most commonly the source for those external relationships.[10]

Beyond the limits of their social networks to help them verify the call and start to take action to leave, the call also reveals their limited access to the means to flee. The Batistes are a prime example of the mobility poor, some-

---

6. Perry and Lindell, "The Effects of Ethnicity on Evacuation Decision-Making," 55.

7. Stephens et al., "Why Did They 'Choose' to Stay?"

8. Ibid.

9. Perry and Lindell, "The Effects of Ethnicity on Evacuation Decision-Making," 64. Also, the adult caveat is essential to mention because the teenagers do have strong friendships, but they are not old enough to fully take on this level of mature decision making.

10. Weber and Peek, *Displaced,* 15.

thing geographer Tim Cresswell discusses in relationship to this same historical storm. As he shows, the lack of mobility was a key problem for the 15 percent of New Orleans residents who did not leave; the politics of mobility are strongly associated with issues of identity such as race and class.[11] Without access to mass transportation, the money to acquire any transportation, or housing outside the city, many were in effect deserted there. A disproportionately high number of the city's populace did not own a car: one-third of the city's population as opposed to the national average of one-tenth, with the percentage of carless black households more than twice that of white ones.[12] As the storm approached and the buses and trains shut down, about 200,000 people had no way out of the city.[13] Even with a car, Ward explains that it is not financially viable to evacuate for every storm in an area prone to hurricanes. Instead, she says that individuals hope that each impending disturbance will change direction even as they board up the house and get food, water, and preparations: "We survived like that for generations, that's what we do, we don't evacuate."[14] These studies and Ward's personal narrative point to another kind of formation of community through (non-)movement, one based on economic and regional exploitation as well as the sensible response of individuals over time. For a family where all share clothes and struggle to afford food, the idea of fleeing a storm should start to be understood as a luxury they, and many others in the path of the actual storm, cannot and could not afford.[15] Although class and its intersection with racial and gender demographics are clearly configured here in the statistics and the stories of the storm as a reason why some did not leave, Ward still says that part of her motivation for the novel was the "really awful ideas" people had about those who stayed, implying she felt the same blame that readers can hear in the prerecorded voice of the government in her novel as well as reflected in studies.[16] Ward's story potentially can alter the presumed narrative of ignorance and obstinance derived from prevailing notions of movement—in this case the choice to leave

11. Cresswell, *On the Move*, 262.

12. O'Toole quoted in Cresswell, *On the Move*, 260.

13. Cresswell, *On the Move*, 261.

14. Masters, "Interview Jesmyn Ward," n.p.

15. For more details on race and class in relationship to the evacuation of Hurricane Katrina, see Elder et al., "African Americans' Decisions Not to Evacuate." Specially in relationship to class the study stated: "One barrier to evacuation was financial: being of low socioeconomic status and having little cash on hand. This barrier reflected in 2 subareas: personal transportation and cash for travel and incidentals. Many possessed personal transportation, but the availability of cash for gas to evacuate at the end of the month before payday was a constraint (the hurricane struck on August 29)" (S126).

16. Masters, "Interview: Jesmyn Ward," n.p. For more on observer responses, see Stephens et al., "Why Did They 'Choose' to Stay?"

the path of the storm—that fails to consider economic limits and differing responses based on gender and racial disparities.

This specific narrative shows not a simple continuation of the dominant white view that restricted black movement during slavery but an assumption now that African Americans can and should move whenever it is necessary while that potential remains limited. The earlier oppressive ideology viewed black movement as a threat, but in this instance non-movement is thought to be a sign of ignorance; instead, it shows how movement is still being controlled and other tactics for survival are being utilized. In each era, the same abstract, impersonal commands demand that they have the ultimate control of one's body and movement, whether that call is to stay on the plantation or to leave one's house immediately. Recall the words of a slave law from 1680, "It shall not be lawfull for any negroe [. . .] to goe or depart from of his masters ground without a certificate," versus the contemporary "Mandatory Evacuation. [. . .] You have been warned."[17] Though the commands are contradictory, the overall configuration of authority is the same.

Preceding chapters have shown how individuals are often forced to move while also disclosing how some can be considered part of the mobility poor, either through economic or legal means. This limitation is true for both the historical migrants and the literary characters discussed: *Whose Names Are Unknown* and *Under the Feet of Jesus* show how a lack of money directly affects migrant laborers' ability to buy gas and get to work, *When the Emperor Was Divine* reveals how enemy status can imprison because people of Japanese descent cannot legally move from their incarcerated spot, and *Their Eyes Were Watching God* articulates the same issue when the characters have trouble fleeing the hurricane in the heart of the narrative. Hence, the status of being mobility poor, of being unable to move, rather than existing in opposition to histories of migration, is in effect another component of the governmentalities studied throughout this book from the earliest slave laws. The lack of access to transportation and its inhibiting effects becomes clear when, as seen with Katrina, the mobility poor may remain unmoved only until a critical combination of discrimination and disaster is reached.

In many respects, the issues of racism and classism raised in Ward's presentation of a recent hurricane can be usefully read through this book's earliest environmental migration and its literary representation. The historical Okeechobee Hurricane of 1928 and its description in *Their Eyes Were Watching God* demonstrate the difficulty of travel for black migrant workers during a catastrophe and also display how those outside oppressors have been in

---

17. Cited in Camp, *Closer to Freedom*, 30.

some ways internalized. This storm acts as the most direct literary and histori-cal "precedent" of Hurricane Katrina seventy-seven years later, with even the number of dead, marked at 1,836 for years, uncannily close to the 1,833 esti-mated for the later storm.[18] During the Okeechobee Hurricane, Hurston's main characters, Tea Cake and Janie, discuss the lack of access to transportation:

> Tea Cake says, "Tain't no cars, Janie."
> And she responds, "Ah thought not! Whut we gointuh do now?"
> "We got tuh walk." (161)

Their legs are their only means of transportation, but Hurston also shows the characters' own difficult choices and influences prior to that moment in the midst of the storm. Hurston's characters do contemplate leaving earlier but reject it for a variety of reasons, including that the fleeing Indians are "dumb," that there is too much money on the muck for there to be a storm to disrupt it, and that the white landowners do not seem to be leaving, so "if the castles thought themselves secure, the cabins needn't worry" (158). In part these excuses mask the difficulty of finding a way out, as Ward articulated, but importantly, Janie and Tea Cake have a chance to get a ride from a friend. Even in this brief moment of possibility, though, the limited access to mobility is revealed—two seats are available with many possible takers.

Additionally, though, all of the presented reasons disclose the systemic racism and classism that has been accepted by Hurston's characters to create a hierarchy of power and a considerably flawed logic. Because of the world in which these characters live, Native Americans are not worth listening to, "else dey'd own dis country still" (156), even as white landowners and the presence of money weigh more heavily in their decisions. Martyn Bone also argues that Tea Cake's "dismissive attitude" when offered a ride by Lias and his uncle may be because Lias is a "Bahaman boy" (155), adding yet another group that Tea Cake does not heed.[19] With each of these examples, Hurston lets us see the mystifications of ideology. For instance, while it may have seemed that the white individuals stayed, there is a big difference between a "castle" and a "cabin" both in its fortitude and location, so there is every reason to be fear-ful in a cabin. After all, the proportion of deaths were predominantly black—three out of every four, and even during Hurricane Katrina, the low return

---

18. The estimate for the Okeechobee Hurricane has since been revised to between 2,500 and 3,000, and that is only for those killed on the mainland United States (Mykle, *Killer 'Cane*, 213). See also Knabb, Rhome, and Brown, "Tropical Cyclone Report," 11; Louisiana Department of Health and Hospitals, "Hurricane Katrina"; and Brunkard, Namulanda, and Ratard, "Hur-ricane Katrina Deaths, Louisiana, 2005."

19. Bone, "The (Extended) South of Black Folk," 770.

rate of African Americans to New Orleans has been tied to the fact that their neighborhoods were hardest hit by the storm.[20] Therefore, the Okeechobee storm and the novel show us the paradoxical lack of mobility available to these migrant laborers and that the power structure that lauds the whites and diminishes everyone else is detrimental on many levels.

A hint of a solution to how the storm should have been handled to minimize death and destruction in *Their Eyes* appears in a symbolic critique of human hierarchical structures through the human and animal interactions during the storm. The text shows that predator versus prey relationships should be equalized and territory shared, at the very least during a crisis, just like white and black relationships should not be built upon a hierarchy that gives safe haven to only the economically and socially powerful. During the storm, Tea Cake and Janie encounter several scenarios in which human beings and wild animals take shelter together without the usual fear or hostility as everyone attempts to survive, including a snake who does not bite a human and a rabbit who is not hunted by humans. The text tells us, "Common danger made common friends. Nothing sought a conquest over the other" (164), but when humans are involved, this symbolic presentation falls to the reality of race relations. This contrast is shown by Tea Cake and Janie's exclusion from a hill where the whites "had preempted that point of elevation and there was no more room. They could climb up one of its high sides and down the other, that was all" (164). The white people have claimed this territory and are unwilling to share it, something borne out in America's longer history of conquest, but this desire to control all the valuable terrain is also reflected in the one animal that acts more like a possessive human—the rabid dog that bites Tea Cake. The dog, having claimed the real estate of a cow, a ridiculous location, will not even let the characters hang onto the cow's tail. The text is stating that only a diseased thing would fight for dominance and conquest in such a moment, and yet it does. Thus, Hurston's treatment long ago presented us with knowledge that could be applied to more contemporary storms and movements when we consider what is lost if, even during the most difficult moments, those in power continue to grasp for that sense of superiority through territory.

In *Salvage the Bones,* Esch presents a similar symbolic sentiment about animals as representing the problems of humans in relationship to space, with her argument developing the need for empathy and respect. She makes this

---

20. Mykle, *Killer 'Cane,* 211; Kleinberg, *Black Cloud,* xiv; Fuller, Sastry, and VanLandingham, "Race, Socioeconomic Status, and Return Migration to New Orleans after Hurricane Katrina."

argument when moving from her initial assumption that all animals flee hurricanes to determining that some cannot flee, eventually concluding:

> Maybe the small don't run. [. . .] They prepare like us[, . . .] tunnel[ing] down [. . .] until they have dug great halls so deep that they sit right above the underground reservoirs we tap into with our wells, and during the hurricane, they hear water lapping above and below while they sit safe in the hand of the earth. (215–16)

Esch describes herself and her family as the small animals, the prey to the predatory world around them. She empathizes with these creatures and foreshadows her own future surrounded by water, although with a less clear sense of safety because she knows that staying is the only possibility for her family as well. Because the automated call to flee immediately follows Esch's statement, the book argues that a better escape plan could have been developed with a more empathetic understanding of the people being told to leave and of their different sense of agency as defined through resilience and interdependence. For instance, more understanding of the prohibitive cost of escape, of the general lack of personal transportation, and of "public" ownership and responsibility should have led officials to acknowledge an ethic of interdependence and employ some of the city's school buses for public egress, instead of leaving them parked, unused, soon to be submerged by the floodwaters.

Overall, these mass displacements and their texts have demonstrated the problems created by larger governmental and corporate entities that present their dominance over people and spaces in ways that exacerbate seemingly natural happenings and seek to diminish people to a precarious, bare life; they also have demonstrated how individuals respond with their own stories as well as the potential empowerment of disadvantaged groups, including women and people of color. All of these stories about race, gender, discrimination, migration (or inaccessibility to it), community, and survival, Ward would see as central; they need to be "salvaged." *Migrating Fictions* has shown the importance of stories about and by women across racial categories in understanding the causes and results of mass migration in twentieth-century history and literature. The Thirdspaces they imagine offer us a way of reexamining the problem of the internally displaced person legally, politically, and ethically, without relieving the state of its responsibilities for all of its citizens.

BIBLIOGRAPHY

Acuña, Rodolfo. *Occupied America: A History of Chicanos*. New York: Harper, 1988.

Agamben, Giorgio. *Homo Sacer: Sovereign Power and Bare Life*. Translated by Daniel Heller-Roazen. Palo Alto, CA: Stanford University Press, 1998.

Alarcón, Norma. "Traddutora, Traditora: A Paradigmatic Figure of Chicana Feminism." *Cultural Critique*, no. 13, The Construction of Gender and Modes of Social Division (Autumn 1989): 57–87.

Aleinikoff, T. Alexander. "State-Centered Refugee Law: From Resettlement to Containment." In *Mistrusting Refugees*, edited by E. Valentine Daniel and John Chr. Knudsen, 257–78. Berkeley: University of California Press, 1995.

Alexandre, Sandy. *The Properties of Violence: Claims to Ownership in Representations of Lynching*. Jackson: University Press of Mississippi, 2012.

Ancheta, Angelo N. *Race, Rights, and the Asian American Experience*. New Brunswick, NJ: Rutgers University Press, 1998.

Anzaldúa, Gloria. *Borderland/La Frontera: The New Mestiza*. 2nd ed. San Francisco: Aunt Lute, 1999.

Arrizón, Alicia. "Mythical Performativity: Relocating Aztlán in Chicana Feminist Cultural Productions." *Theatre Journal* 52, no. 1 (March 2000): 23–49.

Auerbach, Jerold S. *Labor and Liberty: The La Follette Committee and the New Deal*. Indianapolis, IN: Bobbs-Merrill Company, 1966.

Austin, Alfredo López. "Myth of the Half-Man Who Descended from the Sky." In *To Change Place: Aztec Ceremonial Landscapes*, edited by David Carrasco, 152–57. Norman: University of Oklahoma Press, 1991.

Azuma, Eiichiro. *Between Two Empires: Race, History, and Transnationalism in Japanese America*. New York: Oxford University Press, 2005.

Babb, Sanora. "Farmers without Farms." *The New Masses*, June 21, 1938, 15–17.

———. *An Owl on Every Post*. Albuquerque: University of New Mexico Press, 1994.

———. *Whose Names Are Unknown*. Norman: Oklahoma University Press, 2004.

Babb, Sanora, and Dorothy Babb. *On the Dirty Plate Trail: Remembering the Dust Bowl Refugee Camps*. Edited by Douglas Wixson. Austin: University of Texas Press, 2007.

Bailey, Rayna. *Immigration and Migration.* New York: Infobase Publishing, 2008.

Bakhtin, M. M. *The Dialogic Imagination, Four Essays.* Edited by Michael Holquist. Translated by Michael Holquist and Caryl Emerson. Austin: University of Texas Press, 1981.

Balderrama, Francisco E., and Raymond Rodríguez. *Decade of Betrayal: Mexican Repatriation in the 1930s.* Rev. ed. Albuquerque: University of New Mexico Press, 2006.

Barker, Joanne. "For Whom Sovereignty Matters." In *Sovereignty Matters: Locations of Contestation and Possibility in Indigenous Struggles for Self-Determination,* edited by Joanne Barker, 1–31. Lincoln: University of Nebraska, 2005.

Battat, Erin Royston. *Ain't Got No Home: America's Great Migration and the Making of an Interracial Left.* Chapel Hill: University of North Carolina Press, 2014.

Bebout, Lee. *Mythohistorical Interventions: The Chicano Movement and Its Legacies.* Minneapolis: University of Minnesota Press, 2011.

Berenson, Alex, and John M. Broder. "Police Begin Seizing Guns of Civilians." *New York Times,* September 9, 2005. http://www.nytimes.com/2005/09/09/us/nationalspecial/police-begin-seizing-guns-of-civilians.html.

Bergal, Jenni, Sara Shipley Hiles, Frank Koughan, John McQuaid, Jim Morris, Curtis Wilkie, and Katy Reckdahl. *City Adrift: New Orleans before and after Katrina.* Baton Rouge: Louisiana State University Press, 2007.

Bhabha, Homi K. *The Location of Culture.* New York: Routledge, 1994.

———. "The Third Space: Interview with Homi Bhabha." *Identity, Community, Culture, Difference,* edited by Jonathan Rutherford, 207–21. London: Lawrence and Wishart, 1990.

Blake, Debbie, and Carmen Abrego. "Doing Gigs: Speaking, Writing, and Change." In *Gloria E. Anzaldúa: Interviews/Entrevistas,* edited by AnaLouise Keating, 211–33. New York: Routledge, 2000.

Blake, Eric S., Edward N. Rappaport, Jerry D. Jarrell, and Christopher W. Landsea. "The Deadliest, Costliest, and Most Intense United States Tropical Cyclones from 1851 to 2004." August 2005 (updated). National Hurricane Center, Miami, FL. http://www.nhc.noaa.gov/pdf/NWS-TPC-4.pdf.

Bone, Martyn. "The (Extended) South of Black Folk: Intraregional and Transnational Migrant Labor in *Jonah's Gourd Vine* and *Their Eyes Were Watching God.*" *American Literature* 79, no. 4 (December 2007): 753–79.

Boone, Elizabeth Hill. "Migration Histories as Ritual Performance." In *To Change Place: Aztec Ceremonial Landscapes,* edited by David Carrasco, 121–51. Norman: University of Oklahoma Press, 1991.

Boyd, Valerie. *Wrapped in Rainbows: The Life of Zora Neale Hurston.* New York: Scribner, 2003.

Brading, D. A. *Mexican Phoenix. Our Lady of Guadalupe: Image and Tradition across Five Centuries.* New York: Cambridge University Press, 2001.

Brunkard, Joan, Gonza Namulanda, and Raoult Ratard. "Hurricane Katrina Deaths, Louisiana, 2005." August 28, 2008. *Disaster Medicine and Public Health Preparedness.* http://www.dhh.louisiana.gov/assets/docs/katrina/deceasedreports/KatrinaDeaths_082008.pdf.

Bulosan, Carlos. *America Is in the Heart.* Seattle: University of Washington Press, 1973.

Butler, Judith. "Performativity, Precarity and Sexual Politics." *AIBR: Revista de Anropología Iberoamericana* 4, no. 3. (September–December 2009): i–xiii.

———. *A Precarious Life: The Powers of Mourning and Violence.* New York: Verso, 2004.

Camp, Stephanie. *Closer to Freedom: Enslaved Women and Everyday Resistance in the Plantation South*. Chapel Hill: University of North Carolina Press, 2004.

Carbonell, Ana María. "From Llorona to Gritona: Coatlicue in Feminist Tales by Viramontes and Cisneros." *MELUS* 24, no. 2 (Summer 1999): 53–74.

Carby, Hazel. *Cultures in Babylon: Black Britain and African America*. New York: Verso, 1999.

Chang, Robert. S., and Keith Aoki. "Centering the Immigrant in the Inter/National Imagination." *California Law Review* 85, no. 5 (October 1997): 1395–447.

Chen, Fu-Jen, and Su-Lin Yu. "Reclaiming the Southwest: A Traumatic Space in the Japanese American Internment Narrative." *Journal of the Southwest* 47, no. 4 (2005): 551–70.

Chen, Tina. "Towards an Ethics of Knowledge." *MELUS* 30, no. 2 (Summer 2005): 157–73.

Cheung, King-Kok. "Interview with Hisaye Yamamoto." In *Seventeen Syllables*, edited by King-Kok Cheung, 71–86. New Brunswick, NJ: Rutgers University Press, 1994.

Chin, Frank, Jeffery Paul Chan, Lawson Fusao Inada, and Shawn Wong, eds. *Aiiieeeee! An Anthology of Asian-American Writers*. Washington, DC: Howard University Press, 1974.

Choi, Susan. *American Woman*. New York: HarperCollins, 2003.

Chong, Sylvia. "Exceptionalism." In *Keywords for Southern Studies*, edited by Scott Romine, Jennifer Rae Greeson, Jon Smith, and Riché Richardson, 304–15. Athens: University of Georgia Press, 2016.

Chu, Seo-Young. "Science Fiction and Postmemory Han in Contemporary Korean American Literature." *MELUS* 33, no. 4 (2008): 97–121.

Chuh, Kandice. *Imagine Otherwise: On Asian Americanist Critique*. Durham, NC: Duke University Press, 2003.

Cisneros, Sandra. "Guadalupe the Sex Goddess." In *Goddess of the Americas/La diosa de las Américas: Writings on the Virgin of Guadalupe*, edited by Ana Castillo, 46–51. New York: Riverhead, 1996.

———. "It Ocurs to Me I Am the Creative/Destructive Goddess Coatlicue." *The Massachusetts Review* 36, no. 4 (Winter 1995): 599.

Clifford, James. *Routes: Travel and Translation in the Late Twentieth Century*. Cambridge, MA: Harvard University Press, 1997.

Cooke, Dennis H., Jesse F. Cardwell, and Harris J. Dark. "Local Residents and Married Women as Teachers," 252–61. *Review of Educational Research*. American Education Research Association, 1946.

Cooper, Thomas. *Some Information Respecting America*. Dublin, 1794. *The Making of the Modern World*.

Cresswell, Tim. *On the Move: Mobility in the Modern Western World*. New York: Routledge, 2006.

———. *Place: An Introduction*. 2nd ed. Hoboken, NJ: Wiley-Blackwell, 2014.

Cresswell, Tim, and Tanu Priya Uteng, eds. *Gendered Mobility*. Burlington, VT: Ashgate, 2008.

Cronin, Gloria L., ed. *Critical Essays on Zora Neale Hurston*. New York: G. K. Hall & Co., 1998.

Daniel, Cletus E. *Bitter Harvest: A History of California Farmworkers, 1870–1941*. Berkeley: University of California Press, 1982.

Daniels, Roger. *Concentration Camps, North America: Japanese in the United States and Canada During World War II*. Malabar, FL: Krieger, 1993.

————. *Politics of Prejudice: The Anti-Japanese Movement in California and the Struggle for Japanese Exclusion.* Berkeley: University of California Press, 1999.

————. *Prisoners without Trial: Japanese Americans in World War II.* Rev. ed. New York: Hill and Wang, 2004.

————. "Words Do Matter: A Note on Inappropriate Terminology and the Incarceration of Japanese Americans." In *Nikkei in the Pacific Northwest: Japanese Americans and Japanese Canadians in the Twentieth Century,* edited by Louis Fiset and Gail Nomura, 183–207. Seattle: University of Washington Press, 2005.

Daniels, Roger, Harry H. L. Kitano, and Sandra C. Miller, eds. *Japanese Americans: From Relocation to Redress.* Salt Lake City: University of Utah Press, 1986.

Danticat, Edwidge. "Message to My Daughters." In *The Fire This Time: A New Generation Speaks about Race,* edited by Jesmyn Ward, 205–15. New York: Scribner, 2016.

Davis, Angela Y. *Women, Race, and Class.* New York: Vintage, 1983.

del Castillo, Richard Griswold, and Arnoldo De León. *North to Aztlán: A History of Mexican Americans in the United States.* New York: Twayne, 1996.

Delgadillo, Theresa. *The Spiritual Mestizaje: Religion, Gender, Race, and Nation in Contemporary Chicana Narrative.* Durham: Duke University Press, 2011.

Denning, Michael. *The Cultural Front: The Laboring of American Culture in the Twentieth Century.* New York: Verso, 1996.

DiStasi, Lawrence. *Una Storia Segreta: The Secret History of Italian American Evacuation and Internment during World War II.* Berkeley, CA: Heyday, 2004.

Domosh, Mona, and Joni Seager. *Putting Women in Place: Feminist Geographers Make Sense of the World.* New York: Guilford, 2001.

Douglass, Frederick. *What the Black Man Wants.* Speech at the Annual Meeting of the Massachusetts Anti-Slavery Society in Boston, 1865.

Du Bois, W. E. Burghardt. "The Talented Tenth." In *The Negro Problem: A Series of Articles by Representative American Negroes of To-day,* by Booker T. Washington, 33–75. New York: J Pott & Company, 1903.

DuPlessis, Rachel Blau. "Power, Judgment, and Narrative in a Work of Zora Neale Hurston: Feminist Cultural Studies." In Cronin, *Critical Essays on Zora Neale Hurston,* 79–99.

————. *Writing beyond the Ending: Narrative Strategies of Twentieth-Century Women Writers.* Bloomington: Indiana University Press, 1985.

Dyson, Michael Eric. *Come Hell or High Water: Hurricane Katrina and the Color of Disaster.* Cambridge, MA: Basic Civitas, 2006.

Edwards v. California. 314 U.S. 160. U.S. Supreme Court. 1941.

Egan, Timothy. *The Worst Hard Time: The Untold Story of Those Who Survived the Great American Dust Bowl.* Boston: Houghton Mifflin, 2006.

Eisinger, Chester E. "The Freehold Concept in Eighteenth-Century American Letters." *The William and Mary Quarterly* 4, no. 1 (January 1947): 42–59.

Elder, Keith, Sudha Xirasager, Nancy Miller, Shelly Ann Bowen, Saundra Glove, and Crystal Piper. "African Americans' Decisions Not to Evacuate New Orleans before Hurricane Katrina: A Qualitative Study." *American Journal of Public Health* 97, no. S1 (April 2007): S124–29.

Eng, David L. *Racial Castration: Managing Masculinity in Asian America.* Durham, NC: Duke University Press, 2001.

Evernden, Neil. "Beyond Ecology: Self, Place, and the Pathetic Fallacy." In *The Ecocritical Reader*, edited by Cheryll Glotfelty and Harold Fromm, 92–104. Athens: University of Georgia Press, 1996.

Felski, Rita. *The Gender of Modernity*. Cambridge, MA: Harvard University Press, 1995.

Fletcher, Angus. *Allegory: The Theory of a Symbolic Mode*. 1965. Ithaca, NY: Cornell University Press, 2012.

Foner, Eric. *Reconstruction: America's Unfinished Revolution 1863–1877*. Philadelphia: Harper and Row, 1988.

Ford, Jamie. *Hotel on the Corner of Bitter and Sweet*. New York: Ballatine, 2009.

Foucault, Michel. *Discipline and Punishment: The Birth of the Prison*. Translated by Alan Sheridan. New York: Random House, 1995.

———. "Of Other Spaces." Translated by Jay Miskowiec. *Diacritics* 16, no. 1 (1986): 22–27.

Frankenberg, Ruth. *White Women, Race Matters: The Social Construction of Whiteness*. Minneapolis: University of Minnesota Press, 1993.

Franklin, Benjamin. *Autobiography and Other Writings*. Edited by Ormond Seavey. New York: Oxford University Press, 1998.

Fuller, Elizabeth, Narayan Sastry, and Mark VanLandingham. "Race, Socioeconomic Status, and Return Migration to New Orleans After Hurricane Katrina." *Population and Environment* 31, nos. 1–3 (January 2010): 20–42.

García, Michael Nieto, "Ethnic, Feminist, Universal?: Helena María Viramontes's *Under the Feet of Jesus*." *Phenomena: Journal of Language and Literature* 7, no. 3 (February 2004): 125–34.

Gates, Henry Louis, Jr. "A Negro Way of Saying." *New York Times Book Review*, April 21, 1985.

———. *The Signifying Monkey: A Theory of Afro-American Literary Criticism*. New York: Oxford University Press, 1988.

Gates, Henry Louis, Jr., and K. A. Appiah, eds. *Zora Neale Hurston: Critical Perspectives Past and Present*. New York: Amistad, 1993.

Geaghan, Kimberly A. "Forced to Move: An Analysis of Hurricane Katrina Movers." 2009 American Housing Survey: New Orleans. Working Paper Number 2011–17. U.S. Census Bureau, June 2011. https://www.census.gov/content/dam/Census/programs-surveys/ahs/working-papers/HK_Movers-FINAL.pdf.

Geiger, Robert. "If It Rains . . ." *Washington Evening Star*, April 15, 1935, A-2.

Gilroy, Paul. *The Black Atlantic: Modernity and Double Consciousness*. Cambridge, MA: Harvard University Press, 1999.

Gómez-Peña, Guillermo. *Warrior for Gringostroika: Essays, Performance Texts, and Poetry*. Saint Paul, MN: Graywolf, 1993.

Gordon, Avery F. *Ghostly Matters: Haunting and the Sociological Imagination*. Minneapolis: University of Minnesota Press, 1997.

Gregory, James N. *American Exodus: The Dust Bowl Migration and Okie Culture in California*. New York: Oxford University Press, 1989.

———. *Southern Diaspora: How the Great Migration of Black and White Southerners Transformed America*. Chapel Hill: University of North Carolina Press, 2005.

Grewe-Volpp, Christa. "'The oil was made from their bones': Environmental (In)Justice in Helena Maria Viramontes's *Under the Feet of Jesus*." *ISLE* 12, no. 1 (Winter 2005): 61–78.

Griffin, Farah Jasmine. *Toward an Intellectual History of Black Women.* Chapel Hill: University of North Carolina Press, 2015.

———. *"Who Set You Flowin'?": The African American Migration Narrative.* New York: Oxford University Press, 1995.

Groen, Jeffrey A., and Anne E. Polivka. "Going Home after Hurricane Katrina: Determinants of Return Migration and Changes in Affected Areas." *Demography* 47, no. 4 (November 2010): 821–44.

Gross, Ariela J. *What Blood Won't Tell: A History of Race on Trial in America.* Cambridge, MA: Harvard University Press, 2008.

Guterson, David. *Snow Falling on Cedars.* San Diego: Harcourt Brace, 1994.

Hahamovitch, Cindy. *The Fruits of Their Labor: Atlantic Coast Farmworkers and the Making of Migrant Poverty, 1870–1945.* Chapel Hill: University of North Carolina Press, 1997.

———. "Slavery's Stale Soil: Indentured Labor, Guestworkers, and the End of Empire." In *Making the Empire Work: Labor and United States Imperialism,* edited by Daniel E. Bender and Jana K. Lipman, 227–66. New York: New York University Press, 2015.

Hale, Grace Elizabeth. *Making Whiteness: The Culture of Segregation in the South, 1890–1940.* New York: Vintage, 1999.

Hansen, Gladys, and Emmett Condon. *Denial of Disaster: The Untold Story and Photographs of the San Francisco Earthquake of 1906.* San Francisco: Cameron & Co., 1989.

Hardt, Michael, and Antonio Negri. *Multitude: War and Democracy in the Age of Empire.* New York: Penguin, 2004.

Harrison, Sheri-Marie. *Jamaica's Difficult Subjects: Negotiating Sovereignty in Anglophone Caribbean Literature and Criticism.* Columbus: Ohio State University Press, 2014.

Hartman, Saidiya V. *Scenes of Subjection: Terror, Slavery, and Self-Making in Nineteenth-Century America.* New York: Oxford University Press, 1997.

Henderson, George, and Thompson Olasiji. *Migrants, Immigrants, and Slaves: Racial & Ethnic Groups in America.* New York: University Press of America, 1995.

Hernández-Ávila, Inés. "Quincentennial: From Victimhood to Active Resistance." In *Gloria E. Anzaldúa: Interviews/Entrevistas,* edited by AnaLouise Keating, 177–94. New York: Routledge, 2000.

Higham, John. *Strangers in the Land: Patterns of American Nativism, 1860–1925.* New York: Atheneum, 1970.

Hirabayashi, Lane Ryo. "Incarceration." In *Keywords for Asian American Studies.* Edited by Cathy J. Schlund-Vials, Linda Trinh Võ, and K. Scott Wong, 133–34. New York: New York University Press, 2015.

Hirabayashi v. United States. 320 U.S. 81. U.S. Supreme Court. 1943.

Hirsch, Marianne. *Family Frames: Photography, Narrative, and Postmemory.* Cambridge, MA: Harvard University Press, 1997.

Hodgson, Godfrey. *The Colonel: The Life and Wars of Henry Stimson, 1867–1950.* New York: Knopf, 1990.

Hori, Makiko, Mark J. Schafer, and David J. Bowman. "Displacement Dynamics in Southern Louisiana after Hurricanes Katrina and Rita." *Population Research and Policy Review* 28, no. 1 (November 2009): 45–65.

Horton, James Oliver, and Lois E. Horton. *Hard Road to Freedom: The Story of African America.* New Brunswick, NJ: Rutgers University Press, 2001.

Hoshida, George and Tamae. *Taken from the Paradise Isle: The Hoshida Family Story, 1912–1945,* edited by Heidi Kim. Boulder: University Press of Colorado, 2015.

Houston, Jeanne Wakatsuki. *The Legend of Fire Horse Woman.* New York: Kensington, 2003.

Houston, Jeanne Wakatsuki, and James D. Houston. *Farewell to Manzanar: A True Story of Japanese American Experience during and after the World War II Internment.* Boston: Houghton Mifflin, 1973.

"How to Tell Japs from the Chinese." *LIFE,* December 22, 1941, 81–82.

Huehls, Mitchum. "Ostension, Simile, Catachresis: Misusing Helena Viramontes's *Under the Feet of Jesus* to Rethink the Globalization-Environmentalism Relation." *Discourse* 29, nos. 2 & 3 (Spring and Fall 2007): 346–66.

Hurston, Lucy Anne. *Speak, So You Can Speak Again: The Life of Zora Neale Hurston.* New York: Doubleday, 2004.

Hurston, Zora Neale. "Characteristics of Negro Expression." 1934. In Mitchell, *Within the Circle,* 79–94.

———. *Dust Tracks on a Road.* 1942. Restored text established by the Library of America. New York: HarperCollins, 1996.

———. "How It Feels to Be Colored Me." 1928. In *Best American Essays of the Century,* edited by Joyce Carol Oates and Robert Atwan, 114–17. Boston: Houghton Mifflin, 2000

———. *Jonah's Gourd Vine.* 1934. New York: HarperCollins, 2008.

———. *Moses, Man on the Mountain.* 1939. Urbana: University of Illinois Press, 1984.

———. *Mules and Men: Negro Folktales and Voodoo Practices in the South.* 1935. New York: Harper & Row, 1970.

———, ed. "The Negro in Florida 1528–1940." Compiled by the Federal Writer's Project in Florida. Jacksonville University of Florida, unpublished scan 2013.

———. *The Sanctified Church.* Berkeley, CA: Turtle Island, 1981.

———. "Stories of Conflict." Review of *Uncle Tom's Children* in *Saturday Review of Literature,* April 2, 1938. In *Richard Wright: The Critical Reception,* edited by John M. Reilly, 9–10. New York: Burt Franklin & Co., 1978.

———. *Their Eyes Were Watching God.* 1937. New York: HarperCollins, 2006.

———. *Their Eyes Were Watching God.* Holograph Manuscript. Beineke Rare Book and Manuscript Library, Yale University.

———. "What White Publishers Won't Print." 1950. In Mitchell, *Within the Circle,* 117–21.

Image 177 of Virginia, 1665–76, Foreign Business and Inquistions. Manuscript/Mixed Material. From the Library of Congress, *The Thomas Jefferson Papers.* http://hdl.loc.gov/loc.mss/mtj .mtjbib026600.

Irons, Peter. *Justice at War.* New York: Oxford University Press, 1983.

Jackson, Blyden. Introduction to *Moses, Man on the Mountain,* by Zora Neale Hurston, vii–xix. Urbana: University of Illinois Press, 1984.

James, Caryn. "Book Award Becomes a Feast of Canapés." *New York Times,* November 11, 2004, 10.

Jameson, Fredric. "Third-World Literature in the Era of Multinational Capitalism." *Social Text* 15 (1986): 65–88.

Jennings, La Vinia Delois, ed. *Zora Neale Hurston, Haiti, and Their Eyes Were Watching God.* Evanston: University of Illinois Press, 2013.

Johnson, Howard. "Bahamian Labor Migration to Florida in the Late Nineteenth and Early Twentieth Century," *International Migration Review* 22, no. 1 (Spring 1988): 84–103.

Johnson, James Weldon. Preface to *The Book of American Negro Poetry,* vii–xlviii. New York: Harcourt, Brace and Company, 1922.

Johnson v. M'Intosh. 21 U.S. 543. U.S. Supreme Court. 1823.

Johnston, Bret Anthony. "Interview with Julie Otsuka." National Book Foundation, 2011. http://www.nationalbook.org/nba2011_f_otsuka_interv.html#.WUwQjSuQxlB.

Jorjani, Raha. "Could Black People in the U.S. Qualify as Refugees?" *Washington Post,* August 14, 2015.

Julian, George W. 31 Cong., 2 Sess. *Congressional Globe,* Appendix, January 29, 1851, 136. The Library of Congress.

Jurado, Kathy. "Alienated Citizens: 'Hispanophobia' and the Mexican Im/migrant Body." PhD diss., University of Michigan, 2008.

Kakutani, Michiko. "War's Outcasts Dream of Small Pleasures." *New York Times,* September 10, 2002, E6.

Kaplan, Caren. *Questions of Travel: Postmodern Discourses of Displacement.* Durham, NC: Duke University Press, 1996.

Kaplan, Carla. *The Erotics of Talk: Women's Writing and Feminist Paradigms.* New York: Oxford University Press, 1996.

———. *Zora Neale Hurston: A Life in Letters.* New York: Anchor, 2007.

Kaufman, Leslie. "Book Awards Seek a Bigger Splash, Red Carpet and All." *New York Times,* November 11, 2012, 1.

Kawano, Kelley. "A Conversation with Julie Otsuka." *Bold Type.* 2002. http://www.randomhouse .com/boldtype/0902/otsuka/interview.html.

Kawash, Samira. "The Homeless Body." *Public Culture* 10, no. 2 (Winter 1998): 319–39.

———. "Safe House?: Body, Building, and the Question of Security." *Cultural Critique* 45 (2000): 185–221.

Keating, AnaLouise. "Making Choices: Writing, Spirituality, Sexuality, and the Political." In *Gloria E. Anzaldúa: Interviews/Entrevistas,* edited by AnaLouise Keating, 151–76. New York: Routledge, 2000.

Kevane, Bridget, and Juanita Heredia. *Latina Self-Portraits: Interviews with Contemporary Women Writers.* Albuquerque: University of New Mexico Press, 2000.

Kleinberg, Eliot. *Black Cloud: The Great Florida Hurricane of 1928.* New York: Carroll & Graff Publishers, 2003.

Klinkenberg, Jeff. "Unmarked but Not Unmourned: 1928 Hurricane's Victims Get Memorial 80 Years Later." *St. Petersburg Times,* September 14, 2008. http://www.nhc.noaa.gov/data/tcr/ AL122005_Katrina.pdf.

Knabb, Richard D., Jamie R. Rhome, and Daniel P. Brown. "Tropical Cyclone Report: Hurricane Katrina, 23–30 August 2005." September 14, 2011 (updated). National Hurricane Center, Miami, FL.

Kogawa, Joy. *Obasan.* Boston: David Godine, 1981.

Kolodny, Annette. *The Lay of the Land: Metaphor as Experience and History in American Life and Letters.* Chapel Hill: University of North Carolina Press, 1975.

Koshy, Susan. *Sexual Naturalization: Asian Americans and Miscegenation.* Palo Alto, CA: Stanford University Press, 2004.

Krammer, Arnold. *Undue Process: The Untold Story of American's German Alien Internees.* Lanham, MD: Rowman & Littlefield, 1997.

Lafaye, Jacques. *Quetzalcóatl and Guadalupe.* Chicago: University of Chicago Press, 1976.

Lange, Dorothea. "Family of Japanese Ancestry Arrives at Assembly Center at Tanforan Race Track." Photograph. April 29, 1942. National Archives, Washington, DC.

Lawless, Cecelia. "Helena María Viramontes' Homing Devices in *Under the Feet of Jesus.*" In *Homemaking: Women Writers and the Politics and Poetics of Home,* edited by Catherine Wiley and Fiona R. Barnes, 361–82. New York: Garland Press, 1996.

Leader, Leonard. *Los Angeles and the Great Depression.* New York: Garland Science, 1992.

Lee, Spike, dir. *When the Levees Broke: A Requiem in Four Acts.* HBO Studios, 2006.

Lefebvre, Henri. *The Production of Space.* Translated by Donald Nicholson-Smith. Oxford: Blackwell, 1991.

"Legal Answers for New Orleans Residents." CNN.com, September 8, 2005. http://www.cnn.com/2005/LAW/09/08/martial.law.qanda/.

Lemann, Nicholas. *The Promised Land: The Great Black Migration and How It Changed America.* New York: Random House, 1992.

León, Luis D. *La Llorona's Children: Religion, Life, and Death in the U.S–Mexico Borderlands.* Berkeley: University of California Press, 2004.

Leong, Karen J., Christopher A. Airriess, Wei Li, Angela Chia-Chen Chen, and Verna M. Keith. "Resilient History and the Rebuilding of a Community: The Vietnamese American Community in New Orleans East," *Journal of American History* 94 (December 2007): 770–79.

LeSeur, Geta J. *Not All Okies Are White: The Lives of Black Cotton Pickers in Arizona.* Columbia: University of Missouri Press, 2000.

Lessin, Tia, and Carl Deal, dirs. *Trouble the Waters.* Zeitgeist Films, 2009.

Levine, Ellen. *A Fence away from Freedom.* New York: G. P. Putnam's Sons, 1995.

Lewis, Tom. "'A Godlike Presence': The Impact of Radio on the 1920s and 1930s." *OAH Magazine of History* 6, no. 4 (Spring 1992): 26–33.

Ling, Jinqi. *Narrating Nationalisms: Ideology and Form in Asian American Literature.* New York: Oxford University Press, 1998.

Litt, Jacquelyn. "'We need to get together with each other': Women's Narratives of Help in Katrina's Displacement." In *Displaced: Life in the Katrina Diaspora,* edited by Lynn Weber and Lori Peek, 167–82. Austin: University of Texas Press, 2012.

Long, Carolyn Morrow. "John the Conqueror: From Root-Charm to Commercial Product." *Pharmacy in History* 39, no. 2 (1997): 47–53.

Long, Katy. *From Refugee to Migrant?: Labor Mobility's Protection Potential.* Washington, DC: Migration Policy Institute, 2015. http://www.migrationpolicy.org/research/refugee-migrant-labor-mobilitys-protection-potential.

Lookingbill, Brad D. *Dust Bowl, USA: Depression America and the Ecological Imagination, 1929–1941.* Athens: Ohio University Press, 2001.

Lorentz, Pare, dir. *The Plow That Broke the Plains* and *The River*. 1936/1937. Naxos, 2007. DVD.

Louisiana Department of Health and Hospitals. "Hurricane Katrina: Reports of Missing and Deceased." State of Louisiana, August 2, 2006. http://www.dhh.louisiana.gov/offices/page.asp?ID=192&Detail=5248.

"Louisiana Laws—RS 14:329.6—Proclamation of State of Emergency; Conditions Therefor; Effect Thereof," 2006. Justia U.S. Law. http://law.justia.com/codes/louisiana/2006/146/78434.html.

Lowe, Lisa. *Immigrant Acts: On Asian American Cultural Politics*. Durham, NC: Duke University Press, 1996.

Lowitt, Richard. *American Outback: The Oklahoma Panhandle in the Twentieth Century*. Lubbock: Texas Tech University Press, 2006.

Lye, Colleen. *America's Asia: Racial Forms and American Literature, 1893–1945*. Princeton, NJ: Princeton University Press, 2004.

Madsen, Deborah. *Allegory in America: From Puritanism to Postmodernism*. New York: St. Martin's Press, 1996.

Mankiewicz, Josh. "The New Diaspora." *Dateline NBC*, September 9, 2005. MSNBC.com video.

Marks, Carole. *Farewell—We're Good and Gone: The Great Black Migration*. Bloomington: Indiana University Press, 1989.

———. "The Great Migration: African Americans Searching for the Promised Land, 1916–1930." In *In Motion: The African American Migration Experience* website, edited by Howard Dodson and Sylviane A. Diouf. Schomburg Center for Research in Black Culture and New York Public Library, 2005.

Marx, Leo. *The Machine in the Garden: Technology and the Pastoral Ideal in America*. New York: Oxford University Press, 1973.

Mass, Amy Iwasaki. "Psychological Effects of the Camps on the Japanese Americans." In *Japanese Americans: From Relocation to Redress*, edited by Roger Daniels, Harry H. L. Kitano, and Sandra C. Miller, 159–62. Salt Lake City: University of Utah Press, 1986.

Massey, Doreen. *Race, Space and Gender*. Minneapolis: University of Minnesota Press, 1994.

Massey, Douglas S. "Understanding America's Immigration 'Crisis.'" *Proceedings of the American Philosophical Society* 151, no. 3 (September 2007): 309–27.

Masters, Catherine. "Interview: Jesmyn Ward." *The New Zealand Herald*, May 12, 2012.

McDonell, Keelin. "What Is Martial Law?: And Is New Orleans Under It." Slate.com, September 2, 2005. http://www.slate.com/articles/news_and_politics/explainer/2005/09/what_is_martial_law.html.

McDowell, Linda. *Gender, Identity and Place: Understanding Feminist Geographies*. Cambridge: Polity Press, 1999.

McGreal, Chris. "New Orleans Police on Trial Over Killing in Chaos Following Hurricane Katrina." *The Guardian*, November 19, 2010. https://www.theguardian.com/world/2010/nov/19/new-orleans-police-trial-hurricane-katrina.

McWilliams, Carey. *Factories in the Field: The Story of Migratory Farm Labor in California*. Berkeley: University of California Press, 2000.

Miller, Laura. "How the National Book Awards Made Themselves Irrelevant." Salon.com, October 12, 2011. http://www.salon.com/2011/10/12/how_the_national_book_awards_made_themselves_irrelevant/.

Miner, Valerie. "Review: Hopes, Fears and Secrets." *The Women's Review of Books* 13, no. 1 (October 1995): 19–20.

Mitchell, Angelyn, ed. *Within the Circle: An Anthology of African American Literary Criticism from the Harlem Renaissance to the Present.* Durham, NC: Duke University Press, 1994.

Mitchell-Kernan, Claudia. "Signifying, Loud-Talking and Marking." 1972. In *Signifyin(g), Sanctifyin,' and Slam Dunking: A Reader in African American Expressive Culture,* edited by Gena Dagel Caponi, 309–30. Amherst: University of Massachusetts Press, 1999.

Miyake, Perry. *21st Century Manzanar.* Los Angeles: Really Great Book, 2002.

Mohl, Raymond A. "Black Immigrants: Bahamians in Early Twentieth-Century Miami." *Florida Historical Quarterly* 65, no. 3 (January 1987): 271–97.

Morrison, Toni. *The Bluest Eye.* 1970. New York: Knopf, 1993.

Munson, Curtis B. *Report on Japanese on the West Coast of the United States,* Hearings, 79th Congress, 1st sess., Joint Committee on the Investigation of the Pearl Harbor Attack. Washington, DC: Government Printing Office, 1946.

Mykle, Robert. *Killer 'Cane: The Deadly Hurricane of 1928.* New York: Cooper Square, 2002.

National JACL Power of Words II Committee. *Power of Words Handbook. A Guide to Language about Japanese Americans in World War II: Understanding Euphemisms and Preferred Terminology.* April 27, 2013. https://jacl.org/wordpress/wp-content/uploads/2015/08/Power-of -Words-Rev.-Term.-Handbook.pdf.

Ngai, Mae M. *Impossible Subjects: Illegal Aliens and the Making of Modern America.* Princeton, NJ: Princeton University Press, 2004.

Nguyen, Marguerite. "Vietnamese American New Orleans," *Minnesota Review* 85 (May 2015): 114–28.

Ogawa, Dennis M., and Evarts C. Fox Jr. "Japanese Internment and Relocation: The Hawaii Experience." In *Japanese Americans, from Relocation to Redress,* edited by Roger Daniels, Sandra C. Taylor, Harry H. L. Kitano, and Leonard J. Arrington, 135–38. Salt Lake City: University of Utah Press, 1986.

Okada, John. *No-No Boy.* 1957. Seattle: University of Washington Press, 1979.

Okubo, Miné. *Citizen 13660.* 1946. Seattle: University of Washington Press, 2001.

Otsuka, Julie. *The Buddha in the Attic.* New York: Knopf, 2011.

———. "Diem Perdidi." *Granta* 117, October 27, 2011.

———. The Gluckauf-Haahr Annual Lecture in Literature. Yeshiva University, April 17, 2013.

———. "Julie Otsuka on Her Family's Wartime Internment in Topaz, Utah." *Newsweek,* October 16, 2012 (updated).

———. *When the Emperor Was Divine.* New York: Anchor, 2002.

The Oxford Study Bible: Revised English Bible with the Apocrypha, edited by M. Jack Suggs, Katharine Doob Sakenfeld, and James R. Mueller. New York: Oxford University Press, 1992.

Ozawa v. United States. 260 U.S. 178. U.S. Supreme Court. 1922.

Painter, Neil Irvin. *Exodusters: Black Migration to Kansas after Reconstruction.* New York: Norton, 1992.

Palumbo-Liu, David. *Asian/American: Historical Crossings of a Racial Frontier.* Palo Alto, CA: Stanford University Press, 1999.

Patterson, Tiffany Ruby. *Zora Neale Hurston and a History of Southern Life*. Philadelphia: Temple University Press, 2005.

Paquet, Sandra Pouchet. "West Indian Autobiography." *Black American Literature Forum* 24, no. 2 (1990): 357–74.

Pavlić, Edward M. "'Papa Legba Ouvrier Barriere Por Moi Passer': Esu in *Their Eyes* & Zora Neale Hurston's Diasporic Modernism." In *Zora Neale Hurston, Haiti, and Their Eyes Were Watching God*, edited by La Vinia Delois Jennings, 117–52. Evanston: University of Illinois Press, 2013.

Perea, Juan F., ed. *Immigrants Out!: The New Nativism and the Anti-Immigrant Impulse in the United States*. New York: New York University Press, 1997.

Perry, Ronald W., and Michael K. Lindell. "The Effects of Ethnicity on Evacuation Decision-Making." *Internation Journal of Mass Emergencies and Disasters* 9, no. 1 (March 1991): 47–68.

Rabinow, Paul, ed. "Space, Knowledge, and Power." Interview in *The Foucault Reader*, 239–56. New York: Pantheon, 1984.

Rappaport, Edward N., and Jose Fernandez-Partagas. "The Deadliest Atlantic Tropical Cyclones, 1492–2006." National Weather Service, Miami, FL.

Razack, Sherene H., ed. *Race, Space, and the Law: Unmapping a White Settler Society*. Toronto: Between the Lines, 2002.

Reed, Ernest. "Termination Report on the Nature and Extent of Proposed Agricultural Program." *The Japanese-American Evacuation and Resettlement Records, 1930–1974* (bulk 1942–1946). (MSS 67/14C) E2.753. Bancroft Library, University of California at Berkeley.

Reich, Steven A. *A Working People: A History of African American Workers since Emancipation*. New York: Rowman & Littlefield, 2013.

Riney-Kehrberg, Pamela. *Waiting on the Bounty: The Dust Bowl Diary of Mary Knackstedt Dyck*. Iowa City: University of Iowa Press, 1999.

Rodgers, Lawrence R. *Canaan Bound: The African-American Great Migration Novel*. Chicago: University of Illinois Press, 1997.

Sabin, Ashley, and David Redmon, dirs. *Kamp Katrina*. Carnivalesque Films, 2009.

Said, Edward. *Orientalism*. New York: Pantheon, 1978.

Sánchez, Miguel. *Historia de la Virgen de Guadalupe de México*. Edited by Lauro López Beltrán. Cuernavaca, Morelos, México: Editorial "Juan Diego," 1952. Originally *Imagen de la Virgen María, Madre de Dios de Guadalupe*, 1648.

Schlund-Vials, Cathy J. *Modeling Citizenship: Jewish and Asian American Writing*. Philadelphia: Temple University Press, 2011.

Shaw, Randy. *Beyond the Fields: Cesar Chavez, the UFW, and the Struggle for Justice in the 21st Century*. Berkeley: University of California Press, 2008.

Shortridge, James R. "The Emergence of 'Middle West' as an American Regional Label." *Annals of the Association of American Geographers* 74, no. 2 (June 1984): 209–20.

Sibley, David. *Geographies of Exclusion: Society and Difference in the West*. London: Routledge, 1995.

Simpson, Caroline Chung. "Internment." In *Keywords for American Cultural Studies* (2nd ed.), edited by Bruce Burgett and Glenn Hendler. New York: NYU Press, 2014.

Smith, Henry Nash. *Virgin Land: The American West as Symbol and Myth*. Cambridge, MA: Harvard University Press, 1999.

Snodgrass, Michael. "The Bracero Program, 1942–1964." In *Beyond La Frontera: The History of Mexico–U.S. Migration*, edited by Mark Overmyer-Velázquez, 79–102. New York: Oxford University Press, 2011.

Soja, Edward. *Thirdspace: Journeys to Los Angeles and Other Real-and-Imagined Places*. Cambridge, MA: Blackwell, 1996.

Sommers, Samuel R., Evan P. Apfelbaum, Kristin N. Dukes, Negin Toosi, and Elsie J. Wang. "Race and Media Coverage of Hurricane Katrina: Analysis, Implications, and Future Research Questions." *Analyses of Social Issues and Public Policy* 6, no. 1 (December 2006): 39–55.

Sone, Monica. *Nisei Daughter*. Boston: Atlantic Little, Brown, 1953.

Song, Min Hyoung. *The Children of 1965: On Writing, and Not Writing, as an Asian American*. Durham, NC: Duke University Press, 2013.

Southerland, Ellease. "The Influence of Voodoo on the Fiction of Zora Neale Hurston." In *Sturdy Black Bridges: Visions of Black Women in Literature*, edited by Roseanne Bell, Bettye J. Parker, and Beverly Guy-Sheftall, 171–83. Garden City, NY: Anchor Books, 1979.

Srikanth, Rajini. *Constructing the Enemy: Empathy/Antipathy in U.S. Literature and Law*. Philadelphia: Temple University Press, 2012.

Stephens, Nicole M., MarYam G. Hamedani, Hazel Rose Markus, Hilary B. Bergsieker, and Liyam Eloul. "Why Did They 'Choose' to Stay?: Perspectives of Hurricane Katrina Observers and Survivors." *Psychological Science* (July 2009): 878–86.

Stepto, Robert B. *From Behind the Veil: A Study of Afro-American Narrative*. Urbana: University of Illinois Press, 1991.

Stern, Alexandra Minna. "Nationalism on the Line: Masculinity, Race and the Creation of the U.S Border Patrol 1910–1949." In *Continental Crossroads: Remapping U.S-Mexican Borderlands*, edited by Samuel Truett and Elliott Young, 299–323. Durham, NC: Duke University Press, 2004.

Strongman, Roberto. "A Caribbean Response to the Question of Third World National Allegories: Jameson, Ahmad and the Return of the Repressed." *Anthurium: A Caribbean Studies Journal* 6, no. 2 (2008): n.p.

Sturgis, Amy H. *The Trail of Tears and Indian Removal*. Westport, CT: Greenwood, 2006.

Sullivan, Patrick J. *Blue Collar—Roman Collar—White Collar: U.S. Catholic Involvement in Labor Management Controversies, 1960–1980*. Lanham, MD: University Press of America, 1987.

Swyt, Wendy. "Hungry Women: Borderlands Mythos in Two Stories by Helena María Viramontes." *MELUS* 23 no. 2 (Summer 1998): 189–201.

Tajiri, Rea, dir. *History and Memory: For Akiko and Takashige*. New York: Distributed by Women Make Movies, 1991.

Tambling, Jeremy. *Allegory*. New York: Routledge, 2010.

Taylor, Frank J. "The People Nobody Wants." *Saturday Evening Post*, May 9, 1942, 24–25, 64, 66–67.

Taylor, Sandra C. *Jewel of the Desert: Japanese American Internment at Topaz*. Berkeley: University of California Press, 1993.

Terrace v. Thompson. 263 U.S. 197. U.S. Supreme Court. 1923.

Thompson, J. Murray. "The Agricultural Aspects of the Evacuation of Enemy Aliens." The National Defense Migration Hearings before the Select Committee Investigating National Defense Migration. House of Representatives Seventy-Seventh Congress Second Session Pursuant to H. Res. 113. Part 29 San Francisco Hearing February 21 and 23, 1942. https://archive.org/stream/nationaldefensem29unit/nationaldefensem29unit_djvu.txt.

Thornton, Jerome. "The Paradoxical Journey of the African American in African American Fiction." *New Literary History* 21, no. 3 (Spring 1990): 733–45.

Trachtenberg, Alan. *The Incorporation of America and Society in the Gilded Age.* New York: Hill and Wang, 1982.

Truitt, Patricia. *False Images: Law's Construction of the Refugee.* East Haven, CT: Pluto Press, 1996.

Turner, Frederick Jackson. *The Frontier in American History.* New York: H. Holt, 1920.

Tyler, Varro E. "The Elusive History of High John the Conqueror Root." *Pharmacy in History* 33, no. 4 (1991): 164–66.

Uchida, Yoshiko. *Desert Exile: The Uprooting of a Japanese-American Family.* Seattle: University of Washington Press, 1982.

United Nations General Assembly. *Convention Relating to the Status of Refugees.* July 28, 1951, United Nations, Treaty Series, vol. 189, p. 137. http://www.refworld.org/docid/3be01b964.html.

United Nations High Commissioner for Refugees. *Guiding Principles on Internal Displacement.* http://www.unhcr.org/en-us/protection/idps/43ce1cff2/guiding-principles-internal-displacement.html.

———. Introductory note to the *Convention and Protocol Relating to the Status of Refugees: 60 Years.* http://www.unhcr.org/en-us/protection/basic/3b66c2aa10/convention-protocol-relating-status-refugees.html.

United States Commission on Wartime Relocation and Internment of Civilians. *Personal Justice Denied: Report of the Commission on Wartime Relocation and Internment of Civilians.* Seattle: University of Washington Press, 1997.

United States Office of War Information, producer. *Japanese Relocation.* Distributed by the War Activities Committee of the Motion Picture Industry, 1942.

Vials, Chris. *Realism for the Masses: Aesthetics, Popular Front Pluralism, and U.S. Culture, 1935–1947.* Jackson: University Press of Mississippi, 2013.

Vieira de Mello, Sergio. Foreword to the United Nations' *Guiding Principles on Internal Displacement.* http://www.unhcr.org/en-us/protection/idps/43ce1cff2/guiding-principles-internal-displacement.html.

Viramontes, Helena María. "'Nopalitos': The Making of Fiction (Testimonio)." In *Breaking Boundaries: Latina Writing and Critical Readings,* edited by Asunción Horno-Delgado, 33–38. Amherst: University of Massachusetts Press, 1989.

———. "Scripted Language: Writing Is the Only Way I Know How to Pray." Lecture at Sage Hall, Cornell University. November 11, 2009.

———. *Under the Feet of Jesus.* New York: Plume, 1996.

Wallinger, Michael John. "Dispersal of the Japanese Americans: Rhetorical Strategies of the War Relocation Authority 1942–1945." PhD diss., University of Oregon, 1975.

War Relocation Authority. *A Story of Human Conservation.* Washington, DC: United States Department of the Interior, 1946.

Ward, Jesmyn. *Salvage the Bones.* New York: Bloomsbury, 2011.

Weber, Lynn, and Lori Peek, eds. *Displaced: Life in the Katrina Diaspora.* Austin: University of Texas Press, 2012.

Weglyn, Michi Nishiura. *Years of Infamy: The Untold Story of America's Concentration Camps.* Seattle: University of Washington Press, 1996.

Weheliye, Alexander G. *Habeas Viscus: Racializing Assemblages, Biopolitics, and Black Feminist Theories of the Human.* Durham, NC: Duke University Press, 2014.

Weiland, Christine. "Within the Crossroads: Lesbian/Feminist/Spiritual Development." In *Gloria E. Anzaldúa: Interviews/Entrevistas,* edited by AnaLouise Keating, 71–127. New York: Routledge, 2000.

Wheelan, Joseph. *Invading Mexico: America's Continental Dream and the Mexican War 1846–1848.* New York: Carroll and Graf, 2007.

White, G. Edward. "The Lost Internment." *Green Bag* 14, no. 3 (2011): 283–300.

Wilber, C. D. *The Great Valleys and Prairies of Nebraska and the Northwest.* Omaha, NE: Daily Republican Print, 1881.

Willinger, Beth, ed. *Katrina and the Women of New Orleans.* New Orleans: Newcomb College Center for Research on Women at Tulane University, 2008.

Willis, Susan. *Signifying: Black Women Writing the American Experience.* Madison: University of Wisconsin Press, 1987.

Winant, Howard. "The Theoretical Status of the Concept of Race." In *Theories of Race and Racism,* edited by Les Back and John Solomos, 181–90. New York: Routledge, 2000.

Wixson, Douglas. Introduction to *On the Dirty Plate Trail: Remembering the Dust Bowl Refugee Camps,* by Sanora Babb and Dorothy Babb, 1–10. Edited by Douglas Wixson. Austin: University of Texas Press, 2007.

Woo, Elaine. "Sanora Babb, 98; Writer Whose Masterpiece Rivaled Steinbeck's." *Los Angeles Times,* January 8, 2006, B-12.

Wood, W. B. "Ecomigration: Linkages between Environmental Change and Migration." In *Global Migrants, Global Refugees: Problems and Solutions,* edited by Aristide R. Zolberg and Peter Benda, 42–61. New York: Berghahn, 2001.

Wright, Richard. "Between Laughter and Tears." In Cronin, *Critical Essays on Zora Neale Hurston,* 75–76. First published October 5, 1937.

———. "Big Boy Leaves Home." In *The New Caravan Anthology,* vol. 5, edited by Paul Rosenfeld, Lewis Mumford, and Alfred Kreymborg, 124–58. New York: W. W. Norton & Co., 1936.

Yamada, Mitsuke. *Desert Run.* Latham, NY: Kitchen Table/Women of Color, 1988.

Yamamoto, Hisaye. *Seventeen Syllables,* edited by King-Kok Cheung. New Brunswick, NJ: Rutgers University Press, 1994.

Yates, Robert. "Notes of the Secret Debates of the Federal Convention of 1787. Taken by the Late Hon Robert Yates, Chief Justice of the State of New York, and One of the Delegates from That State to the Said Convention." June 26, 1787. http://avalon.law.yale.edu/18th_century/yates.asp.

Young, Iris. *Justice and the Politics of Difference.* Princeton, NJ: Princeton University Press, 1990.

INDEX

CPSIA information can be obtained
at www.ICGtesting.com
Printed in the USA
LVHW071739230623
750622LV00003B/25